PHILOSOPHICAL INVESTIGATIONS

PHILOSOPHICAL INVESTIGATIONS

By
LUDWIG WITTGENSTEIN

Translated by
G. E. M. ANSCOMBE

BASIL BLACKWELL
OXFORD
1978

First Edition 1953
Second Edition 1958
Reprint of English Text alone 1963
Third Edition of English and German Text with index 1967
Reprint of English Text with index 1968, 1972, 1974, 1976, 1978

ISBN 0 631 11900 0 (Cloth)
ISBN 0 631 14670 9 (Paper)

Printed in Great Britain by offset lithography by
Billing & Sons Ltd. Guildford, London and Worcester

TRANSLATOR'S NOTE

My acknowledgments are due to the following, who either checked the translation or allowed me to consult them about German and Austrian usage or read the translation through and helped me to improve the English: Mr. R. Rhees, Professor G. H. von Wright, Mr. P. Geach, Mr. G. Kreisel, Miss L. Labowsky, Mr. D. Paul, Miss I. Murdoch.

NOTE TO SECOND EDITION

THE text has been revised for the new edition. A large number of small changes have been made in the English text. The following passages have been significantly altered:

In Part I: §§ 108, 109, 116, 189, 193, 251, 284, 352, 360, 393, 418, 426, 442, 456, 493, 520, 556, 582, 591, 644, 690, 692.

In Part II: pp. 193e, 211e, 216e, 217e, 220e, 232e.

The text of the Third Edition remains unaltered, but an index has been added.

EDITORS' NOTE

WHAT appears as Part I of this volume was complete by 1945. Part II was written between 1946 and 1949. If Wittgenstein had published his work himself, he would have suppressed a good deal of what is in the last thirty pages or so of Part I and worked what is in Part II, with further material, into its place.

We have had to decide between variant readings for words and phrases throughout the manuscript. The choice never affected the sense.

The passages printed beneath a line at the foot of some pages are written on slips which Wittgenstein had cut from other writings and inserted at these pages, without any further indication of where they were to come in.

Words standing between double brackets are Wittgenstein's references to remarks either in this work or in other writings of his which we hope will appear later.

We are responsible for placing the final fragment of Part II in its present position.

G. E. M. ANSCOMBE
R. RHEES

PREFACE

THE thoughts which I publish in what follows are the precipitate of philosophical investigations which have occupied me for the last sixteen years. They concern many subjects: the concepts of meaning, of understanding, of a proposition, of logic, the foundations of mathematics, states of consciousness, and other things. I have written down all these thoughts as *remarks*, short paragraphs, of which there is sometimes a fairly long chain about the same subject, while I sometimes make a sudden change, jumping from one topic to another.—It was my intention at first to bring all this together in a book whose form I pictured differently at different times. But the essential thing was that the thoughts should proceed from one subject to another in a natural order and without breaks.

After several unsuccessful attempts to weld my results together into such a whole, I realized that I should never succeed. The best that I could write would never be more than philosophical remarks; my thoughts were soon crippled if I tried to force them on in any single direction against their natural inclination.——And this was, of course, connected with the very nature of the investigation. For this compels us to travel over a wide field of thought criss-cross in every direction.— The philosophical remarks in this book are, as it were, a number of sketches of landscapes which were made in the course of these long and involved journeyings.

The same or almost the same points were always being approached afresh from different directions, and new sketches made. Very many of these were badly drawn or uncharacteristic, marked by all the defects of a weak draughtsman. And when they were rejected a number of tolerable ones were left, which now had to be arranged and sometimes cut down, so that if you looked at them you could get a picture of the landscape. Thus this book is really only an album.

Up to a short time ago I had really given up the idea of publishing my work in my lifetime. It used, indeed, to be revived from time to time: mainly because I was obliged to learn that my results (which I had communicated in lectures, typescripts and discussions), variously misunderstood, more or less mangled or watered down, were in circulation. This stung my vanity and I had difficulty in quieting it.

Four* years ago I had occasion to re-read my first book (the *Tractatus Logico-Philosophicus*) and to explain its ideas to someone. It suddenly seemed to me that I should publish those old thoughts and the new ones together: that the latter could be seen in the right light only by contrast with and against the background of my old way of thinking.[1]

For since beginning to occupy myself with philosophy again, sixteen years ago, I have been forced to recognize grave mistakes in what I wrote in that first book. I was helped to realize these mistakes—to a degree which I myself am hardly able to estimate—by the criticism which my ideas encountered from Frank Ramsey, with whom I discussed them in innumerable conversations during the last two years of his life. Even more than to this—always certain and forcible— criticism I am indebted to that which a teacher of this university, Mr. P. Sraffa, for many years unceasingly practised on my thoughts. I am indebted to *this* stimulus for the most consequential ideas of this book.

For more than one reason what I publish here will have points of contact with what other people are writing to-day.—If my remarks do not bear a stamp which marks them as mine,—I do not wish to lay any further claim to them as my property.

I make them public with doubtful feelings. It is not impossible that it should fall to the lot of this work, in its poverty and in the darkness of this time, to bring light into one brain or another—but, of course, it is not likely.

I should not like my writing to spare other people the trouble of thinking. But, if possible, to stimulate someone to thoughts of his own.

I should have liked to produce a good book. This has not come about, but the time is past in which I could improve it.

CAMBRIDGE,
January 1945.

* But cf. G. H. von Wright, 'The Wittgenstein Papers', *The Philosophical Review* 78 1969. It seems that Wittgenstein should have said 'two years'.

[1] It was hoped to carry out this plan in a purely German edition of the present work.

PART I

1. "Cum ipsi (majores homines) appellabant rem aliquam, et cum secundum eam vocem corpus ad aliquid movebant, videbam, et tenebam hoc ab eis vocari rem illam, quod sonabant, cum eam vellent ostendere. Hoc autem eos velle ex motu corporis aperiebatur: tamquam verbis naturalibus omnium gentium, quae fiunt vultu et nutu oculorum, ceterorumque membrorum actu, et sonitu vocis indicante affectionem animi in petendis, habendis, rejiciendis, fugiendisve rebus. Ita verba in variis sententiis locis suis posita, et crebro audita, quarum rerum signa essent, paulatim colligebam, measque jam voluntates, edomito in eis signis ore, per haec enuntiabam." (Augustine, *Confessions*, I. 8.) [1]

These words, it seems to me, give us a particular picture of the essence of human language. It is this: the individual words in language name objects—sentences are combinations of such names.——In this picture of language we find the roots of the following idea: Every word has a meaning. This meaning is correlated with the word. It is the object for which the word stands.

Augustine does not speak of there being any difference between kinds of word. If you describe the learning of language in this way you are, I believe, thinking primarily of nouns like "table", "chair", "bread", and of people's names, and only secondarily of the names of certain actions and properties; and of the remaining kinds of word as something that will take care of itself.

Now think of the following use of language: I send someone shopping. I give him a slip marked "five red apples". He takes the slip to

---

[1] "When they (my elders) named some object, and accordingly moved towards something, I saw this and I grasped that the thing was called by the sound they uttered when they meant to point it out. Their intention was shewn by their bodily movements, as it were the natural language of all peoples: the expression of the face, the play of the eyes, the movement of other parts of the body, and the tone of voice which expresses our state of mind in seeking, having, rejecting, or avoiding something. Thus, as I heard words repeatedly used in their proper places in various sentences, I gradually learnt to understand what objects they signified; and after I had trained my mouth to form these signs, I used them to express my own desires."

the shopkeeper, who opens the drawer marked "apples"; then he looks up the word "red" in a table and finds a colour sample opposite it; then he says the series of cardinal numbers—I assume that he knows them by heart—up to the word "five" and for each number he takes an apple of the same colour as the sample out of the drawer.——It is in this and similar ways that one operates with words.——"But how does he know where and how he is to look up the word 'red' and what he is to do with the word 'five'?"——Well, I assume that he *acts* as I have described. Explanations come to an end somewhere.—But what is the meaning of the word "five"?—No such thing was in question here, only how the word "five" is used.

2.   That philosophical concept of meaning has its place in a primitive idea of the way language functions. But one can also say that it is the idea of a language more primitive than ours.

Let us imagine a language for which the description given by Augustine is right. The language is meant to serve for communication between a builder A and an assistant B. A is building with building-stones: there are blocks, pillars, slabs and beams. B has to pass the stones, and that in the order in which A needs them. For this purpose they use a language consisting of the words "block", "pillar", "slab", "beam". A calls them out;—B brings the stone which he has learnt to bring at such-and-such a call.——Conceive this as a complete primitive language.

3.   Augustine, we might say, does describe a system of communication; only not everything that we call language is this system. And one has to say this in many cases where the question arises "Is this an appropriate description or not?" The answer is: "Yes, it is appropriate, but only for this narrowly circumscribed region, not for the whole of what you were claiming to describe."

It is as if someone were to say: "A game consists in moving objects about on a surface according to certain rules . . ."—and we replied: You seem to be thinking of board games, but there are others. You can make your definition correct by expressly restricting it to those games.

4.   Imagine a script in which the letters were used to stand for sounds, and also as signs of emphasis and punctuation. (A script can be conceived as a language for describing sound-patterns.) Now imagine someone interpreting that script as if there were simply a

correspondence of letters to sounds and as if the letters had not also completely different functions. Augustine's conception of language is like such an over-simple conception of the script.

5.   If we look at the example in §1, we may perhaps get an inkling how much this general notion of the meaning of a word surrounds the working of language with a haze which makes clear vision impossible. It disperses the fog to study the phenomena of language in primitive kinds of application in which one can command a clear view of the aim and functioning of the words.

A child uses such primitive forms of language when it learns to talk. Here the teaching of language is not explanation, but training.

6.   We could imagine that the language of §2 was the *whole* language of A and B; even the whole language of a tribe. The children are brought up to perform *these* actions, to use *these* words as they do so, and to react in *this* way to the words of others.

An important part of the training will consist in the teacher's pointing to the objects, directing the child's attention to them, and at the same time uttering a word; for instance, the word "slab" as he points to that shape. (I do not want to call this "ostensive definition", because the child cannot as yet *ask* what the name is. I will call it "ostensive teaching of words".——I say that it will form an important part of the training, because it is so with human beings; not because it could not be imagined otherwise.) This ostensive teaching of words can be said to establish an association between the word and the thing. But what does this mean? Well, it may mean various things; but one very likely thinks first of all that a picture of the object comes before the child's mind when it hears the word. But now, if this does happen—is it the purpose of the word?—Yes, it *may* be the purpose.—I can imagine such a use of words (of series of sounds). (Uttering a word is like striking a note on the keyboard of the imagination.) But in the language of §2 it is *not* the purpose of the words to evoke images. (It may, of course, be discovered that that helps to attain the actual purpose.)

But if the ostensive teaching has this effect,—am I to say that it effects an understanding of the word? Don't you understand the call "Slab!" if you act upon it in such-and-such a way?—Doubtless the ostensive teaching helped to bring this about; but only together with a particular

12. It is like looking into the cabin of a locomotive. We see handles all looking more or less alike. (Naturally, since they are all supposed to be handled.) But one is the handle of a crank which can be moved continuously (it regulates the opening of a valve); another is the handle of a switch, which has only two effective positions, it is either off or on; a third is the handle of a brake-lever, the harder one pulls on it, the harder it brakes; a fourth, the handle of a pump: it has an effect only so long as it is moved to and fro.

13. When we say: "Every word in language signifies something" we have so far said *nothing whatever;* unless we have explained exactly *what* distinction we wish to make. (It might be, of course, that we wanted to distinguish the words of language (8) from words 'without meaning' such as occur in Lewis Carroll's poems, or words like "Lilliburlero" in songs.)

14. Imagine someone's saying: "*All* tools serve to modify something. Thus the hammer modifies the position of the nail, the saw the shape of the board, and so on."—And what is modified by the rule, the glue-pot, the nails?—"Our knowledge of a thing's length, the temperature of the glue, and the solidity of the box."——Would anything be gained by this assimilation of expressions?—

15. The word "to signify" is perhaps used in the most straightforward way when the object signified is marked with the sign. Suppose that the tools A uses in building bear certain marks. When A shews his assistant such a mark, he brings the tool that has that mark on it.

It is in this and more or less similar ways that a name means and is given to a thing.—It will often prove useful in philosophy to say to ourselves: naming something is like attaching a label to a thing.

16. What about the colour samples that A shews to B: are they part of the *language?* Well, it is as you please. They do not belong among the words; yet when I say to someone: "Pronounce the word 'the' ", you will count the second "the" as part of the sentence. Yet it has a role just like that of a colour-sample in language-game (8); that is, it is a sample of what the other is meant to say.

It is most natural, and causes least confusion, to reckon the samples among the instruments of the language.

((Remark on the reflexive pronoun "*this* sentence".))

17.   It will be possible to say: In language (8) we have different *kinds of word*. For the functions of the word "slab" and the word "block" are more alike than those of "slab" and "d". But how we group words into kinds will depend on the aim of the classification,—and on our own inclination.

Think of the different points of view from which one can classify tools or chess-men.

18.   Do not be troubled by the fact that languages (2) and (8) consist only of orders. If you want to say that this shews them to be incomplete, ask yourself whether our language is complete;—whether it was so before the symbolism of chemistry and the notation of the infinitesimal calculus were incorporated in it; for these are, so to speak, suburbs of our language. (And how many houses or streets does it take before a town begins to be a town?) Our language can be seen as an ancient city: a maze of little streets and squares, of old and new houses, and of houses with additions from various periods; and this surrounded by a multitude of new boroughs with straight regular streets and uniform houses.

19.   It is easy to imagine a language consisting only of orders and reports in battle.—Or a language consisting only of questions and expressions for answering yes and no. And innumerable others.—— And to imagine a language means to imagine a form of life.

But what about this: is the call "Slab!" in example (2) a sentence or a word?—If a word, surely it has not the same meaning as the like-sounding word of our ordinary language, for in §2 it is a call. But if a sentence, it is surely not the elliptical sentence: "Slab!" of our language.——As far as the first question goes you can call "Slab!" a word and also a sentence; perhaps it could be appropriately called a 'degenerate sentence' (as one speaks of a degenerate hyperbola); in fact it *is* our 'elliptical' sentence.—But that is surely only a shortened form of the sentence "Bring me a slab", and there is no such sentence in example (2).—But why should I not on the contrary have called the sentence "Bring me a slab" a *lengthening* of the sentence "Slab!"?— Because if you shout "Slab!" you really mean: "Bring me a slab".— But how do you do this: how do you *mean that* while you *say* "Slab!"? Do you say the unshortened sentence to yourself? And why should I translate the call "Slab!" into a different expression in order to say what someone means by it? And if they mean the same thing—why should I not say: "When he says 'Slab!' hemeans 'Slab!'"? Again, if you can mean "Bring me the slab", why should you not be able to mean "Slab!"?——But when I call "Slab!", then what I want is, *that he should bring me a slab*!——Certainly, but does 'wanting this' consist in thinking in some form or other a different sentence from the one you utter?—

20. But now it looks as if when someone says "Bring me a slab" he could mean this expression as *one* long word corresponding to the single word "Slab!"——Then can one mean it sometimes as one word and sometimes as four? And how does one usually mean it?——I think we shall be inclined to say: we mean the sentence as *four* words when we use it in contrast with other sentences such as "*Hand* me a slab", "Bring *him* a slab", "Bring *two* slabs", etc.; that is, in contrast with sentences containing the separate words of our command in other combinations.——But what does using one sentence in contrast with others consist in? Do the others, perhaps, hover before one's mind? *All* of them? And *while* one is saying the one sentence, or before, or afterwards?—No. Even if such an explanation rather tempts us, we need only think for a moment of what actually happens in order to see that we are going astray here. We say that we use the command in contrast with other sentences because *our language* contains the possibility of those other sentences. Someone who did not understand our language, a foreigner, who had fairly often heard someone giving the order: "Bring me a slab!", might believe that this whole series of sounds was one word corresponding perhaps to the word for "building-stone" in his language. If he himself had then given this order perhaps he would have pronounced it differently, and we should say: he pronounces it so oddly because he takes it for a *single* word.—— But then, is there not also something different going on in him when he pronounces it,—something corresponding to the fact that he con- ceives the sentence as a *single* word?——Either the same thing may go on in him, or something different. For what goes on in you when you give such an order? Are you conscious of its consisting of four words *while* you are uttering it? Of course you have a *mastery* of this language —which contains those other sentences as well—but is this having a mastery something that *happens* while you are uttering the sentence?— And I have admitted that the foreigner will probably pronounce a sentence differently if he conceives it differently; but what we call his wrong conception *need* not lie in anything that accompanies the utterance of the command.

The sentence is 'elliptical', not because it leaves out something that we think when we utter it, but because it is shortened—in comparison with a particular paradigm of our grammar.—Of course one might object here: "You grant that the shortened and the unshortened sentence have the same sense.—What is this sense, then? Isn't there a verbal expression for this sense?"——But doesn't the fact that sentences have the same sense consist in their having the same *use*?—(In Russian one says "stone red" instead of "the stone is red"; do they feel the copula to be missing in the sense, or attach it in *thought*?)

21.   Imagine a language-game in which A asks and B reports the number of slabs or blocks in a pile, or the colours and shapes of the building-stones that are stacked in such-and-such a place.—Such a report might run: "Five slabs". Now what is the difference between the report or statement "Five slabs" and the order "Five slabs!"?—Well, it is the part which uttering these words plays in the language-game. No doubt the tone of voice and the look with which they are uttered, and much else besides, will also be different. But we could also imagine the tone's being the same—for an order and a report can be spoken in a *variety* of tones of voice and with various expressions of face—the difference being only in the application. (Of course, we might use the words "statement" and "command" to stand for grammatical forms of sentence and intonations; we do in fact call "Isn't the weather glorious to-day?" a question, although it is used as a statement.) We could imagine a language in which *all* statements had the form and tone of rhetorical questions; or every command the form of the question "Would you like to . . .?". Perhaps it will then be said: "What he says has the form of a question but is really a command",— that is, has the function of a command in the technique of using the language. (Similarly one says "You will do this" not as a prophecy but as a command. What makes it the one or the other?)

22.   Frege's idea that every assertion contains an assumption, which is the thing that is asserted, really rests on the possibility found in our language of writing every statement in the form: "It is asserted that such-and-such is the case."—But "that such-and-such is the case" is *not* a sentence in our language—so far it is not a *move* in the language-game. And if I write, not "It is asserted that . . . .", but "It is asserted: such-and-such is the case", the words "It is asserted" simply become superfluous.

We might very well also write every statement in the form of a question followed by a "Yes"; for instance: "Is it raining? Yes!" Would this shew that every statement contained a question?

Of course we have the right to use an assertion sign in contrast with a question-mark, for example, or if we want to distinguish an assertion from a fiction or a supposition. It is only a mistake if one thinks that the assertion consists of two actions, entertaining and asserting (assigning the truth-value, or something of the kind), and that in performing these actions we follow the propositional sign roughly as we sing from the musical score. Reading the written sentence loud or soft is indeed comparable with singing from a musical score, but 'meaning' (thinking) the sentence that is read is not.

Frege's assertion sign marks the *beginning of the sentence*. Thus its function is like that of the full-stop. It distinguishes the whole period from a clause *within* the period. If I hear someone say "it's raining" but do not know whether I have heard the beginning and end of the period, so far this sentence does not serve to tell me anything.

23. But how many kinds of sentence are there? Say assertion, question, and command?—There are *countless* kinds: countless different kinds of use of what we call "symbols", "words", "sentences". And this multiplicity is not something fixed, given once for all; but new types of language, new language-games, as we may say, come into existence, and others become obsolete and get forgotten. (We can get a *rough picture* of this from the changes in mathematics.)

Here the term "language-*game*" is meant to bring into prominence the fact that the *speaking* of language is part of an activity, or of a form of life.

Review the multiplicity of language-games in the following examples, and in others:

    Giving orders, and obeying them—
    Describing the appearance of an object, or giving its measurements—
    Constructing an object from a description (a drawing)—
    Reporting an event—
    Speculating about an event—

Imagine a picture representing a boxer in a particular stance. Now, this picture can be used to tell someone how he should stand, should hold himself; or how he should not hold himself; or how a particular man did stand in such-and-such a place; and so on. One might (using the language of chemistry) call this picture a proposition-radical. This will be how Frege thought of the "assumption".

Forming and testing a hypothesis—
Presenting the results of an experiment in tables and diagrams—
Making up a story; and reading it—
Play-acting—
Singing catches—
Guessing riddles—
Making a joke; telling it—
Solving a problem in practical arithmetic—
Translating from one language into another—
Asking, thanking, cursing, greeting, praying.

—It is interesting to compare the multiplicity of the tools in language and of the ways they are used, the multiplicity of kinds of word and sentence, with what logicians have said about the structure of language. (Including the author of the *Tractatus Logico-Philosophicus*.)

24. If you do not keep the multiplicity of language-games in view you will perhaps be inclined to ask questions like: "What is a question?" —Is it the statement that I do not know such-and-such, or the statement that I wish the other person would tell me . . . .? Or is it the description of my mental state of uncertainty?—And is the cry "Help!" such a description?

Think how many different kinds of thing are called "description": description of a body's position by means of its co-ordinates; description of a facial expression; description of a sensation of touch; of a mood.

Of course it is possible to substitute the form of statement or description for the usual form of question: "I want to know whether . . . ." or "I am in doubt whether . . . ."—but this does not bring the different language-games any closer together.

The significance of such possibilities of transformation, for example of turning all statements into sentences beginning "I think" or "I believe" (and thus, as it were, into descriptions of *my* inner life) will become clearer in another place. (Solipsism.)

25. It is sometimes said that animals do not talk because they lack the mental capacity. And this means: "they do not think, and that is why they do not talk." But—they simply do not talk. Or to put it better: they do not use language—if we except the most primitive forms of language.—Commanding, questioning, recounting, chatting, are as much a part of our natural history as walking, eating, drinking, playing.

26. One thinks that learning language consists in giving names to objects. Viz, to human beings, to shapes, to colours, to pains, to

moods, to numbers, etc. . To repeat—naming is something like attaching a label to a thing. One can say that this is preparatory to the use of a word. But *what* is it a preparation *for*?

27. "We name things and then we can talk about them: can refer to them in talk."—'As if what we did next were given with the mere act of naming. As if there were only one thing called "talking about a thing". Whereas in fact we do the most various things with our sentences. Think of exclamations alone, with their completely different functions.

> Water!
> Away!
> Ow!
> Help!
> Fine!
> No!

Are you inclined still to call these words "names of objects"?

In languages (2) and (8) there was no such thing as asking something's name. This, with its correlate, ostensive definition, is, we might say, a language-game on its own. That is really to say: we are brought up, trained, to ask: "What is that called?"—upon which the name is given. And there is also a language-game of inventing a name for something, and hence of saying, "This is . . . ." and then using the new name. (Thus, for example, children give names to their dolls and then talk about them and to them. Think in this connexion how singular is the use of a person's name to *call* him!)

28. Now one can ostensively define a proper name, the name of a colour, the name of a material, a numeral, the name of a point of the compass and so on. The definition of the number two, "That is called 'two' "—pointing to two nuts—is perfectly exact.—But how can two be defined like that? The person one gives the definition to doesn't know what one wants to call "two"; he will suppose that "two" is the name given to *this* group of nuts!——He *may* suppose this; but perhaps he does not. He might make the opposite mistake; when I want to assign a name to this group of nuts, he might understand it as a numeral. And he might equally well take the name of a person, of which I give an ostensive definition, as that of a colour, of a race, or even of a point

of the compass. That is to say: an ostensive definition can be variously interpreted in *every* case.

29. Perhaps you say: two can only be ostensively defined in *this* way: "This *number* is called 'two'". For the word "number" here shews what place in language, in grammar, we assign to the word. But this means that the word "number" must be explained before the ostensive definition can be understood.—The word "number" in the definition does indeed shew this place; does shew the post at which we station the word. And we can prevent misunderstandings by saying: "This *colour* is called so-and-so", "This *length* is called so-and-so", and so on. That is to say: misunderstandings are sometimes averted in this way. But is there only *one* way of taking the word "colour" or "length"?—Well, they just need defining.—Defining, then, by means of other words! And what about the last definition in this chain? (Do not say: "There isn't a 'last' definition". That is just as if you chose to say: "There isn't a last house in this road; one can always build an additional one".)

Whether the word "number" is necessary in the ostensive definition depends on whether without it the other person takes the definition otherwise than I wish. And that will depend on the circumstances under which it is given, and on the person I give it to.

And how he 'takes' the definition is seen in the use that he makes of the word defined.

30. So one might say: the ostensive definition explains the use—the meaning—of the word when the overall role of the word in language is clear. Thus if I know that someone means to explain a colour-word to me the ostensive definition "That is called 'sepia'" will help me to understand the word.—And you can say this, so long as

---

Could one define the word "red" by pointing to something that was *not red*? That would be as if one were supposed to explain the word "modest" to someone whose English was weak, and one pointed to an arrogant man and said "That man is *not* modest". That it is ambiguous is no argument against such a method of definition. Any definition can be misunderstood.

But it might well be asked: are we still to call this "definition"?—For, of course, even if it has the same practical consequences, the same *effect* on the learner, it plays a different part in the calculus from what we ordinarily call "ostensive definition" of the word "red".

you do not forget that all sorts of problems attach to the words "to know" or "to be clear".

One has already to know (or be able to do) something in order to be capable of asking a thing's name. But what does one have to know?

31. When one shews someone the king in chess and says: "This is the king", this does not tell him the use of this piece—unless he already knows the rules of the game up to this last point: the shape of the king. You could imagine his having learnt the rules of the game without ever having been shewn an actual piece. The shape of the chessman corresponds here to the sound or shape of a word.

One can also imagine someone's having learnt the game without ever learning or formulating rules. He might have learnt quite simple board-games first, by watching, and have progressed to more and more complicated ones. He too might be given the explanation "This is the king",—if, for instance, he were being shewn chessmen of a shape he was not used to. This explanation again only tells him the use of the piece because, as we might say, the place for it was already prepared. Or even: we shall only say that it tells him the use, if the place is already prepared. And in this case it is so, not because the person to whom we give the explanation already knows rules, but because in another sense he is already master of a game.

Consider this further case: I am explaining chess to someone; and I begin by pointing to a chessman and saying: "This is the king; it can move like this, ... and so on."—In this case we shall say: the words "This is the king" (or "This is called the 'king' ") are a definition only if the learner already 'knows what a piece in a game is'. That is, if he has already played other games, or has watched other people playing 'and understood'—*and similar things*. Further, only under these conditions will he be able to ask relevantly in the course of learning the game: "What do you call this?"—that is, this piece in a game.

We may say: only someone who already knows how to do something with it can significantly ask a name.

And we can imagine the person who is asked replying: "Settle the name yourself"—and now the one who asked would have to manage everything for himself.

32. Someone coming into a strange country will sometimes learn the language of the inhabitants from ostensive definitions that they give him; and he will often have to *guess* the meaning of these definitions; and will guess sometimes right, sometimes wrong.

And now, I think, we can say: Augustine describes the learning of human language as if the child came into a strange country and did not understand the language of the country; that is, as if it already had a language, only not this one. Or again: as if the child could already *think*, only not yet speak. And "think" would here mean something like "talk to itself".

33. Suppose, however, someone were to object: "It is not true that you must already be master of a language in order to understand an ostensive definition: all you need—of course!—is to know or guess what the person giving the explanation is pointing to. That is, whether for example to the shape of the object, or to its colour, or to its number, and so on."——And what does 'pointing to the shape', 'pointing to the colour' consist in? Point to a piece of paper.—And now point to its shape—now to its colour—now to its number (that sounds queer).—How did you do it?—You will say that you 'meant' a different thing each time you pointed. And if I ask how that is done, you will say you concentrated your attention on the colour, the shape, etc. But I ask again: how is *that* done?

Suppose someone points to a vase and says "Look at that marvellous blue—the shape isn't the point."—Or: "Look at the marvellous shape—the colour doesn't matter." Without doubt you will do something *different* when you act upon these two invitations. But do you always do the *same* thing when you direct your attention to the colour? Imagine various different cases. To indicate a few:

"Is this blue the same as the blue over there? Do you see any difference?"—

You are mixing paint and you say "It's hard to get the blue of this sky."

"It's turning fine, you can already see blue sky again."

"Look what different effects these two blues have."

"Do you see the blue book over there? Bring it here."

"This blue signal-light means . . . ."

"What's this blue called?—Is it 'indigo'?"

You sometimes attend to the colour by putting your hand up to keep the outline from view; or by not looking at the outline of the thing; sometimes by staring at the object and trying to remember where you saw that colour before.

You attend to the shape, sometimes by tracing it, sometimes by screwing up your eyes so as not to see the colour clearly, and in many other ways. I want to say: This is the sort of thing that happens *while* one 'directs one's attention to this or that'. But it isn't these things by themselves that make us say someone is attending to the shape, the colour, and so on. Just as a move in chess doesn't consist simply in moving a piece in such-and-such a way on the board—nor yet in one's thoughts and feelings as one makes the move: but in the circumstances that we call "playing a game of chess", "solving a chess problem", and so on.

34. But suppose someone said: "I always do the same thing when I attend to the shape: my eye follows the outline and I feel . . . .". And suppose this person to give someone else the ostensive definition "That is called a 'circle' ", pointing to a circular object and having all these experiences——cannot his hearer still interpret the definition differently, even though he sees the other's eyes following the outline, and even though he feels what the other feels? That is to say: this 'interpretation' may also consist in how he now makes use of the word; in what he points to, for example, when told: "Point to a circle".—For neither the expression "to intend the definition in such-and-such a way" nor the expression "to interpret the definition in such-and-such a way" stands for a process which accompanies the giving and hearing of the definition.

35. There are, of course, what can be called "characteristic experiences" of pointing to (e.g.) the shape. For example, following the outline with one's finger or with one's eyes as one points.—But *this* does not happen in all cases in which I 'mean the shape', and no more does any other one characteristic process occur in all these cases.— Besides, even if something of the sort did recur in all cases, it would still depend on the circumstances—that is, on what happened before and after the pointing—whether we should say "He pointed to the shape and not to the colour".

For the words "to point to the shape", "to mean the shape", and so on, are not used in the same way as *these*: "to point to this book (not to that one), "to point to the chair, not to the table", and so on.— Only think how differently we *learn* the use of the words "to point to this thing", "to point to that thing", and on the other hand "to point to the colour, not the shape", "to mean the colour", and so on.

To repeat: in certain cases, especially when one points 'to the shape' or 'to the number' there are characteristic experiences and ways of pointing—'characteristic' because they recur often (not always) when shape or number are 'meant'. But do you also know of an experience characteristic of pointing to a piece in a game *as a piece in a game*?

All the same one can say: "I mean that this *piece* is called the 'king', not this particular bit of wood I am pointing to". (Recognizing, wishing, remembering, etc. .)

36. And we do here what we do in a host of similar cases: because we cannot specify any *one* bodily action which we call pointing to the shape (as opposed, for example, to the colour), we say that a *spiritual* [mental, intellectual] activity corresponds to these words.

Where our language suggests a body and there is none: there, we should like to say, is a *spirit*.

37. What is the relation between name and thing named?—Well, what *is* it? Look at language-game (2) or at another one: there you can see the sort of thing this relation consists in. This relation may also consist, among many other things, in the fact that hearing the name calls before our mind the picture of what is named; and it also consists, among other things, in the name's being written on the thing named or being pronounced when that thing is pointed at.

38. But what, for example, is the word "this" the name of in language-game (8) or the word "that" in the ostensive definition "that is called . . . ."?—If you do not want to produce confusion you will do best not to call these words names at all.—Yet, strange to say, the word "this" has been called the only *genuine* name; so that anything else we call a name was one only in an inexact, approximate sense.

This queer conception springs from a tendency to sublime the logic of our language—as one might put it. The proper answer to it is: we call very different things "names"; the word "name" is used to

---

What is it to *mean* the words "*That* is blue" at one time as a statement about the object one is pointing to—at another as an explanation of the word "blue"? Well, in the second case one really means "That is called 'blue' ".—Then can one at one time mean the word "is" as "is called" and the word "blue" as " 'blue' ", and another time mean "is" really as "is"?

It is also possible for someone to get an explanation of the words out of what was intended as a piece of information. [Marginal note: Here lurks a crucial superstition.]

Can I say "bububu" and mean "If it doesn't rain I shall go for a walk"?—It is only in a language that I can mean something by something. This shews clearly that the grammar of "to mean" is not like that of the expression "to imagine" and the like.

characterize many different kinds of use of a word, related to one another in many different ways;—but the kind of use that "this" has is not among them.

It is quite true that, in giving an ostensive definition for instance, we often point to the object named and say the name. And similarly, in giving an ostensive definition for instance, we say the word "this" while pointing to a thing. And also the word "this" and a name often occupy the same position in a sentence. But it is precisely characteristic of a name that it is defined by means of the demonstrative expression "That is N" (or "That is called 'N' "). But do we also give the definitions: "That is called 'this' ", or "This is called 'this' "?

This is connected with the conception of naming as, so to speak, an occult process. Naming appears as a *queer* connexion of a word with an object.—And you really get such a queer connexion when the philosopher tries to bring out *the* relation between name and thing by staring at an object in front of him and repeating a name or even the word "this" innumerable times. For philosophical problems arise when language *goes on holiday*. And *here* we may indeed fancy naming to be some remarkable act of mind, as it were a baptism of an object. And we can also say the word "this" *to* the object, as it were *address* the object as "this"—a queer use of this word, which doubtless only occurs in doing philosophy.

39. But why does it occur to one to want to make precisely this word into a name, when it evidently is *not* a name?—That is just the reason. For one is tempted to make an objection against what is ordinarily called a name. It can be put like this: *a name ought really to signify a simple*. And for this one might perhaps give the following reasons: The word "Excalibur", say, is a proper name in the ordinary sense. The sword Excalibur consists of parts combined in a particular way. If they are combined differently Excalibur does not exist. But it is clear that the sentence "Excalibur has a sharp blade" makes *sense* whether Excalibur is still whole or is broken up. But if "Excalibur" is the name of an object, this object no longer exists when Excalibur is broken in pieces; and as no object would then correspond to the name it would have no meaning. But then the sentence "Excalibur has a sharp blade" would contain a word that had no meaning, and hence the sentence would be nonsense. But it does make sense; so there must always be something corresponding to the words of which it consists. So the word "Excalibur" must disappear when the sense is

analysed and its place be taken by words which name simples. It will be reasonable to call these words the real names.

40. Let us first discuss *this* point of the argument: that a word has no meaning if nothing corresponds to it.—It is important to note that the word "meaning" is being used illicitly if it is used to signify the thing that 'corresponds' to the word. That is to confound the meaning of a name with the *bearer* of the name. When Mr. N. N. dies one says that the bearer of the name dies, not that the meaning dies. And it would be nonsensical to say that, for if the name ceased to have meaning it would make no sense to say "Mr. N. N. is dead."

41. In §15 we introduced proper names into language (8). Now suppose that the tool with the name "N" is broken. Not knowing this, A gives B the sign "N". Has this sign meaning now or not?— What is B to do when he is given it?—We have not settled anything about this. One might ask: what *will* he do? Well, perhaps he will stand there at a loss, or shew A the pieces. Here one *might* say: "N" has become meaningless; and this expression would mean that the sign "N" no longer had a use in our language-game (unless we gave it a new one). "N" might also become meaningless because, for whatever reason, the tool was given another name and the sign "N" no longer used in the language-game.—But we could also imagine a convention whereby B has to shake his head in reply if A gives him the sign belonging to a tool that is broken.—In this way the command "N" might be said to be given a place in the language-game even when the tool no longer exists, and the sign "N" to have meaning even when its bearer ceases to exist.

42. But has for instance a name which has *never* been used for a tool also got a meaning in that game?——Let us assume that "X" is such a sign and that A gives this sign to B—well, even such signs could be given a place in the language-game, and B might have, say, to answer them too with a shake of the head. (One could imagine this as a sort of joke between them.)

43. For a *large* class of cases—though not for all—in which we employ the word "meaning" it can be defined thus: the meaning of a word is its use in the language.

And the *meaning* of a name is sometimes explained by pointing to its *bearer*.

44. We said that the sentence "Excalibur has a sharp blade" made sense even when Excalibur was broken in pieces. Now this is so because in this language-game a name is also used in the absence of its bearer. But we can imagine a language-game with names (that is, with signs which we should certainly include among names) in which they are used only in the presence of the bearer; and so could *always* be replaced by a demonstrative pronoun and the gesture of pointing.

45. The demonstrative "this" can never be without a bearer. It might be said: "so long as there is a *this*, the word 'this' has a meaning too, whether *this* is simple or complex."——But that does not make the word into a name. On the contrary: for a name is not used with, but only explained by means of, the gesture of pointing.

46. What lies behind the idea that names really signify simples?——
Socrates says in the Theaetetus: "If I make no mistake, I have heard some people say this: there is no definition of the primary elements—so to speak—out of which we and everything else are composed; for everything that exists[1] in its own right can only be *named*, no other determination is possible, neither that it *is* nor that it *is not* . . . . . But what exists[1] in its own right has to be . . . . . named without any other determination. In consequence it is impossible to give an account of any primary element; for it, nothing is possible but the bare name; its name is all it has. But just as what consists of these primary elements is itself complex, so the names of the elements become descriptive language by being compounded together. For the essence of speech is the composition of names."
Both Russell's 'individuals' and my 'objects' (*Tractatus Logico-Philosophicus*) were such primary elements.

47. But what are the simple constituent parts of which reality is composed?—What are the simple constituent parts of a chair?—The bits of wood of which it is made? Or the molecules, or the atoms?—"Simple" means: not composite. And here the point is: in what sense 'composite'? It makes no sense at all to speak absolutely of the 'simple parts of a chair'.

---

[1] I have translated the German translation which Wittgenstein used rather than the original. Tr.

Again: Does my visual image of this tree, of this chair, consist of parts? And what are its simple component parts? Multi-colouredness is one kind of complexity; another is, for example, that of a broken outline composed of straight bits. And a curve can be said to be composed of an ascending and a descending segment.

If I tell someone without any further explanation: "What I see before me now is composite", he will have the right to ask: "What do you mean by 'composite'? For there are all sorts of things that that can mean!"—The question "Is what you see composite?" makes good sense if it is already established what kind of complexity—that is, which particular use of the word—is in question. If it had been laid down that the visual image of a tree was to be called "composite" if one saw not just a single trunk, but also branches, then the question "Is the visual image of this tree simple or composite?", and the question "What are its simple component parts?", would have a clear sense—a clear use. And of course the answer to the second question is not "The branches" (that would be an answer to the *grammatical* question: "What are here called 'simple component parts'?") but rather a description of the individual branches.

But isn't a chessboard, for instance, obviously, and absolutely, composite?—You are probably thinking of the composition out of thirty-two white and thirty-two black squares. But could we not also say, for instance, that it was composed of the colours black and white and the schema of squares? And if there are quite different ways of looking at it, do you still want to say that the chessboard is absolutely 'composite'?—Asking "Is this object composite?" *outside* a particular language-game is like what a boy once did, who had to say whether the verbs in certain sentences were in the active or passive voice, and who racked his brains over the question whether the verb "to sleep" meant something active or passive.

We use the word "composite" (and therefore the word "simple") in an enormous number of different and differently related ways. (Is the colour of a square on a chessboard simple, or does it consist of pure white and pure yellow? And is white simple, or does it consist of the colours of the rainbow?—Is this length of 2 cm. simple, or does it consist of two parts, each 1 cm. long? But why not of one bit 3 cm. long, and one bit 1 cm. long measured in the opposite direction?)

To the *philosophical* question: "Is the visual image of this tree composite, and what are its component parts?" the correct answer is: "That depends on what you understand by 'composite'." (And that is of course not an answer but a rejection of the question.)

48. Let us apply the method of §2 to the account in the *Theaetetus*. Let us consider a language-game for which this account is really valid. The language serves to describe combinations of coloured squares on a surface. The squares form a complex like a chessboard. There are red, green, white and black squares. The words of the language are (correspondingly) "R", "G", "W", "B", and a sentence is a series of these words. They describe an arrangement of squares in the order:

1	2	3
4	5	6
7	8	9

And so for instance the sentence "RRBGGGRWW" describes an arrangement of this sort:

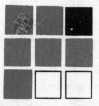

Here the sentence is a complex of names, to which corresponds a complex of elements. The primary elements are the coloured squares. "But are these simple?"—I do not know what else you would have me call "the simples", what would be more natural in this language-game. But under other circumstances I should call a monochrome square "composite", consisting perhaps of two rectangles, or of the elements colour and shape. But the concept of complexity might also be so extended that a smaller area was said to be 'composed' of a greater area and another one subtracted from it. Compare the 'composition of forces', the 'division' of a line by a point outside it; these expressions shew that we are sometimes even inclined to conceive the smaller as the result of a composition of greater parts, and the greater as the result of a division of the smaller.

But I do not know whether to say that the figure described by our sentence consists of four or of nine elements! Well, does the sentence consist of four letters or of nine?—And which are *its* elements, the types of letter, or the letters? Does it matter which we say, so long as we avoid misunderstandings in any particular case?

49. But what does it mean to say that we cannot define (that is, describe) these elements, but only name them? This might mean, for instance, that when in a limiting case a complex consists of only *one* square, its description is simply the name of the coloured square.

Here we might say—though this easily leads to all kinds of philosophical superstition—that a sign "R" or "B", etc. may be sometimes a word and sometimes a proposition. But whether it 'is a word or a proposition' depends on the situation in which it is uttered or written. For instance, if A has to describe complexes of coloured squares to B and he uses the word "R" *alone*, we shall be able to say that the word is a description—a proposition. But if he is memorizing the words and their meanings, or if he is teaching someone else the use of the words and uttering them in the course of ostensive teaching, we shall not say that they are propositions. In this situation the word "R", for instance, is not a description; it *names* an element——but it would be queer to make that a reason for saying that an element can *only* be named! For naming and describing do not stand on the same level: naming is a preparation for description. Naming is so far not a move in the language-game—any more than putting a piece in its place on the board is a move in chess. We may say: *nothing* has so far been done, when a thing has been named. It has not even *got* a name except in the language-game. This was what Frege meant too, when he said that a word had meaning only as part of a sentence.

50. What does it mean to say that we can attribute neither being nor non-being to elements?—One might say: if everything that we call "being" and "non-being" consists in the existence and non-existence of connexions between elements, it makes no sense to speak of an element's being (non-being); just as when everything that we call "destruction" lies in the separation of elements, it makes no sense to speak of the destruction of an element.

One would, however, like to say: existence cannot be attributed to an element, for if it did not *exist*, one could not even name it and so one could say nothing at all of it.—But let us consider an analogous case. There is *one* thing of which one can say neither that it is one metre long, nor that it is not one metre long, and that is the standard metre in Paris.—But this is, of course, not to ascribe any extraordinary property to it, but only to mark its peculiar role in the language-game of measuring with a metre-rule.—Let us imagine samples of colour being preserved in Paris like the standard metre. We define: "sepia" means the colour of the standard sepia which is there kept hermetically sealed. Then it will make no sense to say of this sample either that it is of this colour or that it is not.

We can put it like this: This sample is an instrument of the language used in ascriptions of colour. In this language-game it is not something that is represented, but is a means of representation.—And just this goes for an element in language-game (48) when we name it by uttering the word "R": this gives this object a role in our language-game; it is now a *means* of representation. And to say "If it did not *exist*, it could have no name" is to say as much and as little as: if this thing did not exist, we could not use it in our language-game.—What looks as if it *had* to exist, is part of the language. It is a paradigm in our language-game; something with which comparison is made. And this may be an important observation; but it is none the less an observation concerning our language-game—our method of representation.

51. In describing language-game (48) I said that the words "R", "B", etc. corresponded to the colours of the squares. But what does this correspondence consist in; in what sense can one say that certain colours of squares correspond to these signs? For the account in (48) merely set up a connexion between those signs and certain words of our language (the names of colours).—Well, it was presupposed that the use of the signs in the language-game would be taught in a different way, in particular by pointing to paradigms. Very well; but what does it mean to say that in the *technique of using the language* certain elements correspond to the signs?—Is it that the person who is describing the complexes of coloured squares always says "R" where there is a red square; "B" when there is a black one, and so on? But what if he goes wrong in the description and mistakenly says "R" where he sees a black square——what is the criterion by which this is a *mistake*?— Or does "R"'s standing for a red square consist in this, that when the

people whose language it is use the sign "R" a red square always comes before their minds?

In order to see more clearly, here as in countless similar cases, we must focus on the details of what goes on; must look at them *from close to*.

52.   If I am inclined to suppose that a mouse has come into being by spontaneous generation out of grey rags and dust, I shall do well to examine those rags very closely to see how a mouse may have hidden in them, how it may have got there and so on. But if I am convinced that a mouse cannot come into being from these things, then this investigation will perhaps be superfluous.

But first we must learn to understand what it is that opposes such an examination of details in philosophy.

53.   Our language-game (48) has *various* possibilities; there is a variety of cases in which we should say that a sign in the game was the name of a square of such-and-such a colour. We should say so if, for instance, we knew that the people who used the language were taught the use of the signs in such-and-such a way. Or if it were set down in writing, say in the form of a table, that this element corresponded to this sign, and if the table were used in teaching the language and were appealed to in certain disputed cases.

We can also imagine such a table's being a tool in the use of the language. Describing a complex is then done like this: the person who describes the complex has a table with him and looks up each element of the complex in it and passes from this to the sign (and the one who is given the description may also use a table to translate it into a picture of coloured squares). This table might be said to take over here the role of memory and association in other cases. (We do not usually carry out the order "Bring me a red flower" by looking up the colour red in a table of colours and then bringing a flower of the colour that we find in the table; but when it is a question of choosing or mixing a particular shade of red, we do sometimes make use of a sample or table.)

If we call such a table the expression of a rule of the language-game, it can be said that what we call a rule of a language-game may have very different roles in the game.

54.   Let us recall the kinds of case where we say that a game is played according to a definite rule.

The rule may be an aid in teaching the game. The learner is told it and given practice in applying it.—Or it is an instrument of the game itself.—Or a rule is employed neither in the teaching nor in the game itself; nor is it set down in a list of rules. One learns the game by watching how others play. But we say that it is played according to such-and-such rules because an observer can read these rules off from the practice of the game—like a natural law governing the play.—— But how does the observer distinguish in this case between players' mistakes and correct play?—There are characteristic signs of it in the players' behaviour. Think of the behaviour characteristic of correcting a slip of the tongue. It would be possible to recognize that someone was doing so even without knowing his language.

55. "What the names in language signify must be indestructible; for it must be possible to describe the state of affairs in which everything destructible is destroyed. And this description will contain words; and what corresponds to these cannot then be destroyed, for otherwise the words would have no meaning." I must not saw off the branch on which I am sitting.

One might, of course, object at once that this description would have to except itself from the destruction.—But what corresponds to the separate words of the description and so cannot be destroyed if it is true, is what gives the words their meaning—is that without which they would have no meaning.——In a sense, however, this man is surely what corresponds to his name. But he is destructible, and his name does not lose its meaning when the bearer is destroyed.—An example of something corresponding to the name, and without which it would have no meaning, is a paradigm that is used in connexion with the name in the language-game.

56. But what if no such sample is part of the language, and we *bear in mind* the colour (for instance) that a word stands for?——"And if we bear it in mind then it comes before our mind's eye when we utter the word. So, if it is always supposed to be possible for us to remember it, it must be in itself indestructible."——But what do we regard as the criterion for remembering it right?—When we work with a sample instead of our memory there are circumstances in which we say that the sample has changed colour and we judge of this by memory. But can we not sometimes speak of a darkening (for example) of our memory-image? Aren't we as much at the mercy of memory as of a sample? (For someone might feel like saying: "If we

had no memory we should be at the mercy of a sample".)—Or perhaps of some chemical reaction. Imagine that you were supposed to paint a particular colour "C", which was the colour that appeared when the chemical substances X and Y combined.—Suppose that the colour struck you as brighter on one day than on another; would you not sometimes say: "I must be wrong, the colour is certainly the same as yesterday"? This shews that we do not always resort to what memory tells us as the verdict of the highest court of appeal.

57. "Something red can be destroyed, but red cannot be destroyed, and that is why the meaning of the word 'red' is independent of the existence of a red thing."—Certainly it makes no sense to say that the colour red is torn up or pounded to bits. But don't we say "The red is vanishing"? And don't clutch at the idea of our always being able to bring red before our mind's eye even when there is nothing red any more. That is just as if you chose to say that there would still always be a chemical reaction producing a red flame.—For suppose you cannot remember the colour any more?—When we forget which colour this is the name of, it loses its meaning for us; that is, we are no longer able to play a particular language-game with it. And the situation then is comparable with that in which we have lost a paradigm which was an instrument of our language.

58. "I want to restrict the term 'name' to what cannot occur in the combination 'X exists'.—Thus one cannot say 'Red exists', because if there were no red it could not be spoken of at all."—Better: If "X exists" is meant simply to say: "X" has a meaning,—then it is not a proposition which treats of X, but a proposition about our use of language, that is, about the use of the word "X".

It looks to us as if we were saying something about the nature of red in saying that the words "Red exists" do not yield a sense. Namely that red does exist 'in its own right'. The same idea—that this is a metaphysical statement about red—finds expression again when we say such a thing as that red is timeless, and perhaps still more strongly in the word "indestructible".

But what we really *want* is simply to take "Red exists" as the statement: the word "red" has a meaning. Or perhaps better: "Red does not exist" as " 'Red' has no meaning". Only we do not want to say that that expression *says* this, but that *this* is what it would have to be saying *if* it meant anything. But that it contradicts itself in the attempt to say it—just because red exists 'in its own right'. Whereas the only contradiction lies in something like this: the proposition looks as if it were about the colour, while it is supposed to be saying something about the use of the word "red".—In reality, however, we quite readily say that a particular colour exists; and that is as much as to say that something exists that has that colour. And the first expression is no less accurate than the second; particularly where 'what has the colour' is not a physical object.

59. "A *name* signifies only what is an *element* of reality. What cannot be destroyed; what remains the same in all changes."—But what is that?—Why, it swam before our minds as we said the sentence! This was the very expression of a quite particular image: of a particular picture which we want to use. For certainly experience does not shew us these elements. We see *component parts* of something composite (of a chair, for instance). We say that the back is part of the chair, but is in turn itself composed of several bits of wood; while a leg is a simple component part. We also see a whole which changes (is destroyed) while its component parts remain unchanged. These are the materials from which we construct that picture of reality.

60. When I say: "My broom is in the corner",—is this really a statement about the broomstick and the brush? Well, it could at any rate be replaced by a statement giving the position of the stick and the position of the brush. And this statement is surely a further analysed form of the first one.—But why do I call it "further analysed"?— Well, if the broom is there, that surely means that the stick and brush must be there, and in a particular relation to one another; and this was as it were hidden in the sense of the first sentence, and is *expressed* in the analysed sentence. Then does someone who says that the broom is in the corner really mean: the broomstick is there, and so is the brush, and the broomstick is fixed in the brush?—If we were to ask anyone if he meant this he would probably say that he had not thought specially of the broomstick or specially of the brush at all. And that would be the *right* answer, for he meant to speak neither of the stick nor of the brush in particular. Suppose that, instead of saying "Bring me the broom", you said "Bring me the broomstick and the brush which is fitted on to it."!—Isn't the answer: "Do you want the broom? Why do you put it so oddly?"——Is he going to understand the further analysed sentence better?—This sentence, one might say, achieves the same as the ordinary one, but in a more roundabout way.—

Imagine a language-game in which someone is ordered to bring certain objects which are composed of several parts, to move them about, or something else of the kind. And two ways of playing it: in one (a) the composite objects (brooms, chairs, tables, etc.) have names, as in (15); in the other (b) only the parts are given names and the wholes are described by means of them.—In what sense is an order in the second game an analysed form of an order in the first? Does the former lie concealed in the latter, and is it now brought out by analysis?— True, the broom is taken to pieces when one separates broomstick and brush; but does it follow that the order to bring the broom also consists of corresponding parts?

61. "But all the same you will not deny that a particular order in (a) means the same as one in (b); and what would you call the second one, if not an analysed form of the first?"—Certainly I too should say that an order in (a) had the same meaning as one in (b); or, as I expressed it earlier: they achieve the same. And this means that if I were shewn an order in (a) and asked: "Which order in (b) means the same as this?" or again "Which order in (b) does this contradict?" I should give such-and-such an answer. But that is not to say that we have come to a *general* agreement about the use of the expression "to have the same meaning" or "to achieve the same". For it can be asked in what cases we say: "These are merely two forms of the same game."

62. Suppose for instance that the person who is given the orders in (a) and (b) has to look up a table co-ordinating names and pictures before bringing what is required. Does he do *the same* when he carries out an order in (a) and the corresponding one in (b)?—Yes and no. You may say: "The *point* of the two orders is the same". I should say so too.—But it is not everywhere clear what should be called the 'point' of an order. (Similarly one may say of certain objects that they have this or that purpose. The essential thing is that this is a *lamp*, that it serves to give light;——that it is an ornament to the room, fills an empty space, etc., is not essential. But there is not always a sharp distinction between essential and inessential.)

63. To say, however, that a sentence in (b) is an 'analysed' form of one in (a) readily seduces us into thinking that the former is the more fundamental form; that it alone shews what is meant by the other, and so on. For example, we think: If you have only the unanalysed form you miss the analysis; but if you know the analysed form that

gives you everything.—But can I not say that an aspect of the matter is lost on you in the *latter* case as well as the former?

64. Let us imagine language game (48) altered so that names signify not monochrome squares but rectangles each consisting of two such squares. Let such a rectangle, which is half red half green, be called "U"; a half green half white one, "V"; and so on. Could we not imagine people who had names for such combinations of colour, but not for the individual colours? Think of the cases where we say: "This arrangement of colours (say the French tricolor) has a quite special character."

In what sense do the symbols of this language-game stand in need of analysis? How far is it even *possible* to replace this language-game by (48)?—It is just *another* language-game; even though it is related to (48).

65. Here we come up against the great question that lies behind all these considerations.—For someone might object against me: "You take the easy way out! You talk about all sorts of language-games, but have nowhere said what the essence of a language-game, and hence of language, is: what is common to all these activities, and what makes them into language or parts of language. So you let yourself off the very part of the investigation that once gave you yourself most headache, the part about the *general form of propositions* and of language."

And this is true.—Instead of producing something common to all that we call language, I am saying that these phenomena have no one thing in common which makes us use the same word for all,—but that they are *related* to one another in many different ways. And it is because of this relationship, or these relationships, that we call them all "language". I will try to explain this.

66. Consider for example the proceedings that we call "games". I mean board-games, card-games, ball-games, Olympic games, and so on. What is common to them all?—Don't say: "There *must* be something common, or they would not be called 'games' "—but *look and see* whether there is anything common to all.—For if you look at them you will not see something that is common to *all*, but similarities, relationships, and a whole series of them at that. To repeat: don't think, but look!—Look for example at board-games, with their multifarious relationships. Now pass to card-games; here you find many correspondences with the first group, but many common

features drop out, and others appear. When we pass next to ball-games, much that is common is retained, but much is lost.—Are they all 'amusing'? Compare chess with noughts and crosses. Or is there always winning and losing, or competition between players? Think of patience. In ball games there is winning and losing; but when a child throws his ball at the wall and catches it again, this feature has disappeared. Look at the parts played by skill and luck; and at the difference between skill in chess and skill in tennis. Think now of games like ring-a-ring-a-roses; here is the element of amusement, but how many other characteristic features have disappeared! And we can go through the many, many other groups of games in the same way; can see how similarities crop up and disappear.

And the result of this examination is: we see a complicated network of similarities overlapping and criss-crossing: sometimes overall similarities, sometimes similarities of detail.

67. I can think of no better expression to characterize these similarities than "family resemblances"; for the various resemblances between members of a family: build, features, colour of eyes, gait, temperament, etc. etc. overlap and criss-cross in the same way.—And I shall say: 'games' form a family.

And for instance the kinds of number form a family in the same way. Why do we call something a "number"? Well, perhaps because it has a—direct—relationship with several things that have hitherto been called number; and this can be said to give it an indirect relationship to other things we call the same name. And we extend our concept of number as in spinning a thread we twist fibre on fibre. And the strength of the thread does not reside in the fact that some one fibre runs through its whole length, but in the overlapping of many fibres.

But if someone wished to say: "There is something common to all these constructions—namely the disjunction of all their common properties"—I should reply: Now you are only playing with words. One might as well say: "Something runs through the whole thread—namely the continuous overlapping of those fibres".

68. "All right: the concept of number is defined for you as the logical sum of these individual interrelated concepts: cardinal numbers, rational numbers, real numbers, etc.; and in the same way the concept of a game as the logical sum of a corresponding set of sub-concepts."——It need not be so. For I *can* give the concept 'number' rigid limits

in this way, that is, use the word "number" for a rigidly limited concept, but I can also use it so that the extension of the concept is *not* closed by a frontier. And this is how we do use the word "game". For how is the concept of a game bounded? What still counts as a game and what no longer does? Can you give the boundary? No. You can *draw* one; for none has so far been drawn. (But that never troubled you before when you used the word "game".)

"But then the use of the word is unregulated, the 'game' we play with it is unregulated."——It is not everywhere circumscribed by rules; but no more are there any rules for how high one throws the ball in tennis, or how hard; yet tennis is a game for all that and has rules too.

69. How should we explain to someone what a game is? I imagine that we should describe *games* to him, and we might add: "This *and similar things* are called 'games' ". And do we know any more about it ourselves? Is it only other people whom we cannot tell exactly what a game is?—But this is not ignorance. We do not know the boundaries because none have been drawn. To repeat, we can draw a boundary—for a special purpose. Does it take that to make the concept usable? Not at all! (Except for that special purpose.) No more than it took the definition: 1 pace = 75 cm. to make the measure of length 'one pace' usable. And if you want to say "But still, before that it wasn't an exact measure", then I reply: very well, it was an inexact one.—Though you still owe me a definition of exactness.

70. "But if the concept 'game' is uncircumscribed like that, you don't really know what you mean by a 'game'."——When I give the description: "The ground was quite covered with plants"—do you want to say I don't know what I am talking about until I can give a definition of a plant?

My meaning would be explained by, say, a drawing and the words "The ground looked roughly like this". Perhaps I even say "it looked *exactly* like this."—Then were just *this* grass and *these* leaves there, arranged just like this? No, that is not what it means. And I should not accept any picture as exact in *this* sense.

Someone says to me: "Shew the children a game." I teach them gaming with dice, and the other says "I didn't mean that sort of game." Must the exclusion of the game with dice have come before his mind when he gave me the order?

71.   One might say that the concept 'game' is a concept with blurred edges.—"But is a blurred concept a concept at all?"—Is an indistinct photograph a picture of a person at all? Is it even always an advantage to replace an indistinct picture by a sharp one? Isn't the indistinct one often exactly what we need?

Frege compares a concept to an area and says that an area with vague boundaries cannot be called an area at all. This presumably means that we cannot do anything with it.—But is it senseless to say: "Stand roughly there"? Suppose that I were standing with someone in a city square and said that. As I say it I do not draw any kind of boundary, but perhaps point with my hand—as if I were indicating a particular *spot*. And this is just how one might explain to someone what a game is. One gives examples and intends them to be taken in a particular way.—I do not, however, mean by this that he is supposed to see in those examples that common thing which I—for some reason—was unable to express; but that he is now to *employ* those examples in a particular way. Here giving examples is not an *indirect* means of explaining—in default of a better. For any general definition can be misunderstood too. The point is that *this* is how we play the game. (I mean the language-game with the word "game".)

72.   *Seeing what is common.* Suppose I shew someone various multi-coloured pictures, and say: "The colour you see in all these is called 'yellow ochre' ".—This is a definition, and the other will get to understand it by looking for and seeing what is common to the pictures. Then he can look *at*, can point *to*, the common thing.

Compare with this a case in which I shew him figures of different shapes all painted the same colour, and say: "What these have in common is called 'yellow ochre' ".

And compare this case: I shew him samples of different shades of blue and say: "The colour that is common to all these is what I call 'blue' ".

73.   When someone defines the names of colours for me by pointing to samples and saying "This colour is called 'blue', this 'green' . . . . . " this case can be compared in many respects to putting a table in my hands, with the words written under the colour-samples.— Though this comparison may mislead in many ways.—One is now inclined to extend the comparison: to have understood the definition means to have in one's mind an idea of the thing defined, and that is a sample or picture. So if I am shewn various different leaves and told

"This is called a 'leaf' ", I get an idea of the shape of a leaf, a picture
of it in my mind.—But what does the picture of a leaf look like
when it does not shew us any particular shape, but 'what is common
to all shapes of leaf'? Which shade is the 'sample in my mind' of the
colour green—the sample of what is common to all shades of green?

"But might there not be such 'general' samples? Say a schematic
leaf, or a sample of *pure* green?"—Certainly there might. But for
such a schema to be understood as a *schema*, and not as the shape of a
particular leaf, and for a slip of pure green to be understood as a
sample of all that is greenish and not as a sample of pure green—this
in turn resides in the way the samples are used.

Ask yourself: what *shape* must the sample of the colour green be?
Should it be rectangular? Or would it then be the sample of a green
rectangle?—So should it be 'irregular' in shape? And what is to
prevent us then from regarding it—that is, from using it—only as a
sample of irregularity of shape?

74. Here also belongs the idea that if you see this leaf as a sample
of 'leaf shape in general' you *see* it differently from someone who
regards it as, say, a sample of this particular shape. Now this might
well be so—though it is not so—for it would only be to say that, as a
matter of experience, if you *see* the leaf in a particular way, you use it
in such-and-such a way or according to such-and-such rules. Of course,
there is such a thing as seeing in *this* way or *that*; and there are also
cases where whoever sees a sample like *this* will in general use it in
this way, and whoever sees it otherwise in another way. For example,
if you see the schematic drawing of a cube as a plane figure consisting
of a square and two rhombi you will, perhaps, carry out the order
"Bring me something like this" differently from someone who sees
the picture three-dimensionally.

75. What does it mean to know what a game is? What does it
mean, to know it and not be able to say it? Is this knowledge somehow equivalent to an unformulated definition? So that if it were
formulated I should be able to recognize it as the expression of my
knowledge? Isn't my knowledge, my concept of a game, completely
expressed in the explanations that I could give? That is, in my describing examples of various kinds of game; shewing how all sorts of other
games can be constructed on the analogy of these; saying that I should
scarcely include this or this among games; and so on.

76. If someone were to draw a sharp boundary I could not acknowledge it as the one that I too always wanted to draw, or had drawn in my mind. For I did not want to draw one at all. His concept can then be said to be not the same as mine, but akin to it. The kinship is that of two pictures, one of which consists of colour patches with vague contours, and the other of patches similarly shaped and distributed, but with clear contours. The kinship is just as undeniable as the difference.

77. And if we carry this comparison still further it is clear that the degree to which the sharp picture *can* resemble the blurred one depends on the latter's degree of vagueness. For imagine having to sketch a sharply defined picture 'corresponding' to a blurred one. In the latter there is a blurred red rectangle: for it you put down a sharply defined one. Of course—several such sharply defined rectangles can be drawn to correspond to the indefinite one.—But if the colours in the original merge without a hint of any outline won't it become a hopeless task to draw a sharp picture corresponding to the blurred one? Won't you then have to say: "Here I might just as well draw a circle or heart as a rectangle, for all the colours merge. Anything—and nothing—is right."——And this is the position you are in if you look for definitions corresponding to our concepts in aesthetics or ethics.

In such a difficulty always ask yourself: How did we *learn* the meaning of this word ("good" for instance)? From what sort of examples? in what language-games? Then it will be easier for you to see that the word must have a family of meanings.

78. Compare *knowing* and *saying*:
  how many feet high Mont Blanc is—
  how the word "game" is used—
  how a clarinet sounds.

If you are surprised that one can know something and not be able to say it, you are perhaps thinking of a case like the first. Certainly not of one like the third.

79. Consider this example. If one says "Moses did not exist", this may mean various things. It may mean: the Israelites did not have a *single* leader when they withdrew from Egypt——or: their leader was not called Moses——or: there cannot have been anyone who accomplished all that the Bible relates of Moses——or: etc. etc.—— We may say, following Russell: the name "Moses" can be defined by

means of various descriptions. For example, as "the man who led the Israelites through the wilderness", "the man who lived at that time and place and was then called 'Moses' ", "the man who as a child was taken out of the Nile by Pharaoh's daughter" and so on. And according as we assume one definition or another the proposition "Moses did not exist" acquires a different sense, and so does every other proposition about Moses.—And if we are told "N did not exist", we do ask: "What do you mean? Do you want to say . . . . . . or . . . . . . etc.?"

But when I make a statement about Moses,—am I always ready to substitute some *one* of these descriptions for "Moses"? I shall perhaps say: By "Moses" I understand the man who did what the Bible relates of Moses, or at any rate a good deal of it. But how much? Have I decided how much must be proved false for me to give up my proposition as false? Has the name "Moses" got a fixed and unequivocal use for me in all possible cases?—Is it not the case that I have, so to speak, a whole series of props in readiness, and am ready to lean on one if another should be taken from under me and vice versa?——Consider another case. When I say "N is dead", then something like the following may hold for the meaning of the name "N": I believe that a human being has lived, whom I (1) have seen in such-and-such places, who (2) looked like this (pictures), (3) has done such-and-such things, and (4) bore the name "N" in social life.—Asked what I understand by "N", I should enumerate all or some of these points, and different ones on different occasions. So my definition of "N" would perhaps be "the man of whom all this is true".—But if some point now proves false?—Shall I be prepared to declare the proposition "N is dead" false—even if it is only something which strikes me as incidental that has turned out false? But where are the bounds of the incidental?— If I had given a definition of the name in such a case, I should now be ready to alter it.

And this can be expressed like this: I use the name "N" without a *fixed* meaning. (But that detracts as little from its usefulness, as it detracts from that of a table that it stands on four legs instead of three and so sometimes wobbles.)

Should it be said that I am using a word whose meaning I don't know, and so am talking nonsense?—Say what you choose, so long as it does not prevent you from seeing the facts. (And when you see them there is a good deal that you will not say.)

(The fluctuation of scientific definitions: what to-day counts as an observed concomitant of a phenomenon will to-morrow be used to define it.)

80. I say "There is a chair". What if I go up to it, meaning to fetch it, and it suddenly disappears from sight?——"So it wasn't a chair, but some kind of illusion".——But in a few moments we see it again and are able to touch it and so on.——"So the chair was there after all and its disappearance was some kind of illusion".——But suppose that after a time it disappears again—or seems to disappear. What are we to say now? Have you rules ready for such cases—rules saying whether one may use the word "chair" to include this kind of thing? But do we miss them when we use the word "chair"; and are we to say that we do not really attach any meaning to this word, because we are not equipped with rules for every possible application of it?

81. F. P. Ramsey once emphasized in conversation with me that logic was a 'normative science'. I do not know exactly what he had in mind, but it was doubtless closely related to what only dawned on me later: namely, that in philosophy we often *compare* the use of words with games and calculi which have fixed rules, but cannot say that someone who is using language *must* be playing such a game.—— But if you say that our languages only *approximate* to such calculi you are standing on the very brink of a misunderstanding. For then it may look as if what we were talking about were an *ideal* language. As if our logic were, so to speak, a logic for a vacuum.—Whereas logic does not treat of language—or of thought—in the sense in which a natural science treats of a natural phenomenon, and the most that can be said is that we *construct* ideal languages. But here the word "ideal" is liable to mislead, for it sounds as if these languages were better, more perfect, than our everyday language; and as if it took the logician to shew people at last what a proper sentence looked like.

All this, however, can only appear in the right light when one has attained greater clarity about the concepts of understanding, meaning, and thinking. For it will then also become clear what can lead us (and did lead me) to think that if anyone utters a sentence and *means* or *understands* it he is operating a calculus according to definite rules.

82. What do I call 'the rule by which he proceeds'?—The hypothesis that satisfactorily describes his use of words, which we observe; or the rule which he looks up when he uses signs; or the one which he

gives us in reply if we ask him what his rule is?—But what if observation does not enable us to see any clear rule, and the question brings none to light?—For he did indeed give me a definition when I asked him what he understood by "N", but he was prepared to withdraw and alter it.—So how am I to determine the rule according to which he is playing? He does not know it himself.—Or, to ask a better question: What meaning is the expression "the rule by which he proceeds" supposed to have left to it here?

83.   Doesn't the analogy between language and games throw light here? We can easily imagine people amusing themselves in a field by playing with a ball so as to start various existing games, but playing many without finishing them and in between throwing the ball aimlessly into the air, chasing one another with the ball and bombarding one another for a joke and so on. And now someone says: The whole time they are playing a ball-game and following definite rules at every throw.

And is there not also the case where we play and—make up the rules as we go along? And there is even one where we alter them—as we go along.

84.   I said that the application of a word is not everywhere bounded by rules. But what does a game look like that is everywhere bounded by rules? whose rules never let a doubt creep in, but stop up all the cracks where it might?—Can't we imagine a rule determining the application of a rule, and a doubt which *it* removes—and so on?

But that is not to say that we are in doubt because it is possible for us to *imagine* a doubt. I can easily imagine someone always doubting before he opened his front door whether an abyss did not yawn behind it, and making sure about it before he went through the door (and he might on some occasion prove to be right)—but that does not make me doubt in the same case.

85.   A rule stands there like a sign-post.—Does the sign-post leave no doubt open about the way I have to go? Does it shew which direction I am to take when I have passed it; whether along the road or the footpath or cross-country? But where is it said which way I am to follow it; whether in the direction of its finger or (e.g.) in the opposite one?—And if there were, not a single sign-post, but a chain of adjacent ones or of chalk marks on the ground—is there only *one* way of interpreting them?—So I can say, the sign-post does after all

leave no room for doubt. Or rather: it sometimes leaves room for
doubt and sometimes not. And now this is no longer a philosophical
proposition, but an empirical one.

86. Imagine a language-game like (2) played with the help of a
table. The signs given to B by A are now written ones. B has a
table; in the first column are the signs used in the game, in the second
pictures of building stones. A shews B such a written sign; B looks it
up in the table, looks at the picture opposite, and so on. So the table is a
rule which he follows in executing orders.—One learns to look the
picture up in the table by receiving a training, and part of this training
consists perhaps in the pupil's learning to pass with his finger hori-
zontally from left to right; and so, as it were, to draw a series of
horizontal lines on the table.

Suppose different ways of reading a table were now introduced;
one time, as above, according to the schema:

another time like this:

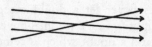

or in some other way.—Such a schema is supplied with the table as
the rule for its use.

Can we not now imagine further rules to explain *this* one? And, on
the other hand, was that first table incomplete without the schema of
arrows? And are other tables incomplete without their schemata?

87. Suppose I give this explanation: "I take 'Moses' to mean the
man, if there was such a man, who led the Israelites out of Egypt,
whatever he was called then and whatever he may or may not have
done besides."—But similar doubts to those about "Moses" are
possible about the words of this explanation (what are you calling
"Egypt", whom the "Israelites" etc.?). Nor would these questions
come to an end when we got down to words like "red", "dark",
"sweet".—"But then how does an explanation help me to under-

stand, if after all it is not the final one? In that case the explanation is never completed; so I still don't understand what he means, and never shall!"—As though an explanation as it were hung in the air unless supported by another one. Whereas an explanation may indeed rest on another one that has been given, but none stands in need of another—unless *we* require it to prevent a misunderstanding. One might say: an explanation serves to remove or to avert a misunderstanding——one, that is, that would occur but for the explanation; not every one that I can imagine.

It may easily look as if every doubt merely *revealed* an existing gap in the foundations; so that secure understanding is only possible if we first doubt everything that *can* be doubted, and then remove all these doubts.

The sign-post is in order—if, under normal circumstances, it fulfils its purpose.

88. If I tell someone "Stand roughly here"—may not this explanation work perfectly? And cannot every other one fail too?

But isn't it an inexact explanation?—Yes; why shouldn't we call it "inexact"? Only let us understand what "inexact" means. For it does not mean "unusable". And let us consider what we call an "exact" explanation in contrast with this one. Perhaps something like drawing a chalk line round an area? Here it strikes us at once that the line has breadth. So a colour-edge would be more exact. But has this exactness still got a function here: isn't the engine idling? And remember too that we have not yet defined what is to count as overstepping this exact boundary; how, with what instruments, it is to be established. And so on.

We understand what it means to set a pocket watch to the exact time or to regulate it to be exact. But what if it were asked: is this exactness ideal exactness, or how nearly does it approach the ideal?—Of course, we can speak of measurements of time in which there is a different, and as we should say a greater, exactness than in the measurement of time by a pocket-watch; in which the words "to set the clock to the exact time" have a different, though related meaning, and 'to tell the time' is a different process and so on.—Now, if I tell someone: "You should come to dinner more punctually; you know it begins at one o'clock exactly"—is there really no question of *exactness* here? because it is possible to say: "Think of the determination of time in the laboratory or the observatory; *there* you see what 'exactness' means"?

"Inexact" is really a reproach, and "exact" is praise. And that is to say that what is inexact attains its goal less perfectly than what is more exact. Thus the point here is what we call "the goal". Am I inexact when I do not give our distance from the sun to the nearest foot, or tell a joiner the width of a table to the nearest thousandth of an inch?

No *single* ideal of exactness has been laid down; we do not know what we should be supposed to imagine under this head—unless you yourself lay down what is to be so called. But you will find it difficult to hit upon such a convention; at least any that satisfies you.

89. These considerations bring us up to the problem: In what sense is logic something sublime?

For there seemed to pertain to logic a peculiar depth—a universal significance. Logic lay, it seemed, at the bottom of all the sciences.— For logical investigation explores the nature of all things. It seeks to see to the bottom of things and is not meant to concern itself whether what actually happens is this or that.——It takes its rise, not from an interest in the facts of nature, nor from a need to grasp causal connexions: but from an urge to understand the basis, or essence, of everything empirical. Not, however, as if to this end we had to hunt out new facts; it is, rather, of the essence of our investigation that we do not seek to learn anything *new* by it. We want to *understand* something that is already in plain view. For *this* is what we seem in some sense not to understand.

Augustine says in the *Confessions* "quid est ergo tempus? si nemo ex me quaerat scio; si quaerenti explicare velim, nescio".—This could not be said about a question of natural science ("What is the specific gravity of hydrogen?" for instance). Something that we know when no one asks us, but no longer know when we are supposed to give an account of it, is something that we need to *remind* ourselves of. (And it is obviously something of which for some reason it is difficult to remind oneself.)

90. We feel as if we had to *penetrate* phenomena: our investigation, however, is directed not towards phenomena, but, as one might say, towards the '*possibilities*' of phenomena. We remind ourselves, that is to say, of the *kind of statement* that we make about phenomena. Thus Augustine recalls to mind the different statements that are made about the duration, past present or future, of events. (These are, of course, not *philosophical* statements about time, the past, the present and the future.)

Our investigation is therefore a grammatical one. Such an investigation sheds light on our problem by clearing misunderstandings away. Misunderstandings concerning the use of words, caused, among other things, by certain analogies between the forms of expression in different regions of language.—Some of them can be removed by substituting one form of expression for another; this may be called an "analysis" of our forms of expression, for the process is sometimes like one of taking a thing apart.

91. But now it may come to look as if there were something like a final analysis of our forms of language, and so a *single* completely resolved form of every expression. That is, as if our usual forms of expression were, essentially, unanalysed; as if there were something hidden in them that had to be brought to light. When this is done the expression is completely clarified and our problem solved.

It can also be put like this: we eliminate misunderstandings by making our expressions more exact; but now it may look as if we were moving towards a particular state, a state of complete exactness; and as if this were the real goal of our investigation.

92. This finds expression in questions as to the *essence* of language, of propositions, of thought.—For if we too in these investigations are trying to understand the essence of language—its function, its structure,—yet *this* is not what those questions have in view. For they see in the essence, not something that already lies open to view and that becomes surveyable by a rearrangement, but something that lies *beneath* the surface. Something that lies within, which we see when we look *into* the thing, and which an analysis digs out.

'*The essence is hidden from us*': this is the form our problem now assumes. We ask: "*What is* language?", "*What is* a proposition?" And the answer to these questions is to be given once for all; and independently of any future experience.

93. One person might say "A proposition is the most ordinary thing in the world" and another: "A proposition—that's something very queer!"——And the latter is unable simply to look and see how propositions really work. The forms that we use in expressing ourselves about propositions and thought stand in his way.

Why do we say a proposition is something remarkable? On the one hand, because of the enormous importance attaching to it. (And that is correct). On the other hand this, together with a misunderstanding of the logic of language, seduces us into thinking that something extraordinary, something unique, must be achieved by propositions.—A *misunderstanding* makes it look to us as if a proposition *did* something queer.

94. 'A proposition is a queer thing!' Here we have in germ the subliming of our whole account of logic. The tendency to assume a pure intermediary between the propositional *signs* and the facts. Or even to try to purify, to sublime, the signs themselves.—For our forms of expression prevent us in all sorts of ways from seeing that nothing out of the ordinary is involved, by sending us in pursuit of chimeras.

95. "Thought must be something unique". When we say, and *mean*, that such-and-such is the case, we—and our meaning—do not stop anywhere short of the fact; but we mean: *this—is—so*. But this paradox (which has the form of a truism) can also be expressed in this way: *Thought* can be of what is *not* the case.

96. Other illusions come from various quarters to attach themselves to the special one spoken of here. Thought, language, now appear to us as the unique correlate, picture, of the world. These concepts: proposition, language, thought, world, stand in line one behind the other, each equivalent to each. (But what are these words to be used for now? The language-game in which they are to be applied is missing.)

97. Thought is surrounded by a halo.—Its essence, logic, presents an order, in fact the a priori order of the world: that is, the order of *possibilities*, which must be common to both world and thought. But this order, it seems, must be *utterly simple*. It is *prior* to all experience, must run through all experience; no empirical cloudiness or uncertainty can be allowed to affect it——It must rather be of the purest crystal. But this crystal does not appear as an abstraction; but as something concrete, indeed, as the most concrete, as it were the *hardest* thing there is (*Tractatus Logico-Philosophicus* No. 5.5563).

We are under the illusion that what is peculiar, profound, essential, in our investigation, resides in its trying to grasp the incomparable essence of language. That is, the order existing between the concepts of proposition, word, proof, truth, experience, and so on. This order is a *super*-order between—so to speak—*super*-concepts. Whereas, of course, if the words "language", "experience", "world", have a use, it must be as humble a one as that of the words "table", "lamp", "door".

98.   On the one hand it is clear that every sentence in our language 'is in order as it is'. That is to say, we are not *striving after* an ideal, as if our ordinary vague sentences had not yet got a quite unexceptionable sense, and a perfect language awaited construction by us.—On the other hand it seems clear that where there is sense there must be perfect order.——So there must be perfect order even in the vaguest sentence.

99.   The sense of a sentence—one would like to say—may, of course, leave this or that open, but the sentence must nevertheless have *a* definite sense. An indefinite sense—that would really not be a sense *at all*.—This is like: An indefinite boundary is not really a boundary at all. Here one thinks perhaps: if I say "I have locked the man up fast in the room—there is only one door left open"—then I simply haven't locked him in at all; his being locked in is a sham. One would be inclined to say here: "You haven't done anything at all". An enclosure with a hole in it is as good as *none*.—But is that true?

100.   "But still, it isn't a game, if there is some vagueness *in the rules*".—But *does* this prevent its being a game?—"Perhaps you'll call it a game, but at any rate it certainly isn't a perfect game." This means: it has impurities, and what I am interested in at present is the pure article.—But I want to say: we misunderstand the role of the ideal in our language. That is to say: we too should call it a game, only we are dazzled by the ideal and therefore fail to see the actual use of the word "game" clearly.

101.   We want to say that there can't be any vagueness in logic. The idea now absorbs us, that the ideal '*must*' be found in reality. Meanwhile we do not as yet see *how* it occurs there, nor do we understand the nature of this "must". We think it must be in reality; for we think we already see it there.

102.   The strict and clear rules of the logical structure of propositions appear to us as something in the background—hidden in the medium of the understanding. I already see them (even though through a medium): for I understand the propositional sign, I use it to say something.

103.   The ideal, as we think of it, is unshakable. You can never get outside it; you must always turn back. There is no outside; outside you cannot breathe.—Where does this idea come from? It is like a pair of glasses on our nose through which we see whatever we look at. It never occurs to us to take them off.

104. We predicate of the thing what lies in the method of representing it. Impressed by the possibility of a comparison, we think we are perceiving a state of affairs of the highest generality.

105. When we believe that we must find that order, must find the ideal, in our actual language, we become dissatisfied with what are ordinarily called "propositions", "words", "signs".

The proposition and the word that logic deals with are supposed to be something pure and clear-cut. And we rack our brains over the nature of the *real* sign.—It is perhaps the *idea* of the sign? or the idea at the present moment?

106. Here it is difficult as it were to keep our heads up,—to see that we must stick to the subjects of our every-day thinking, and not go astray and imagine that we have to describe extreme subtleties, which in turn we are after all quite unable to describe with the means at our disposal. We feel as if we had to repair a torn spider's web with our fingers.

107. The more narrowly we examine actual language, the sharper becomes the conflict between it and our requirement. (For the crystalline purity of logic was, of course, not a *result of investigation*: it was a requirement.) The conflict becomes intolerable; the requirement is now in danger of becoming empty.—We have got on to slippery ice where there is no friction and so in a certain sense the conditions are ideal, but also, just because of that, we are unable to walk. We want to walk: so we need *friction*. Back to the rough ground!

108. We see that what we call "sentence" and "language" has not the formal unity that I imagined, but is the family of structures more or less related to one another.——But what becomes of logic now? Its rigour seems to be giving way here.—But in that case doesn't logic altogether disappear?—For how can it lose its rigour? Of course not by our bargaining any of its rigour out of it.—The *preconceived idea* of crystalline purity can only be removed by turning our whole examination round. (One might say: the axis of reference of our examination must be rotated, but about the fixed point of our real need.)

The philosophy of logic speaks of sentences and words in exactly the sense in which we speak of them in ordinary life when we say e.g.

Faraday in *The Chemical History of a Candle*: "Water is one individual thing—it never changes."

"Here is a Chinese sentence", or "No, that only looks like writing; it is actually just an ornament" and so on.

We are talking about the spatial and temporal phenomenon of language, not about some non-spatial, non-temporal phantasm. [Note in margin: Only it is possible to be interested in a phenomenon in a variety of ways]. But we talk about it as we do about the pieces in chess when we are stating the rules of the game, not describing their physical properties.

The question "What is a word really?" is analogous to "What is a piece in chess?"

109. It was true to say that our considerations could not be scientific ones. It was not of any possible interest to us to find out empirically 'that, contrary to our preconceived ideas, it is possible to think such-and-such'—whatever that may mean. (The conception of thought as a gaseous medium.) And we may not advance any kind of theory. There must not be anything hypothetical in our considerations. We must do away with all *explanation*, and description alone must take its place. And this description gets its light, that is to say its purpose, from the philosophical problems. These are, of course, not empirical problems; they are solved, rather, by looking into the workings of our language, and that in such a way as to make us recognize those workings: *in despite of* an urge to misunderstand them. The problems are solved, not by giving new information, but by arranging what we have always known. Philosophy is a battle against the bewitchment of our intelligence by means of language.

110. "Language (or thought) is something unique"—this proves to be a superstition (*not* a mistake!), itself produced by grammatical illusions.

And now the impressiveness retreats to these illusions, to the problems.

111. The problems arising through a misinterpretation of our forms of language have the character of *depth*. They are deep disquietudes; their roots are as deep in us as the forms of our language and their significance is as great as the importance of our language.——Let us ask ourselves: why do we feel a grammatical joke to be *deep*? (And that is what the depth of philosophy is.)

112. A simile that has been absorbed into the forms of our language produces a false appearance, and this disquiets us. "But *this* isn't how it is!"—we say. "Yet *this* is how it has to *be*!"

113. "But *this* is how it is————" I say to myself over and over
again. I feel as though, if only I could fix my gaze absolutely sharply
on this fact, get it in focus, I must grasp the essence of the matter.

114. (*Tractatus Logico-Philosophicus*, 4.5): "The general form of
propositions is: This is how things are."————That is the kind of proposition that one repeats to oneself countless times. One thinks that one is
tracing the outline of the thing's nature over and over again, and one is
merely tracing round the frame through which we look at it.

115. A *picture* held us captive. And we could not get outside it, for
it lay in our language and language seemed to repeat it to us inexorably.

116. When philosophers use a word—"knowledge", "being",
"object", "I", "proposition", "name"—and try to grasp the *essence*
of the thing, one must always ask oneself: is the word ever actually
used in this way in the language-game which is its original home?—
What *we* do is to bring words back from their metaphysical to their
everyday use.

117. You say to me: "You understand this expression, don't
you? Well then—I am using it in the sense you are familiar with."—
As if the sense were an atmosphere accompanying the word, which it
carried with it into every kind of application.
    If, for example, someone says that the sentence "This is here"
(saying which he points to an object in front of him) makes sense to
him, then he should ask himself in what special circumstances this
sentence is actually used. There it does make sense.

118. Where does our investigation get its importance from, since
it seems only to destroy everything interesting, that is, all that is great
and important? (As it were all the buildings, leaving behind only bits
of stone and rubble.) What we are destroying is nothing but houses of
cards and we are clearing up the ground of language on which they
stand.

119. The results of philosophy are the uncovering of one or
another piece of plain nonsense and of bumps that the understanding
has got by running its head up against the limits of language. These
bumps make us see the value of the discovery.

120. When I talk about language (words, sentences, etc.) I must
speak the language of every day. Is this language somehow too coarse
and material for what we want to say? *Then how is another one to be*

constructed?—And how strange that we should be able to do anything at all with the one we have!

In giving explanations I already have to use language full-blown (not some sort of preparatory, provisional one); this by itself shews that I can adduce only exterior facts about language.

Yes, but then how can these explanations satisfy us?—Well, your very questions were framed in this language; they had to be expressed in this language, if there was anything to ask!

And your scruples are misunderstandings.

Your questions refer to words; so I have to talk about words.

You say: the point isn't the word, but its meaning, and you think of the meaning as a thing of the same kind as the word, though also different from the word. Here the word, there the meaning. The money, and the cow that you can buy with it. (But contrast: money, and its use.)

121. One might think: if philosophy speaks of the use of the word "philosophy" there must be a second-order philosophy. But it is not so: it is, rather, like the case of orthography, which deals with the word "orthography" among others without then being second-order.

122. A main source of our failure to understand is that we do not *command a clear view* of the use of our words.—Our grammar is lacking in this sort of perspicuity. A perspicuous representation produces just that understanding which consists in 'seeing connexions'. Hence the importance of finding and inventing *intermediate cases*.

The concept of a perspicuous representation is of fundamental significance for us. It earmarks the form of account we give, the way we look at things. (Is this a 'Weltanschauung'?)

123. A philosophical problem has the form: "I don't know my way about".

124. Philosophy may in no way interfere with the actual use of language; it can in the end only describe it.

For it cannot give it any foundation either.

It leaves everything as it is.

It also leaves mathematics as it is, and no mathematical discovery can advance it. A "leading problem of mathematical logic" is for us a problem of mathematics like any other.

125. It is the business of philosophy, not to resolve a contradiction by means of a mathematical or logico-mathematical discovery, but to make it possible for us to get a clear view of the state of mathematics that troubles us: the state of affairs *before* the contradiction is resolved. (And this does not mean that one is sidestepping a difficulty.)

The fundamental fact here is that we lay down rules, a technique, for a game, and that then when we follow the rules, things do not turn out as we had assumed. That we are therefore as it were entangled in our own rules.

This entanglement in our rules is what we want to understand (i.e. get a clear view of).

It throws light on our concept of *meaning* something. For in those cases things turn out otherwise than we had meant, foreseen. That is just what we say when, for example, a contradiction appears: "I didn't mean it like that."

The civil status of a contradiction, or its status in civil life: there is the philosophical problem.

126. Philosophy simply puts everything before us, and neither explains nor deduces anything.—Since everything lies open to view there is nothing to explain. For what is hidden, for example, is of no interest to us.

One might also give the name "philosophy" to what is possible *before* all new discoveries and inventions.

127. The work of the philosopher consists in assembling reminders for a particular purpose.

128. If one tried to advance *theses* in philosophy, it would never be possible to debate them, because everyone would agree to them.

129. The aspects of things that are most important for us are hidden because of their simplicity and familiarity. (One is unable to notice something—because it is always before one's eyes.) The real foundations of his enquiry do not strike a man at all. Unless *that* fact has at some time struck him.—And this means: we fail to be struck by what, once seen, is most striking and most powerful.

130. Our clear and simple language-games are not preparatory studies for a future regularization of language—as it were first approximations, ignoring friction and air-resistance. The language-games are rather set up as *objects of comparison* which are meant to throw light on the facts of our language by way not only of similarities, but also of dissimilarities.

131. For we can avoid ineptness or emptiness in our assertions only by presenting the model as what it is, as an object of comparison—as, so to speak, a measuring-rod; not as a preconceived idea to which reality *must* correspond. (The dogmatism into which we fall so easily in doing philosophy.)

132. We want to establish an order in our knowledge of the use of language: an order with a particular end in view; one out of many possible orders; not *the* order. To this end we shall constantly be giving prominence to distinctions which our ordinary forms of language easily make us overlook. This may make it look as if we saw it as our task to reform language.

Such a reform for particular practical purposes, an improvement in our terminology designed to prevent misunderstandings in practice, is perfectly possible. But these are not the cases we have to do with. The confusions which occupy us arise when language is like an engine idling, not when it is doing work.

133. It is not our aim to refine or complete the system of rules for the use of our words in unheard-of ways.

For the clarity that we are aiming at is indeed *complete* clarity. But this simply means that the philosophical problems should *completely* disappear.

The real discovery is the one that makes me capable of stopping doing philosophy when I want to.—The one that gives philosophy peace, so that it is no longer tormented by questions which bring *itself* in question.—Instead, we now demonstrate a method, by examples; and the series of examples can be broken off.—Problems are solved (difficulties eliminated), not a *single* problem.

There is not *a* philosophical method, though there are indeed methods, like different therapies.

134. Let us examine the proposition: "This is how things are."— How can I say that this is the general form of propositions?—It is first and foremost *itself* a proposition, an English sentence, for it has a subject and a predicate. But how is this sentence applied—that is, in our everyday language? For I got it from there and nowhere else.

We may say, e.g.: "He explained his position to me, said that this was how things were, and that therefore he needed an advance". So far, then, one can say that that sentence stands for any statement It is employed as a propositional *schema*, but *only* because it has the construction of an English sentence. It would be possible to say instead "such and such is the case", "this is the situation", and so on. It would also be possible here simply to use a letter, a variable, as in symbolic logic. But no one is going to call the letter "p" the general form of propositions. To repeat: "This is how things are" had that position only because it is itself what one calls an English sentence. But though it is a proposition, still it gets employed as a propositional variable. To say that this proposition agrees (or does not agree) with reality would be obvious nonsense. Thus it illustrates the fact that *one* feature of our concept of a proposition is, *sounding like a proposition*.

135. But haven't we got a concept of what a proposition is, of what we take "proposition" to mean?—Yes; just as we also have a concept of what we mean by "game". Asked what a proposition is—whether it is another person or ourselves that we have to answer—we shall give examples and these will include what one may call inductively defined series of propositions. *This* is the kind of way in which we have such a concept as 'proposition'. (Compare the concept of a proposition with the concept of number.)

136. At bottom, giving "This is how things are" as the general form of propositions is the same as giving the definition: a proposition is whatever can be true or false. For instead of "This is how things are" I could have said "This is true". (Or again "This is false".) But we have

'p' is true = p

'p' is false = not-p.

And to say that a proposition is whatever can be true or false amounts to saying: we call something a proposition when *in our language* we apply the calculus of truth functions to it.

Now it looks as if the definition—a proposition is whatever can be true or false—determined what a proposition was, by saying: what fits the concept 'true', or what the concept 'true' fits, is a proposition. So it is as if we had a concept of true and false, which we could use to determine what is and what is not a proposition. What *engages* with the concept of truth (as with a cogwheel), is a proposition.

But this is a bad picture. It is as if one were to say "The king in chess is *the* piece that one can check." But this can mean no more than that in our game of chess we only check the king. Just as the proposition that only a *proposition* can be true or false can say no more than that we only predicate "true" and "false" of what we call a proposition. And what a proposition is is in one sense determined by the rules of sentence formation (in English for example), and in another sense by the use of the sign in the language-game. And the use of the words "true" and "false" may be among the constituent parts of this game; and if so it *belongs* to our concept 'proposition' but does not '*fit*' it. As we might also say, check *belongs* to our concept of the king in chess (as so to speak a constituent part of it). To say that check did not *fit* our concept of the pawns, would mean that a game in which pawns were checked, in which, say, the players who lost their pawns lost, would be uninteresting or stupid or too complicated or something of the kind.

137.   What about learning to determine the subject of a sentence by means of the question "Who or what . . . .?"—Here, surely, there is such a thing as the subject's 'fitting' this question; for otherwise how should we find out what the subject was by means of the question? We find it out much as we find out which letter of the alphabet comes after 'K' by saying the alphabet up to 'K' to ourselves. Now in what sense does 'L' fit on to this series of letters?—In *that* sense "true" and "false" could be said to fit propositions; and a child might be taught to distinguish between propositions and other expressions by being told "Ask yourself if you can say 'is true' after it. If these words fit, it's a proposition." (And in the same way one might have said: Ask yourself if you can put the words "*This* is how things are:" in front of it.)

138.   But can't the meaning of a word that I understand fit the sense of a sentence that I understand? Or the meaning of one word fit the meaning of another?——Of course, if the meaning is the *use* we make of the word, it makes no sense to speak of such 'fitting.' But we *understand* the meaning of a word when we hear or say it; we grasp it in a flash, and what we grasp in this way is surely something different from the 'use' which is extended in time!

Must I *know* whether I understand a word? Don't I also sometimes imagine myself to understand a word (as I may imagine I understand a kind of calculation) and then realize that I did not understand it? ("I thought I knew what 'relative' and 'absolute' motion meant, but I see that I don't know.")

139. When someone says the word "cube" to me, for example, I know what it means. But can the whole *use* of the word come before my mind, when I *understand* it in this way?

Well, but on the other hand isn't the meaning of the word also determined by this use? And can these ways of determining meaning conflict? Can what we grasp *in a flash* accord with a use, fit or fail to fit it? And how can what is present to us in an instant, what comes before our mind in an instant, fit a *use*?

What really comes before our mind when we *understand* a word?—Isn't it something like a picture? Can't it *be* a picture?

Well, suppose that a picture does come before your mind when you hear the word "cube", say the drawing of a cube. In what sense can this picture fit or fail to fit a use of the word "cube"?—Perhaps you say: "It's quite simple;—if that picture occurs to me and I point to a triangular prism for instance, and say it is a cube, then this use of the word doesn't fit the picture."—But doesn't it fit? I have purposely so chosen the example that it is quite easy to imagine a *method of projection* according to which the picture does fit after all.

The picture of the cube did indeed *suggest* a certain use to us, but it was possible for me to use it differently.

(a) "I believe the right word in this case is . . . .". Doesn't this shew that the meaning of a word is a something that comes before our mind, and which is, as it were, the exact picture we want to use here? Suppose I were choosing between the words "imposing", "dignified", "proud", "venerable"; isn't it as though I were choosing between drawings in a portfolio?—No: the fact that one speaks of the *appropriate word* does not *shew* the existence of a something that etc.. One is inclined, rather, to speak of this picture-like something just because one can find a word appropriate; because one often chooses between words as between similar but not identical pictures; because pictures are often used instead of words, or to illustrate words; and so on.

(b) I see a picture; it represents an old man walking up a steep path leaning on a stick.—How? Might it not have looked just the same if he had been sliding downhill in that position? Perhaps a Martian would describe the picture so. I do not need to explain why *we* do not describe it so.

140. Then what sort of mistake did I make; was it what we should like to express by saying: I should have thought the picture forced a particular use on me? How could I think that? What *did* I think? Is there such a thing as a picture, or something like a picture, that forces a particular application on us; so that my mistake lay in confusing one picture with another?—For we might also be inclined to express ourselves like this: we are at most under a psychological, not a logical, compulsion. And now it looks quite as if we knew of two kinds of case.

What was the effect of my argument? It called our attention to (reminded us of) the fact that there are other processes, besides the one we originally thought of, which we should sometimes be prepared to call "applying the picture of a cube". So our 'belief that the picture forced a particular application upon us' consisted in the fact that only the one case and no other occurred to us. "There is another solution as well" means: there is something else that I am also prepared to call a "solution"; to which I am prepared to apply such-and-such a picture, such-and-such an analogy, and so on.

What is essential is to see that the same thing can come before our minds when we hear the word and the application still be different. Has it the *same* meaning both times? I think we shall say not.

141. Suppose, however, that not merely the picture of the cube, but also the method of projection comes before our mind?——How am I to imagine this?—Perhaps I see before me a schema shewing the method of projection: say a picture of two cubes connected by lines of projection.—But does this really get me any further? Can't I now imagine different applications of this schema too?——Well, yes, but then can't an *application come before my mind*?—It can: only we need to get clearer about our application of *this* expression. Suppose I explain various methods of projection to someone so that he may go on to apply them; let us ask ourselves when we should say that *the* method that I intend comes before his mind.

Now clearly we accept two different kinds of criteria for this: on the one hand the picture (of whatever kind) that at some time or other comes before his mind; on the other, the application which—in the course of time—he makes of what he imagines. (And can't it be clearly seen here that it is absolutely inessential for the picture to exist in his imagination rather than as a drawing or model in front of him; or again as something that he himself constructs as a model?)

Can there be a collision between picture and application? There can, inasmuch as the picture makes us expect a different use, because people in general apply *this* picture like *this*.

I want to say: we have here a *normal* case, and abnormal cases.

142. It is only in normal cases that the use of a word is clearly prescribed; we know, are in no doubt, what to say in this or that case. The more abnormal the case, the more doubtful it becomes what we are to say. And if things were quite different from what they actually are——if there were for instance no characteristic expression of pain, of fear, of joy; if rule became exception and exception rule; or if both became phenomena of roughly equal frequency——this would make our normal language-games lose their point.—The procedure of putting a lump of cheese on a balance and fixing the price by the turn of the scale would lose its point if it frequently happened for such lumps to suddenly grow or shrink for no obvious reason. This remark will become clearer when we discuss such things as the relation of expression to feeling, and similar topics.

143. Let us now examine the following kind of language-game: when A gives an order B has to write down series of signs according to a certain formation rule.

The first of these series is meant to be that of the natural numbers in decimal notation.—How does he get to understand this notation?— First of all series of numbers will be written down for him and he will be required to copy them. (Do not balk at the expression "series of numbers"; it is not being used wrongly here.) And here already there is a normal and an abnormal learner's reaction.—At first perhaps we guide his hand in writing out the series o to 9; but then the *possibility of getting him to understand* will depend on his going on to write it down independently.—And here we can imagine, e.g., that he does copy the figures independently, but not in the right order: he writes sometimes one sometimes another at random. And then communication stops at *that* point.—Or again, he makes '*mistakes*'

What we have to mention in order to explain the significance, I mean the importance, of a concept, are often extremely general facts of nature: such facts as are hardly ever mentioned because of their great generality.

n the order.—The difference between this and the first case will of course be one of frequency.—Or he makes a *systematic* mistake; for example, he copies every other number, or he copies the series 0, 1, 2, 3, 4, 5, ... like this: 1, 0, 3, 2, 5, 4, ... Here we shall almost be tempted to say that he has understood *wrong*.

Notice, however, that there is no sharp distinction between a random mistake and a systematic one. That is, between what you are inclined to call "random" and what "systematic".

Perhaps it is possible to wean him from the systematic mistake (as from a bad habit). Or perhaps one accepts his way of copying and tries to teach him ours as an offshoot, a variant of his.—And here too our pupil's capacity to learn may come to an end.

144. What do I mean when I say "the pupil's capacity to learn *may* come to an end here"? Do I say this from my own experience? Of course not. (Even if I have had such experience.) Then what am I doing with that proposition? Well, I should like you to say: "Yes, it's true, you can imagine that too, that might happen too!"—But was I trying to draw someone's attention to the fact that he is capable of imagining that?——I wanted to put that picture before him, and his *acceptance* of the picture consists in his now being inclined to regard a given case differently: that is, to compare it with *this* rather than *that* set of pictures. I have changed his *way of looking at things*. (Indian mathematicians: "Look at this.")

145. Suppose the pupil now writes the series 0 to 9 to our satisfaction.—And this will only be the case when he is often successful, not if he does it right once in a hundred attempts. Now I continue the series and draw his attention to the recurrence of the first series in the units; and then to its recurrence in the tens. (Which only means that I use particular emphases, underline figures, write them one under another in such-and-such ways, and similar things.)—And now at some point he continues the series independently—or he does not.—But why do you say that? *so* much is obvious!—Of course; I only wished to say: the effect of any further *explanation* depends on his *reaction*.

Now, however, let us suppose that after some efforts on the teacher's part he continues the series correctly, that is, as we do it. So now we can say he has mastered the system.—But how far need he continue the series for us to have the right to say that? Clearly you cannot state a limit here.

146.   Suppose I now ask: "Has he understood the system when he continues the series to the hundredth place?" Or—if I should not speak of 'understanding' in connection with our primitive language-game: Has he got the system, if he continues the series correctly so far?—Perhaps you will say here: to have got the system (or, again, to understand it) can't consist in continuing the series up to *this* or *that* number: *that* is only applying one's understanding. The understanding itself is a state which is the *source* of the correct use.

What is one really thinking of here? Isn't one thinking of the derivation of a series from its algebraic formula? Or at least of something analogous?—But this is where we were before. The point is, we can think of more than *one* application of an algebraic formula; and every type of application can in turn be formulated algebraically; but naturally this does not get us any further.—The application is still a criterion of understanding.

147.   "But how can it be? When *I* say I understand the rule of a series, I am surely not saying so because I have *found out* that up to now I have applied the algebraic formula in such-and-such a way! In my own case at all events I surely know that I mean such-and-such a series; it doesn't matter how far I have actually developed it."—

Your idea, then, is that you know the application of the rule of the series quite apart from remembering actual applications to particular numbers. And you will perhaps say: "Of course! For the series is infinite and the bit of it that I can have developed finite."

148.   But what does this knowledge consist in? Let me ask: *When* do you know that application? Always? day and night? or only when you are actually thinking of the rule? do you know it, that is, in the same way as you know the alphabet and the multiplication table? Or is what you call "knowledge" a state of consciousness or a process—say a thought of something, or the like?

149.   If one says that knowing the ABC is a state of the mind, one is thinking of a state of a mental apparatus (perhaps of the brain) by means of which we explain the *manifestations* of that knowledge. Such a state is called a disposition. But there are objections to speaking

of a state of the mind here, inasmuch as there ought to be two different criteria for such a state: a knowledge of the construction of the apparatus, quite apart from what it does. (Nothing would be more confusing here than to use the words "conscious" and "unconscious" for the contrast between states of consciousness and dispositions. For this pair of terms covers up a grammatical difference.)

150. The grammar of the word "knows" is evidently closely related to that of "can", "is able to". But also closely related to that of "understands". ('Mastery' of a technique,)

151. But there is also *this* use of the word "to know": we say "Now I know!"—and similarly "Now I can do it!" and "Now I understand!"

Let us imagine the following example: A writes series of numbers down; B watches him and tries to find a law for the sequence of numbers. If he succeeds he exclaims: "Now I can go on!"——So this capacity, this understanding, is something that makes its appearance in a moment. So let us try and see what it is that makes its appearance here.—A has written down the numbers 1, 5, 11, 19, 29; at this point B says he knows how to go on. What happened here? Various things may have happened; for example, while A was slowly putting one number after another, B was occupied with trying various algebraic formulae on the numbers which had been written down. After A had written the number 19 B tried the formula $a_n = n^2 + n - 1$; and the next number confirmed his hypothesis.

(a) "Understanding a word": a state. But a *mental* state?—Depression, excitement, pain, are called mental states. Carry out a grammatical investigation as follows: we say

"He was depressed the whole day".

"He was in great excitement the whole day".

"He has been in continuous pain since yesterday".—

We also say "Since yesterday I have understood this word". "Continuously", though?—To be sure, one can speak of an interruption of understanding. But in what cases? Compare: "When did your pains get less?" and "When did you stop understanding that word?"

(b) Suppose it were asked: "*When* do you know how to play chess? All the time? or just while you are making a move? And the *whole* of chess during each move?—How queer that knowing how to play chess should take such a short time, and a game so much longer!

Or again, B does not think of formulae. He watches A writing his numbers down with a certain feeling of tension, and all sorts of vague thoughts go through his head. Finally he asks himself: "What is the series of differences?" He finds the series 4, 6, 8, 10 and says: Now I can go on.

Or he watches and says "Yes, I know *that* series"—and continues it, just as he would have done if A had written down the series 1, 3, 5, 7, 9. —Or he says nothing at all and simply continues the series. Perhaps he had what may be called the sensation "that's easy!". (Such a sensation is, for example, that of a light quick intake of breath, as when one is slightly startled.)

152. But are the processes which I have described here *understanding*?

"B understands the principle of the series" surely doesn't mean simply: the formula "$a_n = \ldots$" occurs to B. For it is perfectly imaginable that the formula should occur to him and that he should nevertheless not understand. "He understands" must have more in it than: the formula occurs to him. And equally, more than any of those more or less characteristic *accompaniments* or manifestations of understanding.

153. We are trying to get hold of the mental process of understanding which seems to be hidden behind those coarser and therefore more readily visible accompaniments. But we do not succeed; or, rather, it does not get as far as a real attempt. For even supposing I had found something that happened in all those cases of understanding,— why should *it* be the understanding? And how can the process of understanding have been hidden, when I said "Now I understand" *because* I understood?! And if I say it is hidden—then how do I know what I have to look for? I am in a muddle.

154. But wait—if "Now I understand the principle" does not mean the same as "The formula .... occurs to me" (or "I say the formula", "I write it down", etc.) —does it follow from this that I employ the sentence "Now I understand ....." or "Now I can go on" as a description of a process occurring behind or side by side with that of saying the formula?

If there has to be anything 'behind the utterance of the formula' it is *particular circumstances*, which justify me in saying I can go on—when the formula occurs to me.

Try not to think of understanding as a 'mental process' at all.—
For *that* is the expression which confuses you. But ask yourself: in
what sort of case, in what kind of circumstances, do we say, "Now I
know how to go on," when, that is, the formula *has* occurred to me?—

In the sense in which there are processes (including mental processes)
which are characteristic of understanding, understanding is not a
mental process.

(A pain's growing more and less; the hearing of a tune or a sentence:
these are mental processes.)

155. Thus what I wanted to say was: when he suddenly knew
how to go on, when he understood the principle, then possibly he
had a special experience—and if he is asked: "What was it? What took
place when you suddenly grasped the principle?" perhaps he will
describe it much as we described it above——but for us it is *the circumstances* under which he had such an experience that justify him in
saying in such a case that he understands, that he knows how to go on.

156. This will become clearer if we interpolate the consideration
of another word, namely "reading". First I need to remark that I am
not counting the understanding of what is read as part of 'reading' for
purposes of this investigation: reading is here the activity of rendering
out loud what is written or printed; and also of writing from dictation,
writing out something printed, playing from a score, and so on.

The use of this word in the ordinary circumstances of our life is of
course extremely familiar to us. But the part the word plays in our life,
and therewith the language-game in which we employ it, would be
difficult to describe even in rough outline. A person, let us say an
Englishman, has received at school or at home one of the kinds of
education usual among us, and in the course of it has learned to read
his native language. Later he reads books, letters, newspapers, and
other things.

Now what takes place when, say, he reads a newspaper?——His
eye passes—as we say—along the printed words, he says them out
loud—or only to himself; in particular he reads certain words by taking
in their printed shapes as wholes; others when his eye has taken in
the first syllables; others again he reads syllable by syllable, and an
occasional one perhaps letter by letter.—We should also say that he
had read a sentence if he spoke neither aloud nor to himself during
the reading but was afterwards able to repeat the sentence word for
word or nearly so.—He may attend to what he reads, or again—as we

might put it—function as a mere reading-machine: I mean, read aloud and correctly without attending to what he is reading; perhaps with his attention on something quite different (so that he is unable to say what he has been reading if he is asked about it immediately afterwards).

Now compare a beginner with this reader. The beginner reads the words by laboriously spelling them out.—Some however he guesses from the context, or perhaps he already partly knows the passage by heart. Then his teacher says that he is not really *reading* the words (and in certain cases that he is only pretending to read them).

If we think of *this* sort of reading, the reading of a beginner, and ask ourselves what *reading* consists in, we shall be inclined to say: it is a special conscious activity of mind.

We also say of the pupil: "Of course he alone knows if he is really reading or merely saying the words off by heart". (We have yet to discuss these propositions: "He alone knows . . . .".)

But I want to say: we have to admit that—as far as concerns uttering any *one* of the printed words—the same thing may take place in the consciousness of the pupil who is 'pretending' to read, as in that of the practised reader who is 'reading' it. The word "to read" is applied *differently* when we are speaking of the beginner and of the practised reader.——Now we should of course like to say: What goes on in that practised reader and in the beginner when they utter the word *can't* be the same. And if there is no difference in what they happen to be conscious of there must be one in the unconscious workings of their minds, or, again, in the brain.—So we should like to say: There are at all events two different mechanisms at work here. And what goes on in them must distinguish reading from not reading. —But these mechanisms are only hypotheses, models designed to explain, to sum up, what you observe.

157. Consider the following case. Human beings or creatures of some other kind are used by us as reading-machines. They are trained for this purpose. The trainer says of some that they can already read, of others that they cannot yet do so. Take the case of a pupil who has so far not taken part in the training: if he is shewn a written word he will sometimes produce some sort of sound, and here and there it happens 'accidentally' to be roughly right. A third person hears this pupil on such an occasion and says: "He is reading". But the teacher says: "No, he isn't reading; that was just an accident".—But let us suppose that this pupil continues to react correctly to further words

that are put before him. After a while the teacher says: "Now he can read!"—But what of that first word? Is the teacher to say: "I was wrong, and he *did* read it"—or: "He only began really to read later on"?—When did he begin to read? Which was the first word that he *read*? This question makes no sense here. Unless, indeed, we give a definition: "The first word that a person 'reads' is the first word of the first series of 50 words that he reads correctly" (or something of the sort).

If on the other hand we use "reading" to stand for a certain experience of transition from marks to spoken sounds, then it certainly makes sense to speak of the *first* word that he really read. He can then say, e.g. "At this word for the first time I had the feeling: 'now I am reading'."

Or again, in the different case of a reading machine which translated marks into sounds, perhaps as a pianola does, it would be possible to say: "The machine *read* only after such-and-such had happened to it—after such-and-such parts had been connected by wires; the first word that it read was . . . .".

But in the case of the living reading-machine "reading" meant reacting to written signs in such-and-such ways. This concept was therefore quite independent of that of a mental or other mechanism.— Nor can the teacher here say of the pupil: "Perhaps he was already reading when he said that word". For there is no doubt about what he did.—The change when the pupil began to read was a change in his *behaviour*; and it makes no sense here to speak of 'a first word in his new state'.

158. But isn't that only because of our too slight acquaintance with what goes on in the brain and the nervous system? If we had a more accurate knowledge of these things we should see what connexions were established by the training, and then we should be able to say when we looked into his brain: "Now he has *read* this word, now the reading connexion has been set up".——And it presumably *must* be like that—for otherwise how could we be so sure that there was such a connexion? That it is so is presumably a priori—or is it only probable? And how probable is it? Now, ask yourself: what do you *know* about these things?——But if it is a priori, that means that it is a form of account which is very convincing to us.

159. But when we think the matter over we are tempted to say: the one real criterion for anybody's *reading* is the conscious act of reading, the act of reading the sounds off from the letters. "A man

surely knows whether he is reading or only pretending to read!"—
Suppose A wants to make B believe he can read Cyrillic script. He
learns a Russian sentence by heart and says it while looking at the
printed words as if he were reading them. Here we shall certainly
say that A knows he is not reading, and has a sense of just this while
pretending to read. For there are of course many more or less characteristic sensations in reading a printed sentence; it is not difficult to
call such sensations to mind: think of sensations of hesitating, of looking closer, of misreading, of words following on one another more or
less smoothly, and so on. And equally there are characteristic sensations in reciting something one has learnt by heart. In our example
A will have none of the sensations that are characteristic of reading,
and will perhaps have a set of sensations characteristic of cheating.

160. But imagine the following case: We give someone who can
read fluently a text that he never saw before. He reads it to us—but
with the sensation of saying something he has learnt by heart (this
might be the effect of some drug). Should we say in such a case that
he was not really reading the passage? Should we here allow his
sensations to count as the criterion for his reading or not reading?

Or again: Suppose that a man who is under the influence of a
certain drug is presented with a series of characters (which need not
belong to any existing alphabet). He utters words corresponding to
the number of the characters, as if they were letters, and does so with
all the outward signs, and with the sensations, of reading. (We have
experiences like this in dreams; after waking up in such a case one says
perhaps: "It seemed to me as if I were reading a script, though it was
not writing at all.") In such a case some people would be inclined to
say the man was *reading* those marks. Others, that he was not.—
Suppose he has in this way read (or interpreted) a set of five marks as
A B O V E—and now we shew him the same marks in the reverse
order and he reads *E V O B A*; and in further tests he always retains
the same interpretation of the marks: here we should certainly be
inclined to say he was making up an alphabet for himself *ad hoc* and
then reading accordingly.

161. And remember too that there is a continuous series of tran-
sitional cases between that in which a person repeats from memory
what he is supposed to be reading, and that in which he spells out every
word without being helped at all by guessing from the context or
knowing by heart.

Try this experiment: say the numbers from 1 to 12. Now look at the dial of your watch and *read* them.—What was it that you called "reading" in the latter case? That is to say: what did you do, to make it into *reading*?

162. Let us try the following definition: You are reading when you *derive* the reproduction from the original. And by "the original" I mean the text which you read or copy; the dictation from which you write; the score from which you play; etc. etc..—Now suppose we have, for example, taught someone the Cyrillic alphabet, and told him how to pronounce each letter. Next we put a passage before him and he reads it, pronouncing every letter as we have taught him. In this case we shall very likely say that he derives the sound of a word from the written pattern by the rule that we have given him. And this is also a clear case of *reading*. (We might say that we had taught him the 'rule of the alphabet'.)

But why do we say that he has *derived* the spoken from the printed words? Do we know anything more than that we taught him how each letter should be pronounced, and that he then read the words out loud? Perhaps our reply will be: the pupil shews that he is using the rule we have given him to pass from the printed to the spoken words.— How this can be *shewn* becomes clearer if we change our example to one in which the pupil has to write out the text instead of reading it to us, has to make the transition from print to handwriting. For in this case we can give him the rule in the form of a table with printed letters in one column and cursive letters in the other. And he shews that he is deriving his script from the printed words by consulting the table.

163. But suppose that when he did this he always wrote *b* for *A*, *c* for *B*, *d* for *C*, and so on, and *a* for *Z*?—Surely we should call this too a derivation by means of the table.—He is using it now, we might say, according to the second schema in §86 instead of the first.

It would still be a perfectly good case of derivation according to the table, even if it were represented by a schema of arrows without any simple regularity.

Suppose, however, that he does not stick to a *single* method of transcribing, but alters his method according to a simple rule: if he has once written *n* for *A*, then he writes *o* for the next *A*, *p* for the next, and so on.—But where is the dividing line between this procedure and a random one?

But does this mean that the word "to derive" really has no meaning, since the meaning seems to disintegrate when we follow it up?

164. In case (162) the meaning of the word "to derive" stood out clearly. But we told ourselves that this was only a quite special case of deriving; deriving in a quite special garb, which had to be stripped from it if we wanted to see the essence of deriving. So we stripped those particular coverings off; but then deriving itself disappeared.— In order to find the real artichoke, we divested it of its leaves. For certainly (162) was a special case of deriving; what is essential to deriving, however, was not hidden beneath the surface of this case, but his 'surface' was one case out of the family of cases of deriving.

And in the same way we also use the word "to read" for a family of cases. And in different circumstances we apply different criteria for a person's reading.

165. But surely—we should like to say—reading is a quite particular process! Read a page of print and you can see that something special is going on, something highly characteristic.——Well, what does go on when I read the page? I see printed words and I say words out loud. But, of course, that is not all, for I might see printed words and say words out loud and still not be reading. Even if the words which I say are those which, going by an existing alphabet, are *supposed* to be read off from the printed ones.—And if you say that reading is a particular experience, then it becomes quite unimportant whether or not you read according to some generally recognized alphabetical rule.—And what does the characteristic thing about the experience of reading consist in?—Here I should like to say: "The words that I utter *come* in a special way." That is, they do not come as they would if I were for example making them up.—They come of themselves.—But even that is not enough; for the sounds of words may *occur* to me while I am looking at printed words, but that does not mean that I have read them.—In addition I might say here, neither do the spoken words occur to me as if, say, something reminded me of them. I should for example not wish to say: the printed word "nothing" always reminds me of the sound "nothing"—but the spoken words as it were slip in as one

---

The grammar of the expression "a quite particular" (atmosphere). One says "This face has a quite *particular* expression," and maybe looks for words to characterize it.

reads. And if I so much as look at a German printed word, there occurs a peculiar process, that of hearing the sound inwardly.

166. I said that when one reads the spoken words come 'in a special way': but in what way? Isn't this a fiction? Let us look at individual letters and attend to the way the sound of the letter comes. Read the letter A.—Now, how did the sound come?—We have no idea what to say about it.——Now write a small Roman a.—How did the movement of the hand come as you wrote? Differently from the way the sound came in the previous experiment?—All I know is, I looked at the printed letter and wrote the cursive letter.——Now look

at the mark   ⊙   and let a sound occur to you as you do so; utter it. The sound 'U' occurred to me; but I could not say that there was any essential difference in the kind of way that sound *came*. The difference lay in the difference of situation. I had told myself beforehand that I was to let a sound occur to me; there was a certain tension present before the sound came. And I did not say 'U' automatically as I do when I look at the letter U. Further, that mark was not *familiar* to me in the way the letters of the alphabet are. I looked at it rather intently and with a certain interest in its shape; as I looked I thought of a reversed sigma.——Imagine having to use this mark regularly as a letter; so that you got used to uttering a particular sound at the sight of it, say the sound "sh". Can we say anything but that after a while this sound comes automatically when we look at the mark? That is to say: I no longer ask myself on seeing it "What sort of letter is that?" —nor, of course, do I tell myself "This mark makes me want to utter the sound 'sh' ", nor yet "This mark somehow reminds me of the sound 'sh' ".

(Compare with this the idea that memory images are distinguished from other mental images by some special characteristic.)

167. Now what is there in the proposition that reading is 'a quite particular process'? It presumably means that when we read *one* particular process takes place, which we recognize.—But suppose that I at one time read a sentence in print and at another write it in Morse code—is the mental process really the same?——On the other hand, however, there is certainly some uniformity in the experience of reading a page of print. For the process is a uniform one. And it is quite easy to understand that there is a difference between this process and one of, say, letting words occur to one at the sight of arbitrary marks.—For the mere look of a printed line is itself extremely

characteristic—it presents, that is, a quite special appearance, the letters all roughly the same size, akin in shape too, and always recurring; most of the words constantly repeated and enormously familiar to us, like well-known faces.—Think of the uneasiness we feel when the spelling of a word is changed. (And of the still stronger feelings that questions about the spelling of words have aroused.) Of course, not all signs have impressed themselves on us so *strongly*. A sign in the algebra of logic for instance can be replaced by any other one without exciting a strong reaction in us.—

Remember that the look of a word is familiar to us in the same kind of way as its sound.

168.   Again, our eye passes over printed lines differently from the way it passes over arbitrary pothooks and flourishes. (I am not speaking here of what can be established by observing the movement of the eyes of a reader.) The eye passes, one would like to say, with particular ease, without being held up; and yet it doesn't *skid*. And at the same time involuntary speech goes on in the imagination. That is how it is when I read German and other languages, printed or written, and in various styles.—But what in all this is essential to reading as such? Not any one feature that occurs in all cases of reading. (Compare reading ordinary print with reading words which are printed entirely in capital letters, as solutions of puzzles sometimes are. How different it is!—Or reading our script from right to left.)

169.   But when we read don't we feel the word-shapes somehow causing our utterance?——Read a sentence.—And now look along the following line

$$\&8\S\neq \ \S\neq?\beta \ \ ^{+}\% \ \ 8I'\S^{*}$$

and say a sentence as you do so. Can't one feel that in the first case the utterance was *connected* with seeing the signs and in the second went on side by side with the seeing without any connexion?

But why do you say that we felt a causal connexion? Causation is surely something established by experiments, by observing a regular concomitance of events for example. So how could I say that I *felt* something which is established by experiment? (It is indeed true that observation of regular concomitances is not the only way we establish causation.) One might rather say, I feel that the letters are the *reason* why I read such-and-such. For if someone asks me "Why do you read such-and-such?"—I justify my reading by the letters which are there.

This justification, however, was something that I said, or thought: what does it mean to say that I *feel* it? I should like to say: when I read I feel a kind of *influence* of the letters working on me——but I feel no influence from that series of arbitrary flourishes on what I say.—Let us once more compare an individual letter with such a flourish. Should I also say I feel the influence of "i" when I read it? It does of course make a difference whether I say "i" when I see "i" or when I see "§". The difference is, for instance, that when I see the letter it is automatic for me to hear the sound "i" inwardly, it happens even against my will; and I pronounce the letter more effortlessly when I read it than when I am looking at "§". That is to say: this is how it is when I make the *experiment*; but of course it is not so if I happen to be looking at the mark "§" and at the same time pronounce a word in which the sound "i" occurs.

170.   It would never have occurred to us to think that we *felt the influence* of the letters on us when reading, if we had not compared the case of letters with that of arbitrary marks. And here we are indeed noticing a *difference*. And we interpret it as the difference between being influenced and not being influenced.

In particular, this interpretation appeals to us especially when we make a point of reading slowly—perhaps in order to see what does happen when we read. When we, so to speak, quite intentionally let ourselves be *guided* by the letters. But this 'letting myself be guided' in turn only consists in my looking carefully at the letters—and perhaps excluding certain other thoughts.

We imagine that a feeling enables us to perceive as it were a connecting mechanism between the look of the word and the sound that we utter. For when I speak of the experiences of being influenced, of causal connexion, of being guided, that is really meant to imply that I as it were feel the movement of the lever which connects seeing the letters with speaking.

171.   I might have used other words to hit off the experience I have when I read a word. Thus I might say that the written word *intimates* the sound to me.—Or again, that when one reads, letter and sound form a *unity*—as it were an alloy. (In the same way e.g. the faces of famous men and the sound of their names are fused together. This

name strikes me as the only right one for this face.) When I feel this unity, I might say, I see or hear the sound in the written word.—

But now just read a few sentences in print as you usually do when you are not thinking about the concept of reading; and ask yourself whether you had such experiences of unity, of being influenced and the rest, as you read.—Don't say you had them unconsciously! Nor should we be misled by the picture which suggests that these phenomena came in sight 'on closer inspection'. If I am supposed to describe how an object looks from far off, I don't make the description more accurate by saying what can be noticed about the object on closer inspection.

172. Let us consider the experience of being guided, and ask ourselves: what does this experience consist in when for instance our *course* is guided?—Imagine the following cases:

You are in a playing field with your eyes bandaged, and someone leads you by the hand, sometimes left, sometimes right; you have constantly to be ready for the tug of his hand, and must also take care not to stumble when he gives an unexpected tug.

Or again: someone leads you by the hand where you are unwilling to go, by force.

Or: you are guided by a partner in a dance; you make yourself as receptive as possible, in order to guess his intention and obey the slightest pressure.

Or: someone takes you for a walk; you are having a conversation; you go wherever he does.

Or: you walk along a field-track, simply following it.

All these situations are similar to one another; but what is common to all the experiences?

173. "But being guided is surely a particular experience!"—The answer to this is: you are now *thinking* of a particular experience of being guided.

If I want to realize the experience of the person in one of the earlier examples, whose writing is guided by the printed text and the table, I imagine 'conscientious' looking-up, and so on. As I do this I assume a particular expression of face (say that of a conscientious book-keeper). *Carefulness* is a most essential part of this picture; in another the exclusion of every volition of one's own would be essential. (But take something normal people do quite unconcernedly and imagine someone accompanying it with the expression—and why not the feelings?—of great carefulness.—Does that mean he is careful? Imagine a servant dropping the tea-tray and everything on it with all the outward signs of carefulness.) If I imagine such a particular experience, it seems to me to be *the* experience of being guided (or of reading). But now I ask myself: what are you doing?—You are looking at every letter, you are making this face, you are writing the letters with deliberation (and so on).—So that is the experience of being guided?——Here I should like to say: "No, it isn't that; it is something more inward, more essential."—It is as if at first all these more or less inessential processes were shrouded in a particular atmosphere, which dissipates when I look closely at them.

174. Ask yourself how you draw a line parallel to a given one 'with deliberation'—and another time, with deliberation, one at an angle to it. What is the experience of deliberation? Here a particular look, a gesture, at once occur to you—and then you would like to say: "And it just is a *particular* inner experience". (And that is, of course, to add nothing).

(This is connected with the problem of the nature of intention, of willing.)

175. Make some arbitrary doodle on a bit of paper.——And now make a copy next to it, let yourself be guided by it.——I should like to say: "Sure enough, I was guided here. But as for what was characteristic in what happened—if I say what happened, I no longer find it characteristic."

But now notice this: *while* I am being guided everything is quite simple, I notice nothing *special*; but afterwards, when I ask myself what it was that happened, it seems to have been something indescribable. *Afterwards* no description satisfies me. It's as if I couldn't believe that I merely looked, made such-and-such a face, and drew a line.— But don't I *remember* anything else? No; and yet I feel as if there must have been something else; in particular when I say "*guidance*", "*influence*", and other such words to myself. "For surely," I tell myself, "I was being *guided*."—Only then does the idea of that ethereal, intangible influence arise.

176. When I look back on the experience I have the feeling that what is essential about it is an 'experience of being influenced', of a connexion—as opposed to any mere simultaneity of phenomena: but at the same time I should not be willing to call any experienced phenomenon the "experience of being influenced". (This contains the

germ of the idea that the will is not a *phenomenon*.) I should like to say
that I had experienced the '*because*', and yet I do not want to call
any phenomenon the "experience of the because".

177.   I should like to say: "I experience the because". Not because
I remember such an experience, but because when I reflect on what I
experience in such a case I look at it through the medium of the concept
'because' (or 'influence' or 'cause' or 'connexion').—For of course it
is correct to say I drew the line under the influence of the original:
this, however, does not consist simply in my feelings as I drew the
line—under certain circumstances, it may consist in my drawing it
parallel to the other—even though this in turn is not in general essential
to being guided.—

178.   We also say: "You can *see* that I am guided by it"—and
what do you see, if you see this?

When I say to myself: "But I *am* guided"—I make perhaps a movement with my hand, which expresses guiding.—Make such a movement of the hand as if you were guiding someone along, and then ask
yourself what the *guiding* character of this movement consisted in. For
you were not guiding anyone. But you still want to call the movement
one of 'guiding'. This movement and feeling did not contain the
essence of guiding, but still this word forces itself upon you. It is just
a single form of guiding which forces the expression on us.

179.   Let us return to our case (151). It is clear that we should not
say B had the right to say the words "Now I know how to go on",
just because he thought of the formula—unless experience shewed
that there was a connexion between thinking of the formula—saying it,
writing it down—and actually continuing the series. And obviously
such a connexion does exist.—And now one might think that the
sentence "I can go on" meant "I have an experience which I know
empirically to lead to the continuation of the series." But does B mean
that when he says he can go on? Does that sentence come to his mind,
or is he ready to produce it in explanation of what he meant?

No. The words "Now I know how to go on" were correctly used
when he thought of the formula: that is, given such circumstances as
that he had learnt algebra, had used such formulae before.—But that
does not mean that his statement is only short for a description of all
the circumstances which constitute the scene for our language-game.—
Think how we learn to use the expressions "Now I know how to go

on", "Now I can go on" and others; in what family of language-games we learn their use.

We can also imagine the case where nothing at all occurred in B's mind except that he suddenly said "Now I know how to go on"—perhaps with a feeling of relief; and that he did in fact go on working out the series without using the formula. And in this case too we should say—in certain circumstances—that he did know how to go on.

180. *This is how these words are used*. It would be quite misleading, in this last case, for instance, to call the words a "description of a mental state".—One might rather call them a "signal"; and we judge whether it was rightly employed by what he goes on to do.

181. In order to understand this, we need also to consider the following: suppose B says he knows how to go on—but when he wants to go on he hesitates and can't do it: are we to say that he was wrong when he said he could go on, or rather that he was able to go on then, only now is not?—Clearly we shall say different things in different cases. (Consider both kinds of case.)

182. The grammar of "to fit", "to be able", and "to understand". (Exercises: (1) When is a cylinder C said to fit into a hollow cylinder H? Only while C is stuck into H? (2) Sometimes we say that C ceased to fit into H at such-and-such a time. What criteria are used in such a case for its having happened at that time? (3) What does one regard as criteria for a body's having changed its weight at a particular time if it was not actually on the balance at that time? (4) Yesterday I knew the poem by heart; today I no longer know it. In what kind of case does it make sense to ask: "When did I stop knowing it?" (5) Someone asks me "Can you lift this weight?" I answer "Yes". Now he says "Do it!"—and I can't. In what kind of circumstances would it count as a justification to say "When I answered 'yes' I *could* do it, only now I can't"?

The criteria which we accept for 'fitting', 'being able to', 'understanding', are much more complicated than might appear at first sight. That is, the game with these words, their employment in the linguistic intercourse that is carried on by their means, is more involved—the role of these words in our language other—than we are tempted to think.

(This role is what we need to understand in order to resolve philosophical paradoxes. And hence definitions usually fail to resolve them; and so, *a fortiori* does the assertion that a word is 'indefinable'.)

183. But did "Now I can go on" in case (151) mean the same as "Now the formula has occurred to me" or something different? We may say that, in those circumstances, the two sentences have the same sense, achieve the same thing. But also that *in general* these two sentences do not have the same sense. We do say: "Now I can go on, I mean I know the formula", as we say "I can walk, I mean I have time"; but also "I can walk, I mean I am already strong enough"; or: "I can walk, as far as the state of my legs is concerned", that is, when we are contrasting *this* condition for walking with others. But here we must be on our guard against thinking that there is some *totality* of conditions corresponding to the nature of each case (e.g. for a person's walking) so that, as it were, he *could not but* walk if they were all fulfilled.

184. I want to remember a tune and it escapes me; suddenly I say "Now I know it" and I sing it. What was it like to suddenly know it? Surely it can't have occurred to me *in its entirety* in that moment!— Perhaps you will say: "It's a particular feeling, as if it were *there*"— but *is* it there? Suppose I now begin to sing it and get stuck?—— But may I not have been *certain* at that moment that I knew it? So in some sense or other it was *there* after all!——But in what sense? You would say that the tune was there, if, say, someone sang it through, or heard it mentally from beginning to end. I am not, of course, denying that the statement that the tune is there can also be given a quite different meaning—for example, that I have a bit of paper on which it is written.—And what does his being 'certain', his knowing it, consist in? —Of course we can say: if someone says with conviction that now he knows the tune, then it is (somehow) present to his mind in its entirety at that moment——and this is a definition of the expression "the tune is present to his mind in its entirety".

185. Let us return to our example (143). Now—judged by the usual criteria—the pupil has mastered the series of natural numbers. Next we teach him to write down other series of cardinal numbers and get him to the point of writing down series of the form

$$0, n, 2n, 3n, \text{etc.}$$

at an order of the form "+n"; so at the order "+1" he writes down the series of natural numbers.—Let us suppose we have done exercises and given him tests up to 1000.

Now we get the pupil to continue a series (say +2) beyond 1000—and he writes 1000, 1004, 1008, 1012.

We say to him: "Look what you've done!"—He doesn't understand. We say: "You were meant to add *two*: look how you began the series!" —He answers: "Yes, isn't it right? I thought that was how I was *meant* to do it."——Or suppose he pointed to the series and said: "But I went on in the same way."—It would now be no use to say: "But can't you see . . . . ?"—and repeat the old examples and explanations.—In such a case we might say, perhaps: It comes natural to this person to understand our order with our explanations as *we* should understand the order: "Add 2 up to 1000, 4 up to 2000, 6 up to 3000 and so on."

Such a case would present similarities with one in which a person naturally reacted to the gesture of pointing with the hand by looking in the direction of the line from finger-tip to wrist, not from wrist to finger-tip.

186. "What you are saying, then, comes to this: a new insight—intuition—is needed at every step to carry out the order '+n' correctly."—To carry it out correctly! How is it decided what is the right step to take at any particular stage?—"The right step is the one that accords with the order—as it was *meant*."—So when you gave the order +2 you meant that he was to write 1002 after 1000—and did you also mean that he should write 1868 after 1866, and 100036 after 100034, and so on—an infinite number of such propositions?—"No: what I meant was, that he should write the next but one number after *every* number that he wrote; and from this all those propositions follow in turn."—But that is just what is in question: what, at any stage, does follow from that sentence. Or, again, what, at any stage we are to call "being in accord" with that sentence (and with the *mean*-ing you then put into the sentence—whatever that may have consisted in). It would almost be more correct to say, not that an intuition was needed at every stage, but that a new decision was needed at every stage.

187. "But I already knew, at the time when I gave the order, that he ought to write 1002 after 1000."—Certainly; and you can also say you *meant* it then; only you should not let yourself be misled by the grammar of the words "know" and "mean". For you don't want

to say that you thought of the step from 1000 to 1002 at that time—and even if you did think of this step, still you did not think of other ones. When you said "I already knew at the time . . . . . " that meant something like: "If I had then been asked what number should be written after 1000, I should have replied '1002'." And that I don't doubt. This assumption is rather of the same kind as: "If he had fallen into the water then, I should have jumped in after him".—Now, what was wrong with your idea?

188. Here I should first of all like to say: your idea was that that act of meaning the order had in its own way already traversed all those steps: that when you meant it your mind as it were flew ahead and took all the steps before you physically arrived at this or that one.

Thus you were inclined to use such expressions as: "The steps are *really* already taken, even before I take them in writing or orally or in thought." And it seemed as if they were in some *unique* way pre-determined, anticipated—as only the act of meaning can anticipate reality.

189. "But *are* the steps then *not* determined by the algebraic formula?"—The question contains a mistake.

We use the expression: "The steps are determined by the formula . . . . .". *How* is it used?—We may perhaps refer to the fact that people are brought by their education (training) so to use the formula $y = x^2$, that they all work out the same value for y when they substitute the same number for x. Or we may say: "These people are so trained that they all take the same step at the same point when they receive the order 'add 3' ". We might express this by saying: for these people the order "add 3" completely determines every step from one number to the next. (In contrast with other people who do not know what they are to do on receiving this order, or who react to it with perfect certainty, but each one in a different way.)

On the other hand we can contrast different kinds of formula, and the different kinds of use (different kinds of training) appropriate to them. Then we *call* formulae of a particular kind (with the appropriate methods of use) "formulae which determine a number y for a given value of x", and formulae of another kind, ones which "do not determine the number y for a given value of x". ($y = x^2$ would be of the first kind, $y \neq x^2$ of the second.) The proposition "The formula . . . . determines a number y" will then be a statement about the form of the formula—and now we must distinguish such a proposition as "The formula which I have written down determines y", or "Here is a formula which determines y", from one of the following kind: "The formula $y = x^2$ determines the number y for a given value of x". The question "Is the formula written down there one that determines y?" will then mean the same as "Is what is there a formula of this kind or that?"—but it is not clear off-hand what we are to make of the question "Is $y = x^2$ a formula which determines y for a given value of x?" One might address this question to a pupil in order to test whether he understands the use of the word "to determine"; or it might be a mathematical problem to prove in a particular system that x has only one square.

190. It may now be said: "The way the formula is meant determines which steps are to be taken". What is the criterion for the way the formula is meant? It is, for example, the kind of way we always use it, the way we are taught to use it.

We say, for instance, to someone who uses a sign unknown to us: "If by '$x!2$' you mean x^2, then you get *this* value for y, if you mean $2x$, *that* one."—Now ask yourself: how does one *mean* the one thing or the other by "$x!2$"?

That will be how meaning it can determine the steps in advance.

191. "It is as if we could grasp the whole use of the word in a flash." Like *what* e.g.?—Can't the use—in a certain sense—be grasped in a flash? And in *what* sense can it not?—The point is, that it is as if we could 'grasp it in a flash' in yet another and much more direct sense than that.—But have you a model for this? No. It is just that this expression suggests itself to us. As the result of the crossing of different pictures.

192. You have no model of this superlative fact, but you are seduced into using a super-expression. (It might be called a philosophical superlative.)

193. The machine as symbolizing its action: the action of a machine—I might say at first—seems to be there in it from the start. What does that mean?—If we know the machine, everything else, that is its movement, seems to be already completely determined.

We talk as if these parts could only move in this way, as if they could not do anything else. How is this—do we forget the possibility of their bending, breaking off, melting, and so on? Yes; in many cases we don't think of that at all. We use a machine, or the drawing of a machine, to symbolize a particular action of the machine. For instance, we give someone such a drawing and assume that he will derive the movement of the parts from it. (Just as we can give someone a number by telling him that it is the twenty-fifth in the series 1, 4, 9, 16, ...)

"The machine's action seems to be in it from the start" means: we are inclined to compare the future movements of the machine in their definiteness to objects which are already lying in a drawer and which we then take out.——But we do not say this kind of thing when we are concerned with predicting the actual behaviour of a machine. Then we do not in general forget the possibility of a distortion of the parts and so on.——We *do* talk like that, however, when we are wondering at the way we can use a machine to symbolize a given way of moving—since it can also move in quite *different* ways.

We might say that a machine, or the picture of it, is the first of a series of pictures which we have learnt to derive from this one.

But when we reflect that the machine could also have moved differently it may look as if the way it moves must be contained in the machine-as-symbol far more determinately than in the actual machine. As if it were not enough for the movements in question to be empirically determined in advance, but they had to be really—in a mysterious sense—already *present*. And it is quite true: the movement of the machine-as-symbol is predetermined in a different sense from that in which the movement of any given actual machine is predetermined.

194. When does one have the thought: the possible movements of a machine are already there in it in some mysterious way?—Well, when one is doing philosophy. And what leads us into thinking that? The kind of way in which we talk about machines. We say, for example, that a machine *has* (possesses) such-and-such possibilities of movement; we speak of the ideally rigid machine which *can* only move in such-and-such a way.——What is this *possibility* of movement? It is not the *movement*, but it does not seem to be the mere physical conditions for moving either—as, that there is play between socket and pin, the pin not fitting too tight in the socket. For while this is the empirical condition for movement, one could also imagine it to be otherwise. The possibility of a movement is, rather, supposed to be like a shadow of the movement itself. But do you know of such a shadow? And by a shadow I do not mean some picture of the movement—for such a

icture would not have to be a picture of just *this* movement. But the
ossibility of this movement must be the possibility of just this
novement. (See how high the seas of language run here!)

The waves subside as soon as we ask ourselves: how do we use
he phrase "possibility of movement" when we are talking about a
;iven machine?——But then where did our queer ideas come from?
Vell, I shew you the possibility of a movement, say by means of a
icture of the movement: 'so possibility is something which is like
eality'. We say: "It isn't moving yet, but it already has the possibility
f moving"——'so possibility is something very near reality'. Though
ve may doubt whether such-and-such physical conditions make this
novement possible, we never discuss whether *this* is the possibility
f this or of that movement: 'so the possibility of the movement
tands in a unique relation to the movement itself; closer than that of a
icture to its subject'; for it can be doubted whether a picture is the
icture of this thing or that. We say "Experience will shew whether
his gives the pin this possibility of movement", but we do not say
"Experience will shew whether this is the possibility of this move-
nent": 'so it is not an empirical fact that this possibility is the possibility
f precisely this movement'.

We mind about the kind of expressions we use concerning these
hings; we do not understand them, however, but misinterpret them.
Vhen we do philosophy we are like savages, primitive people, who
ear the expressions of civilized men, put a false interpretation on
hem, and then draw the queerest conclusions from it.

195.   "But I don't mean that what I do now (in grasping a sense)
etermines the future use *causally* and as a matter of experience, but
hat in a *queer* way, the use itself is in some sense present."—But of
ourse it is, 'in *some* sense'! Really the only thing wrong with what you
ay is the expression "in a queer way". The rest is all right; and the
entence only seems queer when one imagines a different language-game
or it from the one in which we actually use it. (Someone once told
ne that as a child he had been surprised that a tailor could 'sew a
ress'—he thought this meant that a dress was produced by sewing
lone, by sewing one thread on to another.)

196.   In our failure to understand the use of a word we take it as
he expression of a queer *process*. (As we think of time as a queer
nedium, of the mind as a queer kind of being.)

197. "It's as if we could grasp the whole use of a word in a flash."–
And that is just what we say we do. That is to say: we sometime
describe what we do in these words. But there is nothing astonishing
nothing queer, about what happens. It becomes queer when we ar
led to think that the future development must in some way already b
present in the act of grasping the use and yet isn't present.—For we sa
that there isn't any doubt that we understand the word, and on th
other hand its meaning lies in its use. There is no doubt that I no\
want to play chess, but chess is the game it is in virtue of all its rule
(and so on). Don't I know, then, which game I want to play until
have played it? or are all the rules contained in my act of intending
Is it experience that tells me that this sort of game is the usual cons\
quence of such an act of intending? so is it impossible for me to b
certain what I am intending to do? And if that is nonsense—wha
kind of super-strong connexion exists between the act of intendin
and the thing intended?——Where is the connexion effected betwee
the sense of the expression "Let's play a game of chess" and all th
rules of the game?—Well, in the list of rules of the game, in the teachin
of it, in the day-to-day practice of playing.

198. "But how can a rule shew me what I have to do at *this* point
Whatever I do is, on some interpretation, in accord with the rule."–
That is not what we ought to say, but rather: any interpretation sti
hangs in the air along with what it interprets, and cannot give
any support. Interpretations by themselves do not determine mear
ing.

"Then can whatever I do be brought into accord with the rule?"–
Let me ask this: what has the expression of a rule—say a sign-post-
got to do with my actions? What sort of connexion is there here?–
Well, perhaps this one: I have been trained to react to this sign in
particular way, and now I do so react to it.

But that is only to give a causal connexion; to tell how it has com
about that we now go by the sign-post; not what this going-by-th\
sign really consists in. On the contrary; I have further indicated th\
a person goes by a sign-post only in so far as there exists a regular u\
of sign-posts, a custom.

199. Is what we call "obeying a rule" something that it would b
possible for only *one* man to do, and to do only *once* in his life?–
This is of course a note on the grammar of the expression "to obey
rule".

It is not possible that there should have been only one occasion on which someone obeyed a rule. It is not possible that there should have been only one occasion on which a report was made, an order given or understood; and so on.—To obey a rule, to make a report, to give an order, to play a game of chess, are *customs* (uses, institutions).

To understand a sentence means to understand a language. To understand a language means to be master of a technique.

200. It is, of course, imaginable that two people belonging to a tribe unacquainted with games should sit at a chess-board and go through the moves of a game of chess; and even with all the appropriate mental accompaniments. And if *we* were to see it we should say they were playing chess. But now imagine a game of chess translated according to certain rules into a series of actions which we do not ordinarily associate with a *game*—say into yells and stamping of feet. And now suppose those two people to yell and stamp instead of playing the form of chess that we are used to; and this in such a way that their procedure is translatable by suitable rules into a game of chess. Should we still be inclined to say they were playing a game? What right would one have to say so?

201. This was our paradox: no course of action could be determined by a rule, because every course of action can be made out to accord with the rule. The answer was: if everything can be made out to accord with the rule, then it can also be made out to conflict with it. And so there would be neither accord nor conflict here.

It can be seen that there is a misunderstanding here from the mere fact that in the course of our argument we give one interpretation after another; as if each one contented us at least for a moment, until we thought of yet another standing behind it. What this shews is that there is a way of grasping a rule which is *not* an *interpretation*, but which is exhibited in what we call "obeying the rule" and "going against it" in actual cases.

Hence there is an inclination to say: every action according to the rule is an interpretation. But we ought to restrict the term "interpretation" to the substitution of one expression of the rule for another.

202. And hence also 'obeying a rule' is a practice. And to *think* one is obeying a rule is not to obey a rule. Hence it is not possible to obey a rule 'privately': otherwise thinking one was obeying a rule would be the same thing as obeying it.

203. Language is a labyrinth of paths. You approach from *one* side and know your way about; you approach the same place from another side and no longer know your way about.

204. As things are I can, for example, invent a game that is never played by anyone.—But would the following be possible too: mankind has never played any games; once, however, someone invented a game —which no one ever played?

205. "But it is just the queer thing about *intention*, about the mental process, that the existence of a custom, of a technique, is not necessary to it. That, for example, it is imaginable that two people should play chess in a world in which otherwise no games existed; and even that they should begin a game of chess—and then be interrupted.'
But isn't chess defined by its rules? And how are these rules present in the mind of the person who is intending to play chess?

206. Following a rule is analogous to obeying an order. We are trained to do so; we react to an order in a particular way. But what if one person reacts in one way and another in another to the order and the training? Which one is right?
Suppose you came as an explorer into an unknown country with a language quite strange to you. In what circumstances would you say that the people there gave orders, understood them, obeyed them, rebelled against them, and so on?
The common behaviour of mankind is the system of reference by means of which we interpret an unknown language.

207. Let us imagine that the people in that country carried on the usual human activities and in the course of them employed, apparently, an articulate language. If we watch their behaviour we find it intelligible, it seems 'logical'. But when we try to learn their language we find it impossible to do so. For there is no regular connexion between what they say, the sounds they make, and their actions; but still these sounds are not superfluous, for if we gag one of the people, it has the same consequences as with us; without the sounds their actions fall into confusion—as I feel like putting it.
Are we to say that these people have a language: orders, reports, and the rest?
There is not enough regularity for us to call it "language".

208. Then am I defining "order" and "rule" by means of "regularity"?—How do I explain the meaning of "regular", "uniform"

"same" to anyone?—I shall explain these words to someone who, say, only speaks French by means of the corresponding French words. But if a person has not yet got the *concepts*, I shall teach him to use the words by means of *examples* and by *practice*.—And when I do this I do not communicate less to him than I know myself.

In the course of this teaching I shall shew him the same colours, the same lengths, the same shapes, I shall make him find them and produce them, and so on. I shall, for instance, get him to continue an ornamental pattern uniformly when told to do so.—And also to continue progressions. And so, for example, when given: . .. ... to go on: ....

I do it, he does it after me; and I influence him by expressions of agreement, rejection, expectation, encouragement. I let him go his way, or hold him back; and so on.

Imagine witnessing such teaching. None of the words would be explained by means of itself; there would be no logical circle.

The expressions "and so on", "and so on ad infinitum" are also explained in this teaching. A gesture, among other things, might serve this purpose. The gesture that means "go on like this", or "and so on" has a function comparable to that of pointing to an object or a place.

We should distinguish between the "and so on" which is, and the "and so on" which is not, an abbreviated notation. "And so on ad inf." is *not* such an abbreviation. The fact that we cannot write down all the digits of π is not a human shortcoming, as mathematicians sometimes think.

Teaching which is not meant to apply to anything but the examples given is different from that which '*points beyond*' them.

209. "But then doesn't our understanding reach beyond all the examples?"—A very queer expression, and a quite natural one!—

But is that *all*? Isn't there a deeper explanation; or mustn't at least the *understanding* of the explanation be deeper?—Well, have I myself a deeper understanding? Have I *got* more than I give in the explanation?—But then, whence the feeling that I have got more?

Is it like the case where I interpret what is not limited as a length that reaches beyond every length?

210. "But do you really explain to the other person what you yourself understand? Don't you get him to *guess* the essential thing? You give him examples,—but he has to guess their drift, to guess your

intention."—Every explanation which I can give myself I give to him too.—"He guesses what I intend" would mean: various interpretations of my explanation come to his mind, and he lights on one of them. So in this case he could ask; and I could and should answer him.

211.   How can he *know* how he is to continue a pattern by himself— whatever instruction you give him?—Well, how do I know?——If that means "Have I reasons?" the answer is: my reasons will soon give out. And then I shall act, without reasons.

212.   When someone whom I am afraid of orders me to continue the series, I act quickly, with perfect certainty, and the lack of reasons does not trouble me.

213.   "But this initial segment of a series obviously admitted of various interpretations (e.g. by means of algebraic expressions) and so you must first have chosen *one* such interpretation."—Not at all. A doubt was possible in certain circumstances. But that is not to say that I did doubt, or even could doubt. (There is something to be said, which is connected with this, about the psychological 'atmosphere' of a process.)

So it must have been intuition that removed this doubt?—If intuition is an inner voice—how do I know *how* I am to obey it? And how do I know that it doesn't mislead me? For if it can guide me right, it can also guide me wrong.

((Intuition an unnecessary shuffle.))

214.   If you have to have an intuition in order to develop the series 1 2 3 4 ... you must also have one in order to develop the series 2 2 2 2 ....

215.   But isn't *the same* at least the same?

We seem to have an infallible paradigm of identity in the identity of a thing with itself. I feel like saying: "Here at any rate there can't be a variety of interpretations. If you are seeing a thing you are seeing identity too."

Then are two things the same when they are what *one* thing is? And how am I to apply what the *one* thing shews me to the case of two things?

216.   "A thing is identical with itself."—There is no finer example of a useless proposition, which yet is connected with a certain play of the imagination. It is as if in imagination we put a thing into its own shape and saw that it fitted.

We might also say: "Every thing fits into itself." Or again: "Every thing fits into its own shape." At the same time we look at a thing and imagine that there was a blank left for it, and that now it fits into it exactly.

Does this spot ♣ '*fit*' into its white surrounding?—*But that is just how it would look* if there had at first been a hole in its place and it then fitted into the hole. But when we say "it fits" we are not simply describing this appearance; not simply this *situation*.

"Every coloured patch fits exactly into its surrounding" is a rather specialized form of the law of identity.

217. "How am I able to obey a rule?"—if this is not a question about causes, then it is about the justification for my following the rule in the way I do.

If I have exhausted the justifications I have reached bedrock, and my spade is turned. Then I am inclined to say: "This is simply what I do."

(Remember that we sometimes demand definitions for the sake not of their content, but of their form. Our requirement is an architectural one; the definition a kind of ornamental coping that supports nothing.)

218. Whence comes the idea that the beginning of a series is a visible section of rails invisibly laid to infinity? Well, we might imagine rails instead of a rule. And infinitely long rails correspond to the unlimited application of a rule.

219. "All the steps are really already taken" means: I no longer have any choice. The rule, once stamped with a particular meaning, traces the lines along which it is to be followed through the whole of space.——But if something of this sort really were the case, how would it help?

No; my description only made sense if it was to be understood symbolically.—I should have said: *This is how it strikes me*.

When I obey a rule, I do not choose.

I obey the rule *blindly*.

220. But what is the purpose of that symbolical proposition? It was supposed to bring into prominence a difference between being causally determined and being logically determined.

221. My symbolical expression was really a mythological description of the use of a rule.

222. "The line intimates to me the way I am to go."—But that is of course only a picture. And if I judged that it intimated this or that as it were irresponsibly, I should not say that I was obeying it like a rule.

223. One does not feel that one has always got to wait upon the nod (the whisper) of the rule. On the contrary, we are not on tenter-hooks about what it will tell us next, but it always tells us the same, and we do what it tells us.

One might say to the person one was training: "Look, I always do the same thing: I . . . . ."

224. The word "agreement" and the word "rule" are *related* to one another, they are cousins. If I teach anyone the use of the one word, he learns the use of the other with it.

225. The use of the word "rule" and the use of the word "same" are interwoven. (As are the use of "proposition" and the use of "true".)

226. Suppose someone gets the series of numbers 1, 3, 5, 7, ... by working out the series $2x + 1$[1]. And now he asks himself: "But am I always doing the same thing, or something different every time?"

If from one day to the next you promise: "To-morrow I will come and see you"—are you saying the same thing every day, or every day something different?

227. Would it make sense to say "If he did something *different* every day we should not say he was obeying a rule"? That makes *no* sense.

228. "We see a series in just *one* way!"—All right, but what is that way? Clearly we see it algebraically, and as a segment of an expansion. Or is there more in it than that?—"But the way we see it surely gives us everything!"—But that is not an observation about the segment of the series; or about anything that we notice in it; it gives expression to the fact that we look to the rule for instruction and *do something*, without appealing to anything else for guidance.

229. I believe that I perceive something drawn very fine in a segment of a series, a characteristic design, which only needs the addition of "and so on", in order to reach to infinity.

230. "The line intimates to me which way I am to go" is only a paraphrase of: it is my *last* arbiter for the way I am to go.

231. "But surely you can see . . . .?" That is just the characteristic expression of someone who is under the compulsion of a rule.

[1] The MSS. have: . . . . der Reihe x = 1, 3, 5, 7, ... indem er die Reihe der $x^2 + 1$ hinschreibt.—Ed.

232.   Let us imagine a rule intimating to me which way I am to
obey it; that is, as my eye travels along the line, a voice within me says:
"*This* way!"—What is the difference between this process of obeying a
kind of inspiration and that of obeying a rule? For they are surely
not the same. In the case of inspiration I *await* direction. I shall not
be able to teach anyone else my 'technique' of following the line.
Unless, indeed, I teach him some way of hearkening, some kind of
receptivity. But then, of course, I cannot require him to follow the line
in the same way as I do.

These are not my experiences of acting from inspiration and according to a rule; they are grammatical notes.

233.   It would also be possible to imagine such a training in a sort
of arithmetic. Children could calculate, each in his own way—as long
as they listened to their inner voice and obeyed it. Calculating in this
way would be like a sort of composing.

234.   Would it not be possible for us, however, to calculate as we
actually do (all agreeing, and so on), and still at every step to have a
feeling of being guided by the rules as by a spell, feeling astonishment
at the fact that we agreed? (We might give thanks to the Deity for our
agreement.)

235.   This merely shews what goes to make up what we call
"obeying a rule" in everyday life.

236.   Calculating prodigies who get the right answer but cannot
say how. Are we to say that they do not calculate? (A family of cases.)

237.   Imagine someone using a line as a rule in the following
way: he holds a pair of compasses, and carries one of its points along
the line that is the 'rule', while the other one draws the line that follows
the rule. And while he moves along the ruling line he alters the opening of the compasses, apparently with great precision, looking at the
rule the whole time as if it determined what he did. And watching him
we see no kind of regularity in this opening and shutting of the compasses. We cannot learn his way of following the line from it. Here
perhaps one really would say: "The original seems to *intimate* to him
which way he is to go. But it is not a rule."

238.   The rule can only seem to me to produce all its consequences
in advance if I draw them as a *matter of course*. As much as it is a matter

of course for me to call this colour "blue". (Criteria for the fact that
something is 'a matter of course' for me.)

239. How is he to know what colour he is to pick out when he
hears "red"?—Quite simple: he is to take the colour whose image
occurs to him when he hears the word.—But how is he to know which
colour it is 'whose image occurs to him'? Is a further criterion needed
for that? (There is indeed such a procedure as choosing the colour
which occurs to one when one hears the word " .... ")

    " 'Red' means the colour that occurs to me when I hear the word
'red' "—would be a *definition*. Not an explanation of *what it is* to use
a word as a name.

240. Disputes do not break out (among mathematicians, say) over
the question whether a rule has been obeyed or not. People don't
come to blows over it, for example. That is part of the framework
on which the working of our language is based (for example, in giving
descriptions).

241. "So you are saying that human agreement decides what is
true and what is false?"—It is what human beings *say* that is true and
false; and they agree in the *language* they use. That is not agreement in
opinions but in form of life.

242. If language is to be a means of communication there must
be agreement not only in definitions but also (queer as this may
sound) in judgments. This seems to abolish logic, but does not do so.—
It is one thing to describe methods of measurement, and another to
obtain and state results of measurement. But what we call "measuring"
is partly determined by a certain constancy in results of measurement.

243. A human being can encourage himself, give himself orders,
obey, blame and punish himself; he can ask himself a question and
answer it. We could even imagine human beings who spoke only in
monologue; who accompanied their activities by talking to themselves.
—An explorer who watched them and listened to their talk might
succeed in translating their language into ours. (This would enable
him to predict these people's actions correctly, for he also hears them
making resolutions and decisions.)

    But could we also imagine a language in which a person could write
down or give vocal expression to his inner experiences—his feelings,
moods, and the rest—for his private use?——Well, can't we do so
in our ordinary language?—But that is not what I mean. The

individual words of this language are to refer to what can only be known to the person speaking; to his immediate private sensations. So another person cannot understand the language.

244. How do words *refer* to sensations?—There doesn't seem to be any problem here; don't we talk about sensations every day, and give them names? But how is the connexion between the name and the thing named set up? This question is the same as: how does a human being learn the meaning of the names of sensations?—of the word "pain" for example. Here is one possibility: words are connected with the primitive, the natural, expressions of the sensation and used in their place. A child has hurt himself and he cries; and then adults talk to him and teach him exclamations and, later, sentences. They teach the child new pain-behaviour.

"So you are saying that the word 'pain' really means crying?"—On the contrary: the verbal expression of pain replaces crying and does not describe it.

245. For how can I go so far as to try to use language to get between pain and its expression?

246. In what sense are my sensations *private*?—Well, only I can know whether I am really in pain; another person can only surmise it.—In one way this is wrong, and in another nonsense. If we are using the word "to know" as it is normally used (and how else are we to use it?), then other people very often know when I am in pain.—Yes, but all the same not with the certainty with which I know it myself!—It can't be said of me at all (except perhaps as a joke) that I *know* I am in pain. What is it supposed to mean—except perhaps that I *am* in pain?

Other people cannot be said to learn of my sensations *only* from my behaviour,—for *I* cannot be said to learn of them. I *have* them.

The truth is: it makes sense to say about other people that they doubt whether I am in pain; but not to say it about myself.

247. "Only you can know if you had that intention." One might tell someone this when one was explaining the meaning of the word "intention" to him. For then it means: *that* is how we use it.

(And here "know" means that the expression of uncertainty is senseless.)

248. The proposition "Sensations are private" is comparable to "One plays patience by oneself".

249. Are we perhaps over-hasty in our assumption that the smile of an unweaned infant is not a pretence?—And on what experience is our assumption based?

(Lying is a language-game that needs to be learned like any other one.)

250. Why can't a dog simulate pain? Is he too honest? Could one teach a dog to simulate pain? Perhaps it is possible to teach him to howl on particular occasions as if he were in pain, even when he is not. But the surroundings which are necessary for this behaviour to be real simulation are missing.

251. What does it mean when we say: "I can't imagine the opposite of this" or "What would it be like, if it were otherwise?"—For example when someone has said that my images are private, or that only myself can know whether I am feeling pain, and similar things.

Of course, here "I can't imagine the opposite" doesn't mean: my powers of imagination are unequal to the task. These words are a defence against something whose form makes it look like an empirical proposition, but which is really a grammatical one.

But why do we say: "I can't imagine the opposite"? Why not "I can't imagine the thing itself"?

Example: "Every rod has a length." That means something like: we call something (or this) "the length of a rod"—but nothing "the length of a sphere." Now can I imagine 'every rod having a length'? Well, I simply imagine a rod. Only this picture, in connexion with this proposition, has a quite different role from one used in connexion with the proposition "This table has the same length as the one over there". For here I understand what it means to have a picture of the opposite (nor need it be a mental picture).

But the picture attaching to the grammatical proposition could only shew, say, what is called "the length of a rod". And what should the opposite picture be?

((Remark about the negation of an a priori proposition.))

252. "This body has extension." To this we might reply: "Nonsense!"—but are inclined to reply "Of course!"—Why is this?

253. "Another person can't have my pains."—Which are *my* pains? What counts as a criterion of identity here? Consider what makes it possible in the case of physical objects to speak of "two exactly the same", for example, to say "This chair is not the one you saw here yesterday, but is exactly the same as it".

In so far as it makes *sense* to say that my pain is the same as his, it is also possible for us both to have the same pain. (And it would also be imaginable for two people to feel pain in the same—not just the corresponding—place. That might be the case with Siamese twins, for instance.)

I have seen a person in a discussion on this subject strike himself on the breast and say: "But surely another person can't have THIS pain!"—The answer to this is that one does not define a criterion of identity by emphatic stressing of the word "this". Rather, what the emphasis does is to suggest the case in which we are conversant with such a criterion of identity, but have to be reminded of it.

254. The substitution of "identical" for "the same" (for instance) is another typical expedient in philosophy. As if we were talking about shades of meaning and all that were in question were to find words to hit on the correct nuance. That is in question in philosophy only where we have to give a psychologically exact account of the temptation to use a particular kind of expression. What we 'are tempted to say' in such a case is, of course, not philosophy; but it is its raw material. Thus, for example, what a mathematician is inclined to say about the objectivity and reality of mathematical facts, is not a philosophy of mathematics, but something for philosophical *treatment*.

255. The philosopher's treatment of a question is like the treatment of an illness.

256. Now, what about the language which describes my inner experiences and which only I myself can understand? *How* do I use words to stand for my sensations?—As we ordinarily do? Then are my words for sensations tied up with my natural expressions of sensation? In that case my language is not a 'private' one. Someone else might understand it as well as I.—But suppose I didn't have any natural expression for the sensation, but only had the sensation? And now I simply *associate* names with sensations and use these names in descriptions.—

257.   "What would it be like if human beings shewed no outwar
signs of pain (did not groan, grimace, etc.)? Then it would be impo
sible to teach a child the use of the word 'tooth-ache'."—Well, let
assume the child is a genius and itself invents a name for the sensatio
—But then, of course, he couldn't make himself understood when h
used the word.—So does he understand the name, without being ab
to explain its meaning to anyone?—But what does it mean to sa
that he has 'named his pain'?—How has he done this naming of pain
And whatever he did, what was its purpose?—When one says "H
gave a name to his sensation" one forgets that a great deal of stag
setting in the language is presupposed if the mere act of naming is t
make sense. And when we speak of someone's having given a nam
to pain, what is presupposed is the existence of the grammar of th
word "pain"; it shews the post where the new word is stationed.

258.   Let us imagine the following case. I want to keep a dia
about the recurrence of a certain sensation. To this end I associa
it with the sign "S" and write this sign in a calendar for every da
on which I have the sensation.——I will remark first of all that
definition of the sign cannot be formulated.—But still I can give myse
a kind of ostensive definition.—How? Can I point to the sensatio
Not in the ordinary sense. But I speak, or write the sign down, an
at the same time I concentrate my attention on the sensation—and s
as it were, point to it inwardly.—But what is this ceremony fo
for that is all it seems to be! A definition surely serves to establis
the meaning of a sign.—Well, that is done precisely by the concentr
ting of my attention; for in this way I impress on myself the connexio
between the sign and the sensation.—But "I impress it on myself
can only mean: this process brings it about that I remember th
connexion *right* in the future. But in the present case I have no criterio
of correctness. One would like to say: whatever is going to seem rig
to me is right. And that only means that here we can't talk abou
'right'.

259.   Are the rules of the private language *impressions* of rules?-
The balance on which impressions are weighed is not the *impressio*
of a balance.

260.   "Well, I *believe* that this is the sensation S again."—Perhap
you *believe* that you believe it!
Then did the man who made the entry in the calendar make a not

nothing whatever?—Don't consider it a matter of course that a person making a note of something when he makes a mark—say in a calendar. For a note has a function, and this "S" so far has none.
(One can talk to oneself.—If a person speaks when no one else is present, does that mean he is speaking to himself?)

261. What reason have we for calling "S" the sign for a *sensation*? For "sensation" is a word of our common language, not of one intelligible to me alone. So the use of this word stands in need of a justification which everybody understands.—And it would not help either to say that it need not be a *sensation*; that when he writes "S", he has *something*—and that is all that can be said. "Has" and "something" also belong to our common language.—So in the end when one is doing philosophy one gets to the point where one would like just to emit an inarticulate sound.—But such a sound is an expression only as it occurs in a particular language-game, which should now be described.

262. It might be said: if you have given yourself a private definition of a word, then you must inwardly *undertake* to use the word in such-and-such a way. And how do you undertake that? Is it to be assumed that you invent the technique of using the word; or that you found it ready-made?

263. "But I can (inwardly) undertake to call THIS 'pain' in the future."—"But is it certain that you have undertaken it? Are you sure that it was enough for this purpose to concentrate your attention on your feeling?"—A queer question.—

264. "Once you know *what* the word stands for, you understand it, you know its whole use."

265. Let us imagine a table (something like a dictionary) that exists only in our imagination. A dictionary can be used to justify the translation of a word X by a word Y. But are we also to call it justification if such a table is to be looked up only in the imagination?—"Well, yes; then it is a subjective justification."—But justification consists in appealing to something independent.—"But surely I can appeal from one memory to another. For example, I don't know if I have remembered the time of departure of a train right and to check it I call to mind how a page of the time-table looked. Isn't it the same here?"—No; for this process has got to produce a memory which is

actually *correct*. If the mental image of the time-table could not itsel
be *tested* for correctness, how could it confirm the correctness of th
first memory? (As if someone were to buy several copies of the morn
ing paper to assure himself that what it said was true.)

Looking up a table in the imagination is no more looking up a tabl
than the image of the result of an imagined experiment is the result o
an experiment.

266. I can look at the clock to see what time it is: but I can als
look at the dial of a clock in order to *guess* what time it is; or for th
same purpose move the hand of a clock till its position strikes me a
right. So the look of a clock may serve to determine the time in mor
than one way. (Looking at the clock in imagination.)

267. Suppose I wanted to justify the choice of dimensions for
bridge which I imagine to be building, by making loading tests o
the material of the bridge in my imagination. This would, of cours
be to imagine what is called justifying the choice of dimensions for
bridge. But should we also call it justifying an imagined choice o
dimensions?

268. Why can't my right hand give my left hand money?—M
right hand can put it into my left hand. My right hand can write
deed of gift and my left hand a receipt.—But the further practic
consequences would not be those of a gift. When the left hand ha
taken the money from the right, etc., we shall ask: "Well, and what o
it?" And the same could be asked if a person had given himself
private definition of a word; I mean, if he has said the word to himse
and at the same time has directed his attention to a sensation.

269. Let us remember that there are certain criteria in a man'
behaviour for the fact that he does not understand a word: that
means nothing to him, that he can do nothing with it. And criteri
for his 'thinking he understands', attaching some meaning to the word
but not the right one. And, lastly, criteria for his understanding th
word right. In the second case one might speak of a subjective under
standing. And sounds which no one else understands but which
'*appear to understand*' might be called a "private language".

270. Let us now imagine a use for the entry of the sign "S" in m
diary. I discover that whenever I have a particular sensation a man

meter shews that my blood-pressure rises. So I shall be able to say that my blood-pressure is rising without using any apparatus. This is a useful result. And now it seems quite indifferent whether I have recognized the sensation *right* or not. Let us suppose I regularly identify it wrong, it does not matter in the least. And that alone shews that the hypothesis that I make a mistake is mere show. (We as it were turned a knob which looked as if it could be used to turn on some part of the machine; but it was a mere ornament, not connected with the mechanism at all.)

And what is our reason for calling "S" the name of a sensation here? Perhaps the kind of way this sign is employed in this language-game.— And why a "particular sensation," that is, the same one every time? Well, aren't we supposing that we write "S" every time?

271. "Imagine a person whose memory could not retain *what* the word 'pain' meant—so that he constantly called different things by that name—but nevertheless used the word in a way fitting in with the usual symptoms and presuppositions of pain"—in short he uses it as we all do. Here I should like to say: a wheel that can be turned though nothing else moves with it, is not part of the mechanism.

272. The essential thing about private experience is really not that each person possesses his own exemplar, but that nobody knows whether other people also have this or something else. The assumption would thus be possible—though unverifiable—that one section of mankind had one sensation of red and another section another.

273. What am I to say about the word "red"?—that it means something 'confronting us all' and that everyone should really have another word, besides this one, to mean his *own* sensation of red? Or is it like this: the word "red" means something known to everyone; and in addition, for each person, it means something known only to him? (Or perhaps rather: it *refers* to something known only to him.)

274. Of course, saying that the word "red" "refers to" instead of "means" something private does not help us in the least to grasp its function; but it is the more psychologically apt expression for a particular experience in doing philosophy. It is as if when I uttered the word I cast a sidelong glance at the private sensation, as it were in order to say to myself: I know all right what I mean by it.

275.   Look at the blue of the sky and say to yourself "How blue the sky is!"—When you do it spontaneously—without philosophical intentions—the idea never crosses your mind that this impression of colour belongs only to *you*. And you have no hesitation in exclaiming that to someone else. And if you point at anything as you say the words you point at the sky. I am saying: you have not the feeling of pointing-into-yourself, which often accompanies 'naming the sensation' when one is thinking about 'private language'. Nor do you think that really you ought not to point to the colour with your hand, but with your attention. (Consider what it means "to point to something with the attention".)

276.   But don't we at least *mean* something quite definite when we look at a colour and name our colour-impression? It is as if we detached the colour-*impression* from the object, like a membrane. (This ought to arouse our suspicions.)

277.   But how is even possible for us to be tempted to think that we use a word to *mean* at one time the colour known to everyone—and at another the 'visual impression' which *I* am getting *now*? How can there be so much as a temptation here?——I don't turn the same kind of attention on the colour in the two cases. When I mean the colour impression that (as I should like to say) belongs to me alone I immerse myself in the colour—rather like when I 'cannot get my fill of a colour'. Hence it is easier to produce this experience when one is looking at a bright colour, or at an impressive colour-scheme.

278.   "I know how the colour green looks to *me*"—surely that makes sense!—Certainly: what use of the proposition are you thinking of?

279.   Imagine someone saying: "But I know how tall I am!" and laying his hand on top of his head to prove it.

280.   Someone paints a picture in order to shew how he imagines a theatre scene. And now I say: "This picture has a double function: it informs others, as pictures or words inform——but for the one who gives the information it is a representation (or piece of information?) of another kind: for him it is the picture of his image, as it can't be for anyone else. To him his private impression of the picture means what he has imagined, in a sense in which the picture cannot mean this to others."—And what right have I to speak in this second

case of a representation or piece of information—if these words were rightly used in the *first* case?

281. "But doesn't what you say come to this: that there is no pain, for example, without *pain-behaviour*?"—It comes to this: only of a living human being and what resembles (behaves like) a living human being can one say: it has sensations; it sees; is blind; hears; is deaf; is conscious or unconscious.

282. "But in a fairy tale the pot too can see and hear!" (Certainly; but it *can* also talk.)

"But the fairy tale only invents what is not the case: it does not talk *nonsense*."—It is not as simple as that. Is it false or nonsensical to say that a pot talks? Have we a clear picture of the circumstances in which we should say of a pot that it talked? (Even a nonsense-poem is not nonsense in the same way as the babbling of a child.)

We do indeed say of an inanimate thing that it is in pain: when playing with dolls for example. But this use of the concept of pain is a secondary one. Imagine a case in which people ascribed pain *only* to inanimate things; pitied *only* dolls! (When children play at trains their game is connected with their knowledge of trains. It would nevertheless be possible for the children of a tribe unacquainted with trains to learn this game from others, and to play it without knowing that it was copied from anything. One might say that the game did not make the same *sense* to them as to us.)

283. What gives us *so much as the idea* that living beings, things, can feel?

Is it that my education has led me to it by drawing my attention to feelings in myself, and now I transfer the idea to objects outside myself? That I recognize that there is something there (in me) which I can call "pain" without getting into conflict with the way other people use this word?—I do not transfer my idea to stones, plants, etc.

Couldn't I imagine having frightful pains and turning to stone while they lasted? Well, how do I know, if I shut my eyes, whether I have not turned into a stone? And if that has happened, in what sense will *the stone* have the pains? In what sense will they be ascribable to the stone? And why need the pain have a bearer at all here?!

And can one say of the stone that it has a soul and *that* is what has the pain? What has a soul, or pain, to do with a stone?

Only of what behaves like a human being can one say that it *has* pains.

For one has to say it of a body, or, if you like of a soul which some body *has*. And how can a body *have* a soul?

284. Look at a stone and imagine it having sensations.—One says to oneself: How could one so much as get the idea of ascribing a *sensation* to a *thing*? One might as well ascribe it to a number!—And now look at a wriggling fly and at once these difficulties vanish and pain seems able to get a foothold here, where before everything was, so to speak, too smooth for it.

And so, too, a corpse seems to us quite inaccessible to pain.—Our attitude to what is alive and to what is dead, is not the same. All our reactions are different.—If anyone says: "That cannot simply come from the fact that a living thing moves about in such-and-such a way and a dead one not", then I want to intimate to him that this is a case of the transition 'from quantity to quality'.

285. Think of the recognition of *facial expressions*. Or of the description of facial expressions—which does not consist in giving the measurements of the face! Think, too, how one can imitate a man's face without seeing one's own in a mirror.

286. But isn't it absurd to say of a *body* that it has pain?——And why does one feel an absurdity in that? In what sense is it true that my hand does not feel pain, but I in my hand?

What sort of issue is: Is it the *body* that feels pain?—How is it to be decided? What makes it plausible to say that it is *not* the body?— Well, something like this: if someone has a pain in his hand, then the hand does not say so (unless it writes it) and one does not comfort the hand, but the sufferer: one looks into his face.

287. How am I filled with pity *for this man*? How does it come out what the object of my pity is? (Pity, one may say, is a form of conviction that someone else is in pain.)

288. I turn to stone and my pain goes on.—Suppose I were in error and it was no longer *pain*?——But I can't be in error here; it means nothing to doubt whether I am in pain!—That means: if anyone said "I do not know if what I have got is a pain or something else", we should think something like, he does not know what the

English word "pain" means; and we should explain it to him.—How? Perhaps by means of gestures, or by pricking him with a pin and saying: "See, that's what pain is!" This explanation, like any other, he might understand right, wrong, or not at all. And he will shew which he does by his use of the word, in this as in other cases.

If he now said, for example: "Oh, I know what 'pain' means; what I don't know is whether *this*, that I have now, is pain"—we should merely shake our heads and be forced to regard his words as a queer reaction which we have no idea what to do with. (It would be rather as if we heard someone say seriously: "I distinctly remember that some time before I was born I believed . . . . .".)

That expression of doubt has no place in the language-game; but if we cut out human behaviour, which is the expression of sensation, it looks as if I might *legitimately* begin to doubt afresh. My temptation to say that one might take a sensation for something other than what it is arises from this: if I assume the abrogation of the normal language-game with the expression of a sensation, I need a criterion of identity for the sensation; and then the possibility of error also exists.

289.   "When I say 'I am in pain' I am at any rate justified *before myself*."—What does that mean? Does it mean: "If someone else could know what I am calling 'pain', he would admit that I was using the word correctly"?

To use a word without a justification does not mean to use it without right.

290.   What I do is not, of course, to identify my sensation by criteria: but to repeat an expression. But this is not the *end* of the language-game: it is the beginning.

But isn't the beginning the sensation—which I describe?—Perhaps this word "describe" tricks us here. I say "I describe my state of mind" and "I describe my room". You need to call to mind the differences between the language-games.

291.   What we call *"descriptions"* are instruments for particular uses. Think of a machine-drawing, a cross-section, an elevation with measurements, which an engineer has before him. Thinking of a description as a word-picture of the facts has something misleading about it: one tends to think only of such pictures as hang on our walls: which seem simply to portray how a thing looks, what it is like. (These pictures are as it were idle.)

292. Don't always think that you read off what you say from the facts; that you portray these in words according to rules. For even so you would have to apply the rule in the particular case without guidance.

293. If I say of myself that it is only from my own case that I know what the word "pain" means—must I not say the same of other people too? And how can I generalize the *one* case so irresponsibly?

Now someone tells me that *he* knows what pain is only from his own case!——Suppose everyone had a box with something in it: we call it a "beetle". No one can look into anyone else's box, and everyone says he knows what a beetle is only by looking at *his* beetle.—Here it would be quite possible for everyone to have something different in his box. One might even imagine such a thing constantly changing.—But suppose the word "beetle" had a use in these people's language?—If so it would not be used as the name of a thing. The thing in the box has no place in the language-game at all; not even as a *something*: for the box might even be empty.—No, one can 'divide through' by the thing in the box; it cancels out, whatever it is.

That is to say: if we construe the grammar of the expression of sensation on the model of 'object and designation' the object drops out of consideration as irrelevant.

294. If you say he sees a private picture before him, which he is describing, you have still made an assumption about what he has before him. And that means that you can describe it or do describe it more closely. If you admit that you haven't any notion what kind of thing it might be that he has before him—then what leads you into saying, in spite of that, that he has something before him? Isn't it as if I were to say of someone: "He *has* something. But I don't know whether it is money, or debts, or an empty till."

295. "I know . . . . only from my *own* case"—what kind of proposition is this meant to be at all? An experiential one? No.—A grammatical one?

Suppose everyone does say about himself that he knows what pain is only from his own pain.—Not that people really say that, or are even prepared to say it. But *if* everybody said it——it might be a kind of exclamation. And even if it gives no information, still it is a picture, and why should we not want to call up such a picture? Imagine an allegorical painting take the place of those words.

When we look into ourselves as we do philosophy, we often get to

e just such a picture. A full-blown pictorial representation of our
rammar. Not facts; but as it were illustrated turns of speech.

296.   "Yes, but there is *something* there all the same accompanying
ny cry of pain. And it is on account of that that I utter it. And this
omething is what is important—and frightful."—Only whom are we
.forming of this? And on what occasion?

297.   Of course, if water boils in a pot, steam comes out of the pot
nd also pictured steam comes out of the pictured pot. But what if one
.sisted on saying that there must also be something boiling in the
.cture of the pot?

298.   The very fact that we should so much like to say: "*This* is
.e important thing"—while we point privately to the sensation—
. enough to shew how much we are inclined to say something which
.ives no information.

299.   Being unable—when we surrender ourselves to philosophical
.ought—to help saying such-and-such; being irresistibly inclined to say
.—does not mean being forced into an *assumption*, or having an
.nmediate perception or knowledge of a state of affairs.

300.   It is—we should like to say—not merely the picture of the
ehaviour that plays a part in the language-game with the words "he
. in pain", but also the picture of the pain. Or, not merely the para-
.igm of the behaviour, but also that of the pain.—It is a misunder-
.tanding to say "The picture of pain enters into the language-game
.ith the word 'pain'." The image of pain is not a picture and *this*
.nage is not replaceable in the language-game by anything that we
.hould call a picture.—The image of pain certainly enters into the
.nguage game in a sense; only not as a picture.

301.   An image is not a picture, but a picture can correspond to it.

302.   If one has to imagine someone else's pain on the model of
.ne's own, this is none too easy a thing to do: for I have to imagine
.ain which I *do not feel* on the model of the pain which I *do feel*. That
., what I have to do is not simply to make a transition in imagination
.rom one place of pain to another. As, from pain in the hand to pain
.i the arm. For I am not to imagine that I feel pain in some region of
.is body. (Which would also be possible.)
Pain-behaviour can point to a painful place—but the subject of pain
. the person who gives it expression.

303. "I can only *believe* that someone else is in pain, but I *know* if I am."—Yes: one can make the decision to say "I believe he is in pain" instead of "He is in pain". But that is all.——What looks lik an explanation here, or like a statement about a mental process, is i truth an exchange of one expression for another which, while we ar doing philosophy, seems the more appropriate one.

Just try—in a real case—to doubt someone else's fear or pain.

304. "But you will surely admit that there is a difference betwee pain-behaviour accompanied by pain and pain-behaviour without an pain?"—Admit it? What greater difference could there be?—"And ye you again and again reach the conclusion that the sensation itself is *nothing*."—Not at all. It is not a *something*, but not a *nothing* either The conclusion was only that a nothing would serve just as well as something about which nothing could be said. We have only rejecte the grammar which tries to force itself on us here.

The paradox disappears only if we make a radical break with th idea that language always functions in one way, always serves th same purpose: to convey thoughts—which may be about houses, pains good and evil, or anything else you please.

305. "But you surely cannot deny that, for example, in remember ing, an inner process takes place."—What gives the impression tha we want to deny anything? When one says "Still, an inner proces does take place here"—one wants to go on: "After all, you *see* it. And it is this inner process that one means by the word "remember ing".—The impression that we wanted to deny something arises fror our setting our faces against the picture of the 'inner process'. Wha we deny is that the picture of the inner process gives us the correc idea of the use of the word "to remember". We say that this pictur with its ramifications stands in the way of our seeing the use of th word as it is.

306. Why should I deny that there is a mental process? Bu "There has just taken place in me the mental process of remember ing . . . ." means nothing more than: "I have just remembered . . . ." To deny the mental process would mean to deny the remembering to deny that anyone ever remembers anything.

307. "Are you not really a behaviourist in disguise? Aren't yo at bottom really saying that everything except human behaviour i

a fiction?"—If I do speak of a fiction, then it is of a *grammatical* fiction.

308. How does the philosophical problem about mental processes and states and about behaviourism arise?——The first step is the one that altogether escapes notice. We talk of processes and states and leave their nature undecided. Sometime perhaps we shall know more about them—we think. But that is just what commits us to a particular way of looking at the matter. For we have a definite concept of what it means to learn to know a process better. (The decisive movement in the conjuring trick has been made, and it was the very one that we thought quite innocent.)—And now the analogy which was to make us understand our thoughts falls to pieces. So we have to deny the yet uncomprehended process in the yet unexplored medium. And now it looks as if we had denied mental processes. And naturally we don't want to deny them.

309. What is your aim in philosophy?—To shew the fly the way out of the fly-bottle.

310. I tell someone I am in pain. His attitude to me will then be that of belief; disbelief; suspicion; and so on.
Let us assume he says: "It's not so bad."—Doesn't that prove that he believes in something behind the outward expression of pain?—— His attitude is a proof of his attitude. Imagine not merely the words "I am in pain" but also the answer "It's not so bad" replaced by instinctive noises and gestures.

311. "What difference could be greater?"—In the case of pain I believe that I can give myself a private exhibition of the difference. But I can give anyone an exhibition of the difference between a broken and an unbroken tooth.—But for the private exhibition you don't have to give yourself actual pain; it is enough to *imagine* it—for instance, you screw up your face a bit. And do you know that what you are giving yourself this exhibition of is pain and not, for example, a facial expression? And how do you know what you are to give yourself an exhibition of before you do it? This *private* exhibition is an illusion.

312. But again, *aren't* the cases of the tooth and the pain similar? For the visual sensation in the one corresponds to the sensation of pain in the other. I can exhibit the visual sensation to myself as little or as well as the sensation of pain.

Let us imagine the following: The surfaces of the things around us (stones, plants, etc.) have patches and regions which produce pain in our skin when we touch them. (Perhaps through the chemical composition of these surfaces. But we need not know that.) In this case we should speak of pain-patches on the leaf of a particular plant just as at present we speak of red patches. I am supposing that it is useful to us to notice these patches and their shapes; that we can infer important properties of the objects from them.

313. I can exhibit pain, as I exhibit red, and as I exhibit straight and crooked and trees and stones.—*That* is what we *call* "exhibiting".

314. It shews a fundamental misunderstanding, if I am inclined to study the headache I have now in order to get clear about the philo- sophical problem of sensation.

315. Could someone understand the word "pain", who had *never* felt pain?—Is experience to teach me whether this is so or not?— And if we say "A man could not imagine pain without having some- time felt it"—how do we know? How can it be decided whether it is true?

316. In order to get clear about the meaning of the word "think" we watch ourselves while we think; what we observe will be what the word means!—But this concept is not used like that. (It would be as if without knowing how to play chess, I were to try and make out what the word "mate" meant by close observation of the last move of some game of chess.)

317. Misleading parallel: the expression of pain is a cry—the expression of thought, a proposition.
As if the purpose of the proposition were to convey to one person how it is with another: only, so to speak, in his thinking part and not in his stomach.

318. Suppose we think while we talk or write—I mean, as we normally do—we shall not in general say that we think quicker than we talk; the thought seems *not to be separate* from the expression. On the other hand, however, one does speak of the speed of thought; of how a thought goes through one's head like lightning; how problems become clear to us in a flash, and so on. So it is natural to ask if the same thing happens in lightning-like thought—only extremely accelerated—as when we talk and 'think while we talk.' So that in the

first case the clockwork runs down all at once, but in the second bit by bit, braked by the words.

319. I can see or understand a whole thought in a flash in exactly the sense in which I can make a note of it in a few words or a few pencilled dashes.

What makes this note into an epitome of this thought?

320. The lightning-like thought may be connected with the spoken thought as the algebraic formula is with the sequence of numbers which I work out from it.

When, for example, I am given an algebraic function, I am CERTAIN that I shall be able to work out its values for the arguments 1, 2, 3, . . . up to 10. This certainty will be called 'well-founded', for I have learned to compute such functions, and so on. In other cases no reasons will be given for it—but it will be justified by success.

321. "What happens when a man suddenly understands?"—The question is badly framed. If it is a question about the meaning of the expression "sudden understanding", the answer is not to point to a process that we give this name to.—The question might mean: what are the tokens of sudden understanding; what are its characteristic psychical accompaniments?

(There is no ground for assuming that a man feels the facial movements that go with his expression, for example, or the alterations in his breathing that are characteristic of some emotion. Even if he feels them as soon as his attention is directed towards them.) ((Posture.))

322. The question what the expression means is not answered by such a description; and this misleads us into concluding that understanding is a specific indefinable experience. But we forget that what should interest us is the question: how do we *compare* these experiences; what criterion of identity *do we fix* for their occurrence?

323. "Now I know how to go on!" is an exclamation; it corresponds to an instinctive sound, a glad start. Of course it does not follow from my feeling that I shall not find I am stuck when I do try to go on.—Here there are cases in which I should say: "When I said I knew how to go on, I *did* know." One will say that if, for example, an unforeseen interruption occurs. But what is unforeseen must not simply be that I get stuck.

We could also imagine a case in which light was always seeming to dawn on someone—he exclaims "Now I have it!" and then can never justify himself in practice.—It might seem to him as if in the twinkling of an eye he forgot again the meaning of the picture that occurred to him.

324. Would it be correct to say that it is a matter of induction, and that I am as certain that I shall be able to continue the series, as I am that this book will drop on the ground when I let it go; and that I should be no less astonished if I suddenly and for no obvious reason got stuck in working out the series, than I should be if the book remained hanging in the air instead of falling?—To that I will reply that we don't need any grounds for *this* certainty either. What could justify the certainty *better* than success?

325. "The certainty that I shall be able to go on after I have had this experience—seen the formula, for instance,—is simply based on induction." What does this mean?—"The certainty that the fire will burn me is based on induction." Does that mean that I argue to myself: "Fire has always burned me, so it will happen now too?" Or is the previous experience the *cause* of my certainty, not its ground? Whether the earlier experience is the cause of the certainty depends on the system of hypotheses, of natural laws, in which we are considering the phenomenon of certainty.

Is our confidence justified?—What people accept as a justification—is shewn by how they think and live.

326. We expect *this*, and are surprised at *that*. But the chain of reasons has an end.

327. "Can one think without speaking?"—And what is *thinking?*—Well, don't you ever think? Can't you observe yourself and see what is going on? It should be quite simple. You do not have to wait for it as for an astronomical event and then perhaps make your observation in a hurry.

328. Well, what does one include in 'thinking'? What has one learnt to use this word for?—If I say I have thought—need I always be right?—What *kind* of mistake is there room for here? Are there circumstances in which one would ask: "Was what I was doing then really thinking; am I not making a mistake?" Suppose someone takes a measurement in the middle of a train of thought: has he interrupted the thought if he says nothing to himself during the measuring?

329. When I think in language, there aren't 'meanings' going
through my mind in addition to the verbal expressions: the language is
itself the vehicle of thought.

330. Is thinking a kind of speaking? One would like to say it is
what distinguishes speech with thought from talking without thinking.
—And so it seems to be an accompaniment of speech. A process,
which may accompany something else, or can go on by itself.
Say: "Yes, this pen is blunt. Oh well, it'll do." First, thinking it;
then without thought; then just think the thought without the words.
—Well, while doing some writing I might test the point of my pen,
make a face—and then go on with a gesture of resignation.—I might
also act in such a way while taking various measurements that an on-
looker would say I had—without words—thought: If two magnitudes
are equal to a third, they are equal to one another.—But what con-
stitutes thought here is not some process which has to accompany
the words if they are not to be spoken without thought.

331. Imagine people who could only think aloud. (As there are
people who can only read aloud.)

332. While we sometimes call it "thinking" to accompany a
sentence by a mental process, that accompaniment is not what we
mean by a "thought".——Say a sentence and think it; say it with understanding.—And now do not say it, and just do what you accompanied
it with when you said it with understanding!—(Sing this tune with
expression. And now don't sing it, but repeat its expression!—And
here one actually might repeat something. For example, motions of
the body, slower and faster breathing, and so on.)

333. "Only someone who is *convinced* can say that."—How does
the conviction help him when he says it?—Is it somewhere at hand by
the side of the spoken expression? (Or is it masked by it, as a soft
sound by a loud one, so that it can, as it were, no longer be heard
when one expresses it out loud?) What if someone were to say "In
order to be able to sing a tune from memory one has to hear it in
one's mind and sing from that"?

334. "So you really wanted to say . . . ."—We use this phrase
in order to lead someone from one form of expression to another.
One is tempted to use the following picture: what he really 'wanted to
say', what he 'meant' was already *present somewhere* in his mind even

before we gave it expression. Various kinds of thing may persuade us to give up one expression and to adopt another in its place. To understand this, it is useful to consider the relation in which the solutions of mathematical problems stand to the context and ground of their formulation. The concept 'trisection of the angle with ruler and compass', when people are trying to do it, and, on the other hand, when it has been proved that there is no such thing.

335. What happens when we make an effort—say in writing a letter—to find the right expression for our thoughts?—This phrase compares the process to one of translating or describing: the thoughts are already there (perhaps were there in advance) and we merely look for their expression. This picture is more or less appropriate in different cases.—But can't all sorts of things happen here?—I surrender to a mood and the expression *comes*. Or a picture occurs to me and I try to describe it. Or an English expression occurs to me and I try to hit on the corresponding German one. Or I make a gesture, and ask myself: What words correspond to this gesture? And so on.

Now if it were asked: "Do you have the thought before finding the expression?" what would one have to reply? And what, to the question: "What did the thought consist in, as it existed before its expression?"

336. This case is similar to the one in which someone imagines that one could not think a sentence with the remarkable word order of German or Latin just as it stands. One first has to think it, and then one arranges the words in that queer order. (A French politician once wrote that it was a peculiarity of the French language that in it words occur in the order in which one thinks them.)

337. But didn't I already intend the whole construction of the sentence (for example) at its beginning? So surely it already existed in my mind before I said it out loud!—If it was in my mind, still it would not normally be there in some different word order. But here we are constructing a misleading picture of 'intending', that is, of the use of this word. An intention is embedded in its situation, in human customs and institutions. If the technique of the game of chess did not exist, I could not intend to play a game of chess. In so far as I do intend the construction of a sentence in advance, that is made possible by the fact that I can speak the language in question.

338. After all, one can only say something if one has learned to talk. Therefore in order to *want* to say something one must also have mastered a language; and yet it is clear that one can want to speak without speaking. Just as one can want to dance without dancing.

And when we think about this, we grasp at the *image* of dancing, speaking, etc. .

339. Thinking is not an incorporeal process which lends life and sense to speaking, and which it would be possible to detach from speaking, rather as the Devil took the shadow of Schlemiehl from the ground.——But how "not an incorporeal process"? Am I acquainted with incorporeal processes, then, only thinking is not one of them? No; I called the expression "an incorporeal process" to my aid in my embarrassment when I was trying to explain the meaning of the word "thinking" in a primitive way.

One might say "Thinking is an incorporeal process", however, if one were using this to distinguish the grammar of the word "think" from that of, say, the word "eat". Only that makes the difference between the meanings look *too slight*. (It is like saying: numerals are actual, and numbers non-actual, objects.) An unsuitable type of expression is a sure means of remaining in a state of confusion. It as it were bars the way out.

340. One cannot guess how a word functions. One has to *look at* its use and learn from that.

But the difficulty is to remove the prejudice which stands in the way of doing this. It is not a *stupid* prejudice.

341. Speech with and without thought is to be compared with the playing of a piece of music with and without thought.

342 William James, in order to shew that thought is possible without speech, quotes the recollection of a deaf-mute, Mr. Ballard, who wrote that in his early youth, even before he could speak, he had had thoughts about God and the world.—What can he have meant?—Ballard writes: "It was during those delightful rides, some two or three years before my initiation into the rudiments of written language, that I began to ask myself the question: how came the world into being?"—Are you sure—one would like to ask—that this is the correct translation of your wordless thought into words? And why does this question—which otherwise seems not to exist—raise its head here? Do I want to say that the writer's memory deceives

him?—I don't even know if I should say *that*. These recollections are a queer memory phenomenon,—and I do not know what conclusions one can draw from them about the past of the man who recounts them.

343.   The words with which I express my memory are my memory-reaction.

344.   Would it be imaginable that people should never speak an audible language, but should still say things to themselves in the imagination?

"If people always said things only to themselves, then they would merely be doing *always* what as it is they do *sometimes*."—So it is quite easy to imagine this: one need only make the easy transition from some to all. (Like: "An infinitely long row of trees is simply one that does *not* come to an end.") Our criterion for someone's saying something to himself is what he tells us and the rest of his behaviour; and we only say that someone speaks to himself if, in the ordinary sense of the words, he *can speak*. And we do not say it of a parrot; nor of a gramophone.

345.   "What sometimes happens might always happen."—What kind of proposition is that? It is like the following: If "$F(a)$" makes sense "$(x).F(x)$" makes sense.

"If it is possible for someone to make a false move in some game, then it might be possible for everybody to make nothing but false moves in every game."—Thus we are under a temptation to misunderstand the logic of our expressions here, to give an incorrect account of the use of our words.

Orders are sometimes not obeyed. But what would it be like if no orders were *ever* obeyed? The concept 'order' would have lost its purpose.

346.   But couldn't we imagine God's suddenly giving a parrot understanding, and its now saying things to itself?—But here it is an important fact that I imagined a deity in order to imagine this.

347.   "But at least I know from my own case what it means 'to say things to oneself'. And if I were deprived of the organs of speech, I could still talk to myself."

If I know it only from my own case, then I know only what *I* call that, not what anyone else does.

348.   "These deaf-mutes have learned only a gesture-language, but each of them talks to himself inwardly in a vocal language."—Now,

don't you understand that?—But how do I know whether I understand it?!—What can I do with this information (if it is such)? The
whole idea of understanding smells fishy here. I do not know whether
I am to say I understand it or don't understand it. I might answer
'It's an English sentence; *apparently* quite in order—that is, until one
wants to do something with it; it has a connexion with other sentences
which makes it difficult for us to say that nobody really knows what
it tells us; but everyone who has not become calloused by doing
philosophy notices that there is something wrong here."

349. "But this supposition surely makes good sense!"—Yes; in
ordinary circumstances these words and this picture have an application
with which we are familiar.—But if we suppose a case in which this
application falls away we become as it were conscious for the first
time of the nakedness of the words and the picture.

350. "But if I suppose that someone has a pain, then I am simply
supposing that he has just the same as I have so often had."—That
gets us no further. It is as if I were to say: "You surely know what
'It is 5 o'clock here' means; so you also know what 'It's 5 o'clock on
the sun' means. It means simply that it is just the same time there as
it is here when it is 5 o'clock."—The explanation by means of *identity*
does not work here. For I know well enough that one can call 5 o'clock
here and 5 o'clock there "the same time", but what I do not know is
in what cases one is to speak of its being the same time here and there.
    In exactly the same way it is no explanation to say: the supposition
that he has a pain is simply the supposition that he has the same as I.
For *that* part of the grammar is quite clear to me: that is, that one will
say that the stove has the same experience as I, *if* one says: it is in pain
and I am in pain.

351. Yet we go on wanting to say: "Pain is pain—whether *he*
has it, or *I* have it; and however I come to know whether he has a
pain or not."—I might agree.—And when you ask me "Don't you
know, then, what I mean when I say that the stove is in pain?"—I
can reply: These words may lead me to have all sorts of images; but
their usefulness goes no further. And I can also imagine something
in connexion with the words: "It was just 5 o'clock in the afternoon
on the sun"—such as a grandfather clock which points to 5.—But a
still better example would be that of the application of "above" and
"below" to the earth. Here we all have a quite clear idea of what

"above" and "below" mean. I see well enough that I am on top
the earth is surely beneath me! (And don't smile at this example
We are indeed all taught at school that it is stupid to talk like that
But it is much easier to bury a problem than to solve it.) And it i
only reflection that shews us that in this case "above" and "below"
cannot be used in the ordinary way. (That we might, for instance, say
that the people at the antipodes are 'below' our part of the earth, bu
it must also be recognized as right for them to use the same expression
about us.)

352. Here it happens that our thinking plays us a queer trick
We want, that is, to quote the law of excluded middle and to say
"Either such an image is in his mind, or it is not; there is no third
possibility!"—We encounter this queer argument also in other region:
of philosophy. "In the decimal expansion of π either the group "7777"
occurs, or it does not—there is no third possibility." That is to say
"God sees—but we don't know." But what does that mean?—We
use a picture; the picture of a visible series which one person sees the
whole of and another not. The law of excluded middle says here
It must either look like this, or like that. So it really—and this is a
truism—says nothing at all, but gives us a picture. And the problem
ought now to be: does reality accord with the picture or not? And thi
picture *seems* to determine what we have to do, what to look for, and
how—but it does not do so, just because we do not know how it is to
be applied. Here saying "There is no third possibility" or "But there
can't be a third possibility!"—expresses our inability to turn our eye
away from this picture: a picture which looks as if it must already
contain both the problem and its solution, while all the time we *fee*
that it is not so.

Similarly when it is said "Either he has this experience, or not"—
what primarily occurs to us is a picture which by itself seems to make
the sense of the expressions *unmistakable*: "Now you know what is in
question"—we should like to say. And that is precisely what it does
not tell him.

353. Asking whether and how a proposition can be verified is only
a particular way of asking "How d'you mean?" The answer is a
contribution to the grammar of the proposition.

354. The fluctuation in grammar between criteria and symptom
makes it look as if there were nothing at all but symptoms. We say

for example: "Experience teaches that there is rain when the barometer falls, but it also teaches that there is rain when we have certain sensations of wet and cold, or such-and-such visual impressions." In defence of this one says that these sense-impressions can deceive us. But here one fails to reflect that the fact that the false appearance is precisely one of rain is founded on a definition.

355. The point here is not that our sense-impressions can lie, but that we understand their language. (And this language like any other is founded on convention.)

356. One is inclined to say: "Either it is raining, or it isn't—how I know, how the information has reached me, is another matter." But then let us put the question like this: What do I call "information that it is raining"? (Or have I only information of this information too?) And what gives this 'information' the character of information about something? Doesn't the form of our expression mislead us here? For isn't it a misleading metaphor to say: "My eyes give me the information that there is a chair over there"?

357. We do not say that *possibly* a dog talks to itself. Is that because we are so minutely acquainted with its soul? Well, one might say this: If one sees the behaviour of a living thing, one sees its soul.— But do I also say in my own case that I am saying something to myself, because I am behaving in such-and-such a way?—I do *not* say it from observation of my behaviour. But it only makes sense because I do behave in this way.—Then it is not because I *mean* it that it makes sense?

358. But isn't it our *meaning* it that gives sense to the sentence? (And here, of course, belongs the fact that one cannot mean a senseless series of words.) And 'meaning it' is something in the sphere of the mind. But it is also something private! It is the intangible *something*; only comparable to consciousness itself.

How could this seem ludicrous? It is, as it were, a dream of our language.

359. Could a machine think?——Could it be in pain?—Well, is the human body to be called such a machine? It surely comes as close as possible to being such a machine.

360. But a machine surely cannot think!—Is that an empirical statement? No. We only say of a human being and what is like one that it thinks. We also say it of dolls and no doubt of spirits too. Look at the word "to think" as a tool.

361. The chair is thinking to itself: . . . . .

WHERE? In one of its parts? Or outside its body; in the air around it? Or not *anywhere* at all? But then what is the difference between this chair's saying something to itself and another one's doing so, next to it?—But then how is it with man: where does *he* say things to himself? How does it come about that this question seems senseless; and that no specification of a place is necessary except just that this man is saying something to himself? Whereas the question *where* the chair talks to itself seems to demand an answer.—The reason is: we want to know *how* the chair is supposed to be like a human being; whether, for instance, the head is at the top of the back and so on.

What is it like to say something to oneself; what happens here?—How am I to explain it? Well, only as you might teach someone the meaning of the expression "to say something to oneself". And certainly we learn the meaning of that as children.—Only no one is going to say that the person who teaches it to us tells us 'what takes place'.

362. Rather it seems to us as though in this case the instructor *imparted* the meaning to the pupil—without telling him it directly; but in the end the pupil is brought to the point of giving himself the correct ostensive definition. And this is where our illusion is.

363. "But when I imagine something, something certainly *happens*!" Well, something happens—and then I make a noise. What for? Presumably in order to tell what happens.—But how is *telling* done? When are we said to *tell* anything?—What is the language-game of telling?

I should like to say: you regard it much too much as a matter of course that one can tell anything to anyone. That is to say: we are so much accustomed to communication through language, in conversation, that it looks to us as if the whole point of communication lay in this: someone else grasps the sense of my words—which is something mental: he as it were takes it into his own mind. If he then does something further with it as well, that is no part of the immediate purpose of language.

One would like to say "Telling brings it about that he *knows* that I am in pain; it produces this mental phenomenon; everything else is inessential to the telling." As for what this queer phenomenon of knowledge is—there is time enough for that. Mental processes just are queer. (It is as if one said: "The clock tells us the time. *What* time is, is not yet settled. And as for what one tells the time *for*—that doesn't come in here.")

364.   Someone does a sum in his head. He uses the result, let's say, for building a bridge or a machine.—Are you trying to say that he has not *really* arrived at this number by calculation? That it has, say, just 'come' to him in the manner of a kind of dream? There surely must have been calculation going on, and there was. For he *knows* that, and how, he calculated; and the correct result he got would be inexplicable without calculation.——But what if I said: "*It strikes him as if* he had calculated. And why should the correct result be explicable? Is it not incomprehensible enough, that without saying a word, without making a note, he was able to CALCULATE?"—
Is calculating in the imagination in some sense less real than calculating on paper? It is *real*—calculation-in-the-head.—Is it like calculation on paper?—I don't know whether to call it like. Is a bit of white paper with black lines on it like a human body?

365.   Do Adelheid and the Bishop play a *real* game of chess?—Of course. They are not merely pretending—which would also be possible as part of a play.—But, for example, the game has no beginning!—Of course it has; otherwise it would not be a game of chess.—

366.   Is a sum in the head less real than a sum on paper?—Perhaps one is inclined to say some such thing; but one can get oneself to think the opposite as well by telling oneself: paper, ink, etc. are only logical constructions out of our sense-data.
"I have done the multiplication . . . . . in my head"—do I perhaps not *believe* such a statement?—But was it really a multiplication? It was not merely 'a' multiplication, but *this* one—in the head. This is the point at which I go wrong. For I now want to say: it was some mental process *corresponding* to the multiplication on paper. So it would make sense to say: "*This* process in the mind corresponds to *his* process on paper." And it would then make sense to talk of a method of projection according to which the image of the sign was a representation of the sign itself.

367.   The mental picture is the picture which is described when someone describes what he imagines.

368.   I describe a room to someone, and then get him to paint an *impressionistic* picture from this description to shew that he has understood it.—Now he paints the chairs which I described as green, dark red; where I said "yellow", he paints blue.—That is the impression

which he got of that room. And now I say: "Quite right! That's what it's like."

369. One would like to ask: "What is it like—what happens—when one does a sum in one's head?"—And in a particular case the answer may be "First I add 17 and 18, then I subtract 39 . . . . ." But that is not the answer to our question. What is called doing sums in one's head is not explained by *such* an answer.

370. One ought to ask, not what images are or what happens when one imagines anything, but how the word "imagination" is used. But that does not mean that I want to talk only about words. For the question as to the nature of the imagination is as much about the word "imagination" as my question is. And I am only saying that this question is not to be decided—neither for the person who does the imagining, nor for anyone else—by pointing; nor yet by a description of any process. The first question also asks for a word to be explained; but it makes us expect a wrong kind of answer.

371. *Essence* is expressed by grammar.

372. Consider: "The only correlate in language to an intrinsic necessity is an arbitrary rule. It is the only thing which one can milk out of this intrinsic necessity into a proposition."

373. Grammar tells what kind of object anything is. (Theology as grammar.)

374. The great difficulty here is not to represent the matter as if there were something one *couldn't* do. As if there really were an object, from which I derive its description, but I were unable to shew it to anyone.——And the best that I can propose is that we should yield to the temptation to use this picture, but then investigate how the *application* of the picture goes.

375. How does one teach anyone to read to himself? How does one know if he can do so? How does he himself know that he is doing what is required of him?

376. When I say the ABC to myself, what is the criterion of my doing the same as someone else who silently repeats it to himself? It might be found that the same thing took place in my larynx and in his. (And similarly when we both think of the same thing, wish the same, and so on.) But then did we learn the use of the words: "to

say such-and-such to oneself" by someone's pointing to a process in
the larynx or the brain? Is it not also perfectly possible that my image
of the sound *a* and his correspond to different physiological processes?
The question is: *How do we compare* images?

377. Perhaps a logician will think: The same is the same—how
identity is established is a psychological question. (High is high—
it is a matter of psychology that one sometimes *sees*, and sometimes
hears it.)

What is the criterion for the sameness of two images?—What is
the criterion for the redness of an image? For me, when it is someone
else's image: what he says and does. For myself, when it is my image:
nothing. And what goes for "red" also goes for "same".

378. "Before I judge that two images which I have are the same,
I must recognize them as the same." And when that has happened,
how am I to know that the word "same" describes what I recognize?
Only if I can express my recognition in some other way, and if it is
possible for someone else to teach me that "same" is the correct word
here.

For if I need a justification for using a word, it must also be one for
someone else.

379. First I am aware of it as *this*; and then I remember what it
is called.—Consider: in what cases is it right to say this?

380. How do I recognize that this is red?—"I see that it is *this*;
and then I know that that is what this is called." This?—What?!
What kind of answer to this question makes sense?

(You keep on steering towards the idea of the private ostensive
definition.)

I could not apply any rules to a *private* transition from what is seen
to words. Here the rules really would hang in the air; for the institution of their use is lacking.

381. How do I know that this colour is red?—It would be an
answer to say: "I have learnt English".

382. At these words I form this image. How can I *justify* this?
Has anyone shewn me the image of the colour blue and told me
that *this* is the image of blue?

What is the meaning of the words: "*This* image"? How does one
point to an image? How does one point twice to the same image?

383. We are not analysing a phenomenon (e.g. thought) but a concept (e.g. that of thinking), and therefore the use of a word. So it may look as if what we were doing were Nominalism. Nominalists make the mistake of interpreting all words as *names*, and so of not really describing their use, but only, so to speak, giving a paper draft on such a description.

384. You learned the *concept* 'pain' when you learned language.

385. Ask yourself: Would it be imaginable for someone to learn to do sums in his head without ever doing written or oral ones?— "Learning it" will mean: being made able to do it. Only the question arises, what will count as a criterion for being able to do it?——But is it also possible for some tribe to know only of calculation in the head, and of no other kind? Here one has to ask oneself: "What will that be like?"—And so one will have to depict it as a limiting case. And the question will then arise whether we are still willing to use the concept of 'calculating in the head' here—or whether in such circumstances it has lost its purpose, because the phenomena gravitate towards another paradigm.

386. "But why have you so little confidence in yourself? Ordinarily you always know well enough what it is to 'calculate.' So if you say you have calculated in imagination, then you will have done so. If you had *not* calculated, you would not have said you had. Equally, if you say that you see something red in imagination, then it will *be* red. You know what 'red' is elsewhere.—And further: you do not always rely on the agreement of other people; for you often report that you have seen something no one else has."——But I do have confidence in myself—I say without hesitation that I have done this sum in my head, have imagined this colour. The difficulty is not that I doubt whether I really imagined anything red. But it is *this*: that we should be able, just like that, to point out or describe the colour we have imagined, **that the projection of the image into reality presents no difficulty** at all. Are they then so alike that one might mix them up?—But I can also recognize a man from a drawing straight off.—Well, but can I ask: "What does a correct image of this colour look like?" or "What sort of thing is it?"; can I *learn* this?

(I cannot accept his testimony because it is not *testimony*. It only tells me what he is *inclined* to say.)

387. The *deep* aspect of this matter readily eludes us.

388. "I don't see anything violet here, but I can shew it you if you give me a paint box." How can one *know* that one can shew it f . . . ., in other words, that one can recognize it if one sees it?

How do I know from my *image*, what the colour really looks like?

How do I know that I shall be able to do something? that is, that the state I am in now is that of being able to do that thing?

389. "The image must be more like its object than any picture. For, however like I make the picture to what it is supposed to represent, it can always be the picture of something else as well. But it is essential to the image that it is the image of *this* and of nothing else." Thus one might come to regard the image as a super-likeness.

390. Could one imagine a stone's having consciousness? And if anyone can do so—why should that not merely prove that such image-nongery is of no interest to us?

391. I can perhaps even imagine (though it is not easy) that each of the people whom I see in the street is in frightful pain, but is artfully concealing it. And it is important that I have to imagine an artful concealment here. That I do not simply say to myself: "Well, his soul is in pain: but what has that to do with his body?" or "After all it need not shew in his body!"—And if I imagine this—what do I do; what do I say to myself; how do I look at the people? Perhaps I look at one and think: "It must be difficult to laugh when one is in such pain", and much else of the same kind. I as it were play a part, *act* as if the others were in pain. When I do this I am said for example to be imagining . . . .

392. "When I imagine he is in pain, all that really goes on in me is . . . ." Then someone else says: "I believe I can imagine it *without* thinking ' . . . .' " ("I believe I can think without words.") This leads to nothing. The analysis oscillates between natural science and grammar.

393. "When I imagine that someone who is laughing is really in pain I don't imagine any pain-behaviour, for I see just the opposite. So *what* do I imagine?"—I have already said what. And I do not necessarily imagine *my* being in pain.——"But then what is the process of imagining it?"——Where (outside philosophy) do we use the

words "I can imagine his being in pain" or "I imagine that . . . ."
or "Imagine that . . . ."?

We say, for example, to someone who has to play a theatrical part:
"Here you must imagine that this man is in pain and is concealing
it"—and now we give him no directions, do not tell him what he
is *actually* to do. For this reason the suggested analysis is not to
the point either.—We now watch the actor who is imagining this
situation.

394. In what sort of circumstances should we ask anyone: "What
actually went on in you as you imagined this?"—And what sort of
answer do we expect?

395. There is a lack of clarity about the role of *imaginability* in our
investigation. Namely about the extent to which it ensures that a
proposition makes sense.

396. It is no more essential to the understanding of a proposition
that one should imagine anything in connexion with it, than that one
should make a sketch from it.

397. Instead of "imaginability" one can also say here: represent-
ability by a particular method of representation. And such a representation *may* indeed safely point a way to further use of a sentence.
On the other hand a picture may obtrude itself upon us and be of no
use at all.

398. "But when I imagine something, or even actually *see* objects,
I have *got* something which my neighbour has not."—I understand
you. You want to look about you and say: "At any rate only I have
got THIS."—What are these words for? They serve no purpose.—
Can one not add: "There is here no question of a 'seeing'—and therefore none of a 'having'—nor of a subject, nor therefore of 'I' either"?
Might I not ask: In what sense have you *got* what you are talking about
and saying that only you have got it? Do you possess it? You do not
even *see* it. Must you not really say that no one has got it? And this too
is clear: if as a matter of logic you exclude other people's having
something, it loses its sense to say that you have it.

But what is the thing you are speaking of? It is true I said that I
knew within myself what you meant. But that meant that I knew
how one thinks to conceive this object, to see it, to make one's looking
and pointing mean it. I know how one stares ahead and looks abou

ne in this case—and the rest. I think we can say: you are talking (if,
or example, you are sitting in a room) of the 'visual room'. The 'visual
oom' is the one that has no owner. I can as little own it as I can walk
bout it, or look at it, or point to it. Inasmuch as it cannot be any one
lse's it is not mine either. In other words, it does not belong to me
ecause I want to use the same form of expression about it as about the
naterial room in which I sit. The description of the latter need not
nention an owner, in fact it need not have any owner. But then the
visual room *cannot* have any owner. "For"—one might say—"it has
o master, outside or in."

Think of a picture of a landscape, an imaginary landscape with a
ouse in it.—Someone asks "Whose house is that?"—The answer,
y the way, might be "It belongs to the farmer who is sitting on the
ench in front of it". But then he cannot for example enter his house.

399.   One might also say: Surely the owner of the visual room
would have to be the same kind of thing as it is; but he is not to be
ound in it, and there is no outside.

400.   The 'visual room' seemed like a discovery, but what its
liscoverer really found was a new way of speaking, a new comparison;
t might even be called a new sensation.

401.   You have a new conception and interpret it as seeing a new
bject. You interpret a grammatical movement made by yourself
s a quasi-physical phenomenon which you are observing. (Think for
xample of the question: "Are sense-data the material of which the
niverse is made?")

But there is an objection to my saying that you have made a 'gram-
natical' movement. What you have primarily discovered is a new way
f looking at things. As if you had invented a new way of painting;
r, again, a new metre, or a new kind of song.—

402.   "It's true I say 'Now I am having such-and-such an image',
ut the words 'I am having' are merely a sign to someone *else*; the
lescription of the image is a *complete* account of the imagined world."—
You mean: the words "I am having" are like "I say! . . . ." You are
nclined to say it should really have been expressed differently. Perhaps
imply by making a sign with one's hand and then giving a description.
—When as in this case, we disapprove of the expressions of ordinary
anguage (which are after all performing their office), we have got a
icture in our heads which conflicts with the picture of our ordinary

way of speaking. Whereas we are tempted to say that our way of speaking does not describe the facts as they really are. As if, for example the proposition "he has pains" could be false in some other way than by that man's *not* having pains. As if the form of expression were saying something false even when the proposition *faute de mieux* asserted something true.

For *this* is what disputes between Idealists, Solipsists and Realists look like. The one party attack the normal form of expression as if they were attacking a statement; the others defend it, as if they were stating facts recognized by every reasonable human being.

403. If I were to reserve the word "pain" solely for what I had hitherto called "my pain", and others "L.W.'s pain", I should do other people no injustice, so long as a notation were provided in which the loss of the word "pain" in other connexions were somehow supplied. Other people would still be pitied, treated by doctors and so on. It would, of course, be *no* objection to this mode of expression to say: "But look here, other people have just the same as you!"

But what should I gain from this new kind of account? Nothing. But after all neither does the solipsist *want* any practical advantage when he advances his view!

404. "When I say 'I am in pain', I do not point to a person who is in pain, since in a certain sense I have no idea *who* is." And this can be given a justification. For the main point is: I did not say that such-and-such a person was in pain, but "I am . . . . ." Now in saying this I don't name any person. Just as I don't name anyone when I *groan* with pain. Though someone else sees who is in pain from the groaning.

What does it mean to know *who* is in pain? It means, for example, to know which man in this room is in pain: for instance, that it is the one who is sitting over there, or the one who is standing in that corner, the tall one over there with the fair hair, and so on.—What am I getting at? At the fact that there is a great variety of criteria for personal '*identity*'.

Now which of them determines my saying that '*I*' am in pain? None.

405. "But at any rate when you say 'I am in pain', you want to draw the attention of others to a particular person."—The answer might be: No, I want to draw their attention to *myself*.—

406. "But surely what you want to do with the words 'I am....'
is to distinguish between *yourself* and *other* people."—Can this be said
in every case? Even when I merely groan? And even if I do 'want
to distinguish' between myself and other people—do I want to distinguish between the person L.W. and the person N.N.?

407. It would be possible to imagine someone groaning out:
"Someone is in pain—I don't know who!"—and our then hurrying
to help him, the one who groaned.

408. "But you aren't in doubt whether it is you or someone else
who has the pain!"—The proposition "I don't know whether I
or someone else is in pain" would be a logical product, and one of its
factors would be: "I don't know whether I am in pain or not"—
and that is not a significant proposition.

409. Imagine several people standing in a ring, and me among them.
One of us, sometimes this one, sometimes that, is connected to the
poles of an electrical machine without our being able to see this. I
observe the faces of the others and try to see which of us has just been
electrified.—Then I say: "Now I *know* who it is; for it's myself."
In this sense I could also say: "Now I know who is getting the shocks;
it is myself." This would be a rather queer way of speaking.—But if I
make the supposition that I can feel the shock even when someone
else is electrified, then the expression "Now I know who ...."
becomes quite unsuitable. It does not belong to this game.

410. "I" is not the name of a person, nor "here" of a place, and
"this" is not a name. But they are connected with names. Names are
explained by means of them. It is also true that it is characteristic of
physics not to use these words.

411. Consider how the following questions can be applied, and
how settled:
(1) "Are these books *my* books?"
(2) "Is this foot *my* foot?"
(3) "Is this body *my* body?"
(4) "Is this sensation *my* sensation?"
Each of these questions has practical (non-philosophical) applications.
(2) Think of cases in which my foot is anaesthetized or paralysed.
Under certain circumstances the question could be settled by determining whether I can feel pain in this foot.

(3) Here one might be pointing to a mirror-image. Under certain circumstances, however, one might touch a body and ask the question. In others it means the same as: "Does my body look like *that*?"

(4) Which sensation does one mean by '*this*' one? That is: how is one using the demonstrative pronoun here? Certainly otherwise than in, say, the first example! Here confusion occurs because one imagines that by directing one's attention to a sensation one is pointing to it.

412. The feeling of an unbridgeable gulf between consciousness and brain-process: how does it come about that this does not come into the considerations of our ordinary life? This idea of a difference in kind is accompanied by slight giddiness,—which occurs when we are performing a piece of logical sleight-of-hand. (The same giddiness attacks us when we think of certain theorems in set theory.) When does this feeling occur in the present case? It is when I, for example, turn my attention in a particular way on to my own consciousness, and, astonished, say to myself: THIS is supposed to be produced by a process in the brain!—as it were clutching my forehead.—But what can it mean to speak of "turning my attention on to my own consciousness"? This is surely the queerest thing there could be! It was a particular act of gazing that I called doing this. I stared fixedly in front of me—but *not* at any particular point or object. My eyes were wide open, the brows not contracted (as they mostly are when I am interested in a particular object). No such interest preceded this gazing. My glance was vacant; or again *like* that of someone admiring the illumination of the sky and drinking in the light.

Now bear in mind that the proposition which I uttered as a paradox (THIS is produced by a brain-process!) has nothing paradoxical about it. I could have said it in the course of an experiment whose purpose was to shew that an effect of light which I see is produced by stimulation of a particular part of the brain.—But I did not utter the sentence in the surroundings in which it would have had an everyday and unparadoxical sense. And my attention was not such as would have accorded with making an experiment. (If it had been, my look would have been intent, not vacant.)

413. Here we have a case of introspection, not unlike that from which William James got the idea that the 'self' consisted mainly of 'peculiar motions in the head and between the head and throat'.

And James' introspection shewed, not the meaning of the word "self" (so far as it means something like "person", "human being", "he himself", "I myself"), nor any analysis of such a thing, but the state of a philosopher's attention when he says the word "self" to himself and tries to analyse its meaning. (And a good deal could be learned from this.)

414. You think that after all you must be weaving a piece of cloth: because you are sitting at a loom—even if it is empty—and going through the motions of weaving.

415. What we are supplying are really remarks on the natural history of human beings; we are not contributing curiosities however, but observations which no one has doubted, but which have escaped remark only because they are always before our eyes.

416. "Human beings agree in saying that they see, hear, feel, and so on (even though some are blind and some are deaf). So they are their own witnesses that they have *consciousness*."—But how strange this is! Whom do I really inform, if I say "I have consciousness"? What is the purpose of saying this to myself, and how can another person understand me?—Now, expressions like "I see", "I hear", "I am conscious" really have their uses. I tell a doctor "Now I am hearing with this ear again", or I tell someone who believes I am in a faint "I am conscious again", and so on.

417. Do I observe myself, then, and perceive that I am seeing or conscious? And why talk about observation at all? Why not simply say "I perceive I am conscious"?—But what are the words "I perceive" for here?—why not say "I am conscious"?—But don't the words "I perceive" here shew that I am attending to my consciousness?—which is ordinarily not the case.—If so, then the sentence "I perceive I am conscious" does not say that I am conscious, but that my attention is disposed in such-and-such a way.

But isn't it a particular experience that occasions my saying "I am conscious again"?—*What* experience? In what situations do we say it?

418. Is my having consciousness a fact of experience?—

But doesn't one say that a man has consciousness, and that a tree or a stone does not?—What would it be like if it were otherwise?—Would human beings all be unconscious?—No; not in the ordinary sense of the word. But I, for instance, should not have consciousness——as I now in fact have it.

419. In what circumstances shall I say that a tribe has a *chief*? And the chief must surely have *consciousness*. Surely we can't have a chief without consciousness!

420. But can't I imagine that the people around me are automata, lack consciousness, even though they behave in the same way as usual?—If I imagine it now—alone in my room—I see people with fixed looks (as in a trance) going about their business—the idea is perhaps a little uncanny. But just try to keep hold of this idea in the midst of your ordinary intercourse with others, in the street, say! Say to yourself, for example: "The children over there are mere automata; all their liveliness is mere automatism." And you will either find these words becoming quite meaningless; or you will produce in yourself some kind of uncanny feeling, or something of the sort.

Seeing a living human being as an automaton is analogous to seeing one figure as a limiting case or variant of another; the cross-pieces of a window as a swastika, for example.

421. It seems paradoxical to us that we should make such a medley, mixing physical states and states of consciousness up together in a *single* report: "He suffered great torments and tossed about restlessly". It is quite usual; so why do we find it paradoxical? Because we want to say that the sentence deals with both tangibles and intangibles at once.—But does it worry you if I say: "These three struts give the building stability"? Are three and stability tangible?——Look at the sentence as an instrument, and at its sense as its employment.

422. What am I believing in when I believe that men have souls? What am I believing in, when I believe that this substance contains two carbon rings? In both cases there is a picture in the foreground, but the sense lies far in the background; that is, the application of the picture is not easy to survey.

423. *Certainly* all these things happen in you.—And now all I ask is to understand the expression we use.—The picture is there. And I am not disputing its validity in any particular case.—Only I also want to understand the application of the picture.

424. The picture is *there*; and I do not dispute its *correctness*. But *what* is its application? Think of the picture of blindness as a darkness in the soul or in the head of the blind man.

425. In numberless cases we exert ourselves to find a picture and once it is found the application as it were comes about of itself. In

his case we already have a picture which forces itself on us at every
urn,—but does not help us out of the difficulty, which only begins
here.

If I ask, for example: "How am I to imagine *this* mechanism going
into *this* box?"—perhaps a drawing reduced in scale may serve to
answer me. Then I can be told: "You see, it goes in like *this*"; or
perhaps even: "Why are you surprised? See how it goes *here*; it is the
same there". Of course the latter does not explain anything more: it
simply invites me to apply the picture I am given.

426. A picture is conjured up which seems to fix the sense *unambiguously*. The actual use, compared with that suggested by the
picture, seems like something muddied. Here again we get the same
thing as in set theory: the form of expression we use seems to have been
designed for a god, who knows what we cannot know; he sees the whole
of each of those infinite series and he sees into human consciousness.
For us, of course, these forms of expression are like pontificals which
we may put on, but cannot do much with, since we lack the effective
power that would give these vestments meaning and purpose.

In the actual use of expressions we make detours, we go by side-
roads. We see the straight highway before us, but of course we
cannot use it, because it is permanently closed.

427. "While I was speaking to him I did not know what was going
on in his head." In saying this, one is not thinking of brain-processes,
but of thought-processes. The picture should be taken seriously.
We should really like to see into his head. And yet we only mean what
elsewhere we should mean by saying: we should like to know what he
is thinking. I want to say: we have this vivid picture—and that use,
apparently contradicting the picture, which expresses the psychical.

428. "This queer thing, thought"—but it does not strike us as
queer when we are thinking. Thought does not strike us as mysterious
while we are thinking, but only when we say, as it were retrospectively:
"How was that possible?" How was it possible for thought to deal
with the very object *itself*? We feel as if by means of it we had caught
reality in our net.

429. The agreement, the harmony, of thought and reality consists
in this: if I say falsely that something is *red*, then, for all that, it isn't *red*.

And when I want to explain the word "red" to someone, in the sentence "That is not red", I do it by pointing to something red.

430. "Put a ruler against this body; it does not say that the body is of such-and-such a length. Rather is it in itself—I should like to say—dead, and achieves nothing of what thought achieves."—It is as if we had imagined that the essential thing about a living man was the outward form. Then we made a lump of wood in that form, and were abashed to see the stupid block, which hadn't even any similarity to a living being.

431. "There is a gulf between an order and its execution. It has to be filled by the act of understanding."

"Only in the act of understanding is it meant that we are to do THIS. The order——why, that is nothing but sounds, ink-marks.—"

432. Every sign *by itself* seems dead. *What* gives it life?—In use it is *alive*. Is life breathed into it there?—Or is the *use* its life?

433. When we give an order, it can look as if the ultimate thing sought by the order had to remain unexpressed, as there is always a gulf between an order and its execution. Say I want someone to make a particular movement, say to raise his arm. To make it quite clear, I do the movement. This picture seems unambiguous till we ask: how does he know that *he is to make that movement*?—How does he know at all what use he is to make of the signs I give him, whatever they are?—Perhaps I shall now try to supplement the order by means of further signs, by pointing from myself to him, making encouraging gestures, etc. . Here it looks as if the order were beginning to stammer.

As if the signs were precariously trying to produce understanding in us.—But if we now understand them, by what token do we understand?

434. The gesture—we should like to say—*tries* to portray, but cannot do it.

435. If it is asked: "How do sentences manage to represent?"—the answer might be: "Don't you know? You certainly see it, when you use them." For nothing is concealed.

How do sentences do it?—Don't you know? For nothing is hidden.

But given this answer: "But you know how sentences do it, for nothing is concealed" one would like to retort "Yes, but it all goes by so quick, and I should like to see it as it were laid open to view."

436.   Here it is easy to get into that dead-end in philosophy, where one believes that the difficulty of the task consists in our having to describe phenomena that are hard to get hold of, the present experience that slips quickly by, or something of the kind. Where we find ordinary language too crude, and it looks as if we were having to do, not with the phenomena of every-day, but with ones that "easily elude us, and, in their coming to be and passing away, produce those others as an average effect". (Augustine: Manifestissima et usitatissima sunt, et eadem rusus nimis latent, et nova est inventio eorum.)

437.   A wish seems already to know what will or would satisfy it; a proposition, a thought, what makes it true—even when that thing is not there at all! Whence this *determining* of what is not yet there? This despotic demand? ("The hardness of the logical must.")

438.   "A plan as such is something unsatisfied." (Like a wish, an expectation, a suspicion, and so on.)
By this I mean: expectation is unsatisfied, because it is the expectation of something; belief, opinion, is unsatisfied, because it is the opinion that something is the case, something real, something outside the process of believing.

439.   In what sense can one call wishes, expectations, beliefs, etc. "unsatisfied"? What is our prototype of nonsatisfaction? Is it a hollow space? And would one call that unsatisfied? Wouldn't this be a metaphor too?—Isn't what we call nonsatisfaction a feeling—say hunger?
In a particular system of expressions we can describe an object by means of the words "satisfied" and "unsatisfied". For example, if we lay it down that we call a hollow cylinder an "unsatisfied cylinder" and the solid cylinder that fills it "its satisfaction".

440.   Saying "I should like an apple" does not mean: I believe an apple will quell my feeling of nonsatisfaction. *This* proposition is not an expression of a wish but of nonsatisfaction.

441.   By nature and by a particular training, a particular education, we are disposed to give spontaneous expression to wishes in certain circumstances. (A *wish* is, of course, not such a 'circumstance'.) In this game the question whether I know what I wish before my wish is

fulfilled cannot arise at all. And the fact that some event stops my wishing does not mean that it fulfills it. Perhaps I should not have been
satisfied if my wish had been satisfied.

On the other hand the word "wish" is also used in this way: ".
don't know myself what I wish for." ("For wishes themselves are a
veil between us and the thing wished for.")

Suppose it were asked "Do I know what I long for before I get it?"
If I have learned to talk, then I do know.

442. I see someone pointing a gun and say "I expect a report"
The shot is fired.—Well, that was what you expected; so did tha
report somehow already exist in your expectation? Or is it just tha
there is some other kind of agreement between your expectation and
what occurred; that that noise was not contained in your expectation
and merely accidentally supervened when the expectation was being
fulfilled?—But no, if the noise had not occurred, my expectation would
not have been fulfilled; the noise fulfilled it; it was not an accompaniment of the fulfilment like a second guest accompanying the one
expected.—Was the thing about the event that was not in the expectation too an accident, an extra provided by fate?—But then what was
not an extra? Did something of the shot already occur in my expectation?—Then what *was* extra? for wasn't I expecting the whole shot.

"The report was not so loud as I had expected."—"Then was there
a louder bang in your expectation?"

443. "The red which you imagine is surely not the same (not the
same thing) as the red which you see in front of you; so how can you
say that it is what you imagined?"—But haven't we an analogous case
with the propositions "Here is a red patch" and "Here there isn't a
red patch"? The word "red" occurs in both; so this word canno
indicate the presence of something red.

444. One may have the feeling that in the sentence "I expect he is
coming" one is using the words "he is coming" in a different sense
from the one they have in the assertion "He is coming". But if it wer
so how could I say that my expectation had been fulfilled? If I wanted
to explain the words "he" and "is coming", say by means of ostensiv
definitions, the same definitions of these words would go for both
sentences.

But it might now be asked: what's it like for him to come?—The
door opens, someone walks in, and so on.—What's it like for me to

expect him to come?—I walk up and down the room, look at the clock now and then, and so on.—But the one set of events has not the smallest similarity to the other! So how can one use the same words in describing them?—But perhaps I say as I walk up and down: "I expect he'll come in"—Now there is a similarity somewhere. But of what kind?!

445. It is in language that an expectation and its fulfilment make contact.

446. It would be odd to say: "A process looks different when it happens from when it doesn't happen." Or "A red patch looks different when it is there from when it isn't there—but language abstracts from this difference, for it speaks of a red patch whether it is there or not."

447. The feeling is as if the negation of a proposition had to make it true in a certain sense, in order to negate it.

(The assertion of the negative proposition contains the proposition which is negated, but not the assertion of it.)

448. "If I say I did *not* dream last night, still I must know where to look for a dream; that is, the proposition 'I dreamt', applied to this actual situation, may be false, but mustn't be senseless."—Does that mean, then, that you did after all feel something, as it were the hint of a dream, which made you aware of the place which a dream would have occupied?

Again: if I say "I have no pain in my arm", does that mean that I have a shadow of the sensation of pain, which as it were indicates the place where the pain might be?

In what sense does my present painless state contain the possibility of pain?

If anyone says: "For the word 'pain' to have a meaning it is necessary that pain should be recognized as such when it occurs"—one can reply: "It is not more necessary than that the absence of pain should be recognized."

449. "But mustn't I know what it would be like if I were in pain?" —We fail to get away from the idea that using a sentence involves imagining something for every word.

We do not realize that we *calculate*, operate, with words, and in the course of time translate them sometimes into one picture, sometimes into another.—It is as if one were to believe that a written order for a

cow which someone is to hand over to me always had to be accompanied
by an image of a cow, if the order was not to lose its meaning.

450. Knowing what someone looks like: being able to call up an
image—but also: being able to *mimic* his expression. Need one imagine
it in order to mimic it? And isn't mimicking it just as good as imagining it?

451. Suppose I give someone the order "Imagine a red circle here"
—and now I say: understanding the order means knowing what it is
like for it to have been carried out—or even: being able to imagine
what it is like . . . . .?

452. I want to say: "If someone could see the mental process of
expectation, he would necessarily be seeing *what* was being expected."
—But that is the case: if you see the expression of an expectation, you
see what is being expected. And in what other way, in what other sense
would it be possible to see it?

453. Anyone who perceived my expectation would necessarily
have a direct perception of *what* was being expected. That is to say, he
would not have to *infer* it from the process he perceived!—But to say
that someone perceives an expectation *makes no sense*. Unless indeed
it means, for example, that he perceives the expression of an expectation. To say of an expectant person that he perceives his expectation
instead of saying that he expects, would be an idiotic distortion of the
expression.

454. "Everything is already there in . . . ." How does it come
about that this arrow ⟫⟫⟫————————→ *points*? Doesn't it seem to
carry in it something besides itself?—"No, not the dead line on paper;
only the psychical thing, the meaning, can do that."—That is both
true and false. The arrow points only in the application that a living
being makes of it.

This pointing is *not* a hocus-pocus which can be performed only by
the soul.

455. We want to say: "When we mean something, it's like going
up to someone, it's not having a dead picture (of any kind)." We go
up to the thing we mean.

456. "When one means something, it is oneself meaning"; so one is
oneself in motion. One is rushing ahead and so cannot also observe
oneself rushing ahead. Indeed not.

457. Yes: meaning something is like going up to someone.

458. "An order orders its own execution." So it knows its execution, then, even before it is there?—But that was a grammatical proposition and it means: If an order runs "Do such-and-such" then executing the order is called "doing such-and-such."

459. We say "The order orders *this*—" and do it; but also "The order orders this: I am to . . . ." We translate it at one time into a proposition, at another into a demonstration, and at another into action.

460. Could the justification of an action as fulfilment of an order run like this: "You said 'Bring me a yellow flower', upon which this one gave me a feeling of satisfaction; that is why I have brought it"? Wouldn't one have to reply: "But I didn't set you to bring me the flower which should give you that sort of feeling after what I said!"?

461. In what sense does an order anticipate its execution? By ordering *just that* which later on is carried out?—But one would have to say "which later on is carried out, or again is not carried out." And that is to say nothing.

"But even if my wish does not determine what is going to be the case, still it does so to speak determine the theme of a fact, whether the fact fulfils the wish or not." We are—as it were—surprised, not at anyone's knowing the future, but at his being able to prophesy at all (right or wrong).

As if the mere prophecy, no matter whether true or false, foreshadowed the future; whereas it knows nothing of the future and cannot know less than nothing.

462. I can look for him when he is not there, but not hang him when he is not there.

One might want to say: "But he must be somewhere there if I am looking for him."—Then he must be somewhere there too if I don't find him and even if he doesn't exist at all.

463. "You were looking for *him*? You can't even have known if he was there!"—But this problem really does arise when one looks for something in mathematics. One can ask, for example, how was it possible so much as to *look for* the trisection of the angle?

464. My aim is: to teach you to pass from a piece of disguised nonsense to something that is patent nonsense.

465. "An expectation is so made that whatever happens has to accord with it, or not."

Suppose you now ask: then are facts defined one way or the other by an expectation—that is, is it defined for whatever event may occur whether it fulfils the expectation or not? The answer has to be: "Yes, unless the expression of the expectation is indefinite; for example, contains a disjunction of different possibilities."

466. What does man think for? What use is it?—Why does he make boilers according to *calculations* and not leave the thickness of their walls to chance? After all it is only a fact of experience that boilers do not explode so often if made according to these calculations. But just as having once been burnt he would do anything rather than put his hand into a fire, so he would do anything rather than not calculate for a boiler.—But as we are not interested in causes,—we shall say: human beings do in fact think: this, for instance, is how they proceed when they make a boiler.—Now, can't a boiler produced in this way explode? Oh, yes.

467. Does man think, then, because he has found that thinking pays?—Because he thinks it advantageous to think?

(Does he bring his children up because he has found it pays?)

468. What would shew *why* he thinks?

469. And yet one can say that thinking has been found to pay. That there are fewer boiler explosions than formerly, now that we no longer go by feeling in deciding the thickness of the walls, but make such-and-such calculations instead. Or since each calculation done by one engineer got checked by a second one.

470. So we do *sometimes* think because it has been found to pay.

471. It often happens that we only become aware of the important *facts*, if we suppress the question "why?"; and then in the course of our investigations these facts lead us to an answer.

472. The character of the belief in the uniformity of nature can perhaps be seen most clearly in the case in which we fear what we expect. Nothing could induce me to put my hand into a flame—although after all it is *only in the past* that I have burnt myself.

473. The belief that fire will burn me is of the same kind as the fear that it will burn me.

474. I shall get burnt if I put my hand in the fire: that is certainty. That is to say: here we see the meaning of certainty. (What it amounts o, not just the meaning of the word "certainty.")

475. On being asked for the grounds of a supposition, one *be-hinks* oneself of them. Does the same thing happen here as when one onsiders what may have been the causes of an event?

476. We should distinguish between the object of fear and the ause of fear.

Thus a face which inspires fear or delight (the object of fear or lelight), is not on that account its cause, but—one might say—its arget.

477. "Why do you believe that you will burn yourself on the 1ot-plate?"—Have you reasons for this belief; and do you need easons?

478. What kind of reason have I to assume that my finger will eel a resistance when it touches the table? What kind of reason to)elieve that it will hurt if this pencil pierces my hand?—When I ask .his, a hundred reasons present themselves, each drowning the voice)f the others. "But I have experienced it myself innumerable times, .nd as often heard of similar experiences; if it were not so, it would
. . . . . .; etc."

479. The question: "On what grounds do you believe this?" might nean: "From what you are now deducing it (have you just deduced ⟨t)?" But it might also mean: "What grounds can you produce for his assumption on thinking it over?"

480. Thus one could in fact take "grounds" for an opinion to nean only what a man had said to himself before he arrived at the)pinion. The calculation that he has actually carried out. If it is 1ow asked: But how *can* previous experience be a ground for issuming that such-and-such will occur later on?—the answer is: Vhat general concept have we of grounds for this kind of assumption? Γhis sort of statement about the past is simply what we call a ground or assuming that this will happen in the future.—And if you are urprised at our playing such a game I refer you to the *effect* of a past :xperience (to the fact that a burnt child fears the fire).

481. If anyone said that information about the past could not convince him that something would happen in the future, I should not understand him. One might ask him: What do you expect to be told, then? What sort of information do you call a ground for such a belief? What do you call "conviction"? In what kind of way do you expect to be convinced?—If *these* are not grounds, then what are grounds?— If you say these are not grounds, then you must surely be able to state what must be the case for us to have the right to say that there are grounds for our assumption.

For note: here grounds are not propositions which logically imply what is believed.

Not that one can say: less is needed for belief than for knowledge.— For the question here is not one of an approximation to logical inference.

482. We are misled by this way of putting it: "This is a good ground, for it makes the occurrence of the event probable." That is as if we had asserted something further about the ground, which justified it as a ground; whereas to say that this ground makes the occurrence probable is to say nothing except that this ground comes up to a particular standard of good grounds—but the standard has no grounds!

483. A good ground is one that looks *like this*.

484. One would like to say: "It is a good ground only because it makes the occurrence *really* probable". Because it, so to speak, really has an influence on the event; as it were an experiential one.

485. Justification by experience comes to an end. If it did not it would not be justification.

486. Does it *follow* from the sense-impressions which I get that there is a chair over there?—How can a *proposition* follow from sense-impressions? Well, does it follow from the propositions which describe the sense-impressions? No.—But don't I infer that a chair is there from impressions, from sense-data?—I make no inference!—and yet I sometimes do. I see a photograph for example, and say "There must have been a chair over there" or again "From what I can see here I infer that there is a chair over there." That is an inference; but not one belonging to logic. An inference is a transition to an assertion; and so also to the behaviour that corresponds to the assertion. 'I draw the consequences' not only in words, but also in action.

Was I justified in drawing these consequences? What is *called* a
justification here?—How is the word "justification" used? Describe
language-games. From these you will also be able to see the importance
of being justified.

487.   "I am leaving the room because you tell me to."
"I am leaving the room, but not because you tell me to."
Does this proposition *describe* a connexion between my action and his
order; or does it make the connexion?
Can one ask: "How do you know that you do it because of this, or
not because of this?" And is the answer perhaps: "I feel it"?

488.   How do I judge whether it is so? By circumstantial evidence?

489.   Ask yourself: On what occasion, for what purpose, do we say
this?
What kind of actions accompany these words? (Think of a greeting.)
In what scenes will they be used; and what for?

490.   How do I know that *this line of thought* has led me to this
action?—Well, it is a particular picture: for example, of a calculation
leading to a further experiment in an experimental investigation. It
looks like *this*——and now I could describe an example.

491.   Not: "without language we could not communicate with
one another"—but for sure: without language we cannot influence
other people in such-and-such ways; cannot build roads and machines,
etc.. And also: without the use of speech and writing people could
not communicate.

492.   To invent a language could mean to invent an instrument for
a particular purpose on the basis of the laws of nature (or consistently
with them); but it also has the other sense, analogous to that in which
we speak of the invention of a game.
Here I am stating something about the grammar of the word
"language", by connecting it with the grammar of the word "invent".

493.   We say: "The cock calls the hens by crowing"—but doesn't a
comparison with our language lie at the bottom of this?—Isn't the
aspect quite altered if we imagine the crowing to set the hens in
motion by some kind of physical causation?
But if it were shewn how the words "Come to me" act on the person
addressed, so that finally, given certain conditions, the muscles of his

legs are innervated, and so on—should we feel that that sentence lost
the character of a *sentence*?

494. I want to say: It is *primarily* the apparatus of our ordinary
language, of our word-language, that we call language; and then other
things by analogy or comparability with this.

495. Clearly, I can establish by experience that a human being (or
animal) reacts to one sign as I want him to, and to another not. That,
e.g., a human being goes to the right at the sign " $\longrightarrow$ " and
goes to the left at the sign " $\longleftarrow$ "; but that he does not react
to the sign " $0\!\!-\!\!|$ ", as to " $\longleftarrow$ ".

I do not even need to fabricate a case, I only have to consider
what is in fact the case; namely, that I can direct a man who has learned
only German, only by using the German language. (For here I am
looking at learning German as adjusting a mechanism to respond to a
certain kind of influence; and it may be all one to us whether someone
else has learned the language, or was perhaps from birth constituted to
react to sentences in German like a normal person who has learned
German.)

496. Grammar does not tell us how language must be constructed
in order to fulfil its purpose, in order to have such-and-such an effect
on human beings. It only describes and in no way explains the use of
signs.

497. The rules of grammar may be called "arbitrary", if that is to
mean that the *aim* of the grammar is nothing but that of the language.
If someone says "If our language had not this grammar, it could not
express these facts"—it should be asked what "*could*" means here.

498. When I say that the orders "Bring me sugar" and "Bring me
milk" make sense, but not the combination "Milk me sugar", that does
not mean that the utterance of this combination of words has no effect.
And if its effect is that the other person stares at me and gapes, I don't
on that account call it the order to stare and gape, even if that was
precisely the effect that I wanted to produce.

499. To say "This combination of words makes no sense" excludes
it from the sphere of language and thereby bounds the domain of
language. But when one draws a boundary it may be for various
kinds of reason. If I surround an area with a fence or a line or other
wise, the purpose may be to prevent someone from getting in or out

but it may also be part of a game and the players be supposed, say, to jump over the boundary; or it may shew where the property of one man ends and that of another begins; and so on. So if I draw a boundary line that is not yet to say what I am drawing it for.

500. When a sentence is called senseless, it is not as it were its sense that is senseless. But a combination of words is being excluded from the language, withdrawn from circulation.

501. "The purpose of language is to express thoughts."—So presumably the purpose of every sentence is to express a thought. Then what thought is expressed, for example, by the sentence "It's raining"?—

502. Asking what the sense is. Compare:
"This sentence makes sense."—"What sense?"
"This set of words is a sentence."—"What sentence?"

503. If I give anyone an order I feel it to be *quite enough* to give him signs. And I should never say: this is only words, and I have got to get behind the words. Equally, when I have asked someone something and he gives me an answer (i.e. a sign) I am content—that was whát I expected—and I don't raise the objection: but that's a mere answer.

504. But if you say: "How am I to know what he means, when I see nothing but the signs he gives?" then I say: "How is *he* to know what he means, when he has nothing but the signs either?"

505. Must I understand an order before I can act on it?—Certainly, otherwise you wouldn't know what you had to do!—But isn't there in turn a jump from *knowing* to doing?—

506. The absent-minded man who at the order "Right turn!" turns left, and then, clutching his forehead, says "Oh! right turn" and does a right turn.—What has struck him? An interpretation?

507. "I am not merely saying this, I mean something by it."—When we consider what is going on in us when we *mean* (and don't merely say) words, it seems to us as if there were something coupled to these words, which otherwise would run idle.—As if they, so to speak, connected with something in us.

508. I say the sentence: "The weather is fine"; but the words are after all arbitrary signs—so let's put "a b c d" in their place. But now when I read this, I can't connect it straight away with the above sense.—

I am not used, I might say, to saying "a" instead of "the", "b" instead
of "weather", etc. . But I don't mean by that that I am not used to
making an immediate association between the word "the" and "a",
but that I am not used to using "a" *in the place* of "the"—and therefore
in the sense of "the". (I have not mastered this language.)

(I am not used to measuring temperatures on the Fahrenheit scale.
Hence such a measure of temperature '*says*' nothing to me.)

509.   Suppose we asked someone "In what sense are these words a
description of what you are seeing?"—and he answers: "I *mean* this
by these words." (Say he was looking at a landscape.) Why is this
answer "I *mean* this . . . ." no answer at all?

How does one use words to *mean* what one sees before one?

Suppose I said "a b c d" and meant: the weather is fine. For as I
uttered these signs I had the experience normally had only by someone
who had year-in year-out used "a" in the sense of "the", "b" in the
sense of "weather", and so on.—Does "a b c d" now mean: the weather
is fine?

What is supposed to be the criterion for my having had *that* experience?

510.   Make the following experiment: *say* "It's cold here" and *mean*
"It's warm here". Can you do it?—And what are you doing as you do
it? And is there only one way of doing it?

511.   What does "discovering that an expression doesn't make
sense" mean?—and what does it mean to say: "If I mean something by
it, surely it must make sense"?—If I mean something by it?—If I
mean *what* by it?!—One wants to say: a significant sentence is one
which one can not merely say, but also think.

512.   It looks as if we could say: "Word-language allows of senseless combinations of words, but the language of imagining does not
allow us to imagine anything senseless."—Hence, too, the language of
drawing doesn't allow of senseless drawings? Suppose they were
drawings from which bodies were supposed to be modelled. In this
case some drawings make sense, some not.—What if I imagine senseless
combinations of words?

513.   Consider the following form of expression: "The number of
pages in my book is equal to a root of the equation $x^3 + 2x - 3 = 0$."
Or: "I have n friends and $n^2 + 2n + 2 = 0$". Does this sentence
make sense? This cannot be seen immediately. This example shews

ow it is that something can look like a sentence which we understand,
nd yet yield no sense.

(This throws light on the concepts 'understanding' and 'meaning'.)

514. A philosopher says that he understands the sentence "I am
ere", that he means something by it, thinks something—even when
e doesn't think at all how, on what occasions, this sentence is used.
nd if I say "A rose is red in the dark too" you positively see this red
1 the dark before you.

515. Two pictures of a rose in the dark. One is quite black; for
he rose is invisible. In the other, it is painted in full detail and sur-
ounded by black. Is one of them right, the other wrong? Don't we
alk of a white rose in the dark and of a red rose in the dark? And
on't we say for all that that they can't be distinguished in the dark?

516. It seems clear that we understand the meaning of the question:
Does the sequence 7777 occur in the development of π ?" It is
n English sentence; it can be shewn what it means for 415 to occur
1 the development of π; and similar things. Well, our understanding
f that question reaches just so far, one may say, as such explanations
each.

517. The question arises: Can't we be mistaken in thinking that
/e understand a question?

For many mathematical proofs do lead us to say that we *cannot*
magine something which we believed we could imagine. (E.g., the
onstruction of the heptagon.) They lead us to revise what counts as
he domain of the imaginable.

518. Socrates to Theaetetus: "And if someone thinks mustn't he
hink *something*?"—Th: "Yes, he must."—Soc.: "And if he thinks
omething, mustn't it be something real?"—Th.: "Apparently."

And mustn't someone who is painting be painting something—and
omeone who is painting something be painting something real!—
Vell, tell me what the object of painting is: the picture of a man (e.g.),
r the man that the picture portrays?

519. One wants to say that an order is a picture of the action
/hich was carried out on the order; but also that it is a picture of the
ction which *is to be* carried out on the order.

520. "If a proposition too is conceived as a picture of a possible
tate of affairs and is said to shew the possibility of the state of affairs,

still the most that the proposition can do is what a painting or relief or film does: and so it can at any rate not set forth what is not the case. So does it depend wholly on our grammar what will be called (logically) possible and what not,—i.e. what that grammar permits?"—But surely that is arbitrary!—Is it arbitrary?—It is not every sentence-like formation that we know how to do something with, not every technique has an application in our life; and when we are tempted in philosophy to count some quite useless thing as a proposition, that is often because we have not considered its application sufficiently.

521. Compare 'logically possible' with 'chemically possible'. One might perhaps call a combination chemically possible if a formula with the right valencies existed (e.g. H - O - O - O - H). Of course such a combination need not exist; but even the formula HO_2 cannot have less than no combination corresponding to it in reality.

522. If we compare a proposition to a picture, we must think whether we are comparing it to a portrait (a historical representation) or to a genre-picture. And both comparisons have point.

When I look at a genre-picture, it 'tells' me something, even though I don't believe (imagine) for a moment that the people I see in it really exist, or that there have really been people in that situation. But suppose I ask: "*What* does it tell me, then?"

523. I should like to say "What the picture tells me is itself." That is, its telling me something consists in its own structure, in its own lines and colours. (What would it mean to say "What this musical theme tells me is itself"?)

524. Don't take it as a matter of course, but as a remarkable fact, that pictures and fictitious narratives give us pleasure, occupy our minds.

("Don't take it as a matter of course" means: find it surprising, as you do some things which disturb you. Then the puzzling aspect of the latter will disappear, by your accepting this fact as you do the other.)

((The transition from patent nonsense to something which is disguised nonsense.))

525. "After he had said this, he left her as he did the day before."- Do I understand this sentence? Do I understand it just as I should if I heard it in the course of a narrative? If it were set down in isolation

should say, I don't know what it's about. But all the same I should
now how this sentence might perhaps be used; I could myself invent
context for it.

(A multitude of familiar paths lead off from these words in every
irection.)

526.   What does it mean to understand a picture, a drawing?
Iere too there is understanding and failure to understand. And here
oo these expressions may mean various kinds of thing. A picture is
erhaps a still-life; but I don't understand one part of it: I cannot
ee solid objects there, but only patches of colour on the canvas.—
Jr I see everything as solid but there are objects that I am not
cquainted with (they look like implements, but I don't know their
se).—Perhaps, however, I am acquainted with the objects, but
1 another sense do not understand the way they are arranged.

527.   Understanding a sentence is much more akin to understanding
theme in music than one may think. What I mean is that understand-
ng a sentence lies nearer than one thinks to what is ordinarily called
inderstanding a musical theme. Why is just *this* the pattern of variation
1 loudness and tempo? One would like to say "Because I know
vhat it's all about." But what is it all about? I should not be able to
ay. In order to 'explain' I could only compare it with something else
vhich has the same rhythm (I mean the same pattern). (One says
'Don't you see, this is as if a conclusion were being drawn" or "This
s as it were a parenthesis", etc. How does one justify such com-
arisons?—There are very different kinds of justification here.)

528.   It would be possible to imagine people who had something
not quite unlike a language: a play of sounds, without vocabulary or
grammar. ('Speaking with tongues.')

529.   "But what would the meaning of the sounds be in such
case?"—What is it in music? Though I don't at all wish to say
hat this language of a play of sounds would have to be compared
o music.

530.   There might also be a language in whose use the 'soul' of the
vords played no part. In which, for example, we had no objection to
eplacing one word by another arbitrary one of our own invention.

531.   We speak of understanding a sentence in the sense in which it
an be replaced by another which says the same; but also in the sense

in which it cannot be replaced by any other. (Any more than on
musical theme can be replaced by another.)

In the one case the thought in the sentence is something commo
to different sentences; in the other, something that is expressed onl
by these words in these positions. (Understanding a poem.)

532. Then has "understanding" two different meanings here?—
would rather say that these kinds of use of "understanding" make u
its meaning, make up my *concept* of understanding.

For I *want* to apply the word "understanding" to all this.

533. But in the second case how can one explain the expressio
transmit one's comprehension? Ask yourself: How does one *lea*
anyone to comprehension of a poem or of a theme? The answer t
this tells us how meaning is explained here.

534. *Hearing* a word in a particular sense. How queer that ther
should be such a thing!

Phrased *like this*, emphasized like this, heard in this way, this sentenc
is the first of a series in which a transition is made to *these* sentence
pictures, actions.

((A multitude of familiar paths lead off from these words in ever
direction.))

535. What happens when we learn to *feel* the ending of a churc
mode as an ending?

536. I say: "I can think of this face (which gives an impression c
timidity) as courageous too." We do not mean by this that I ca
imagine someone with this face perhaps saving someone's life (tha
of course, is imaginable in connexion with any face). I am speakin
rather of an aspect of the face itself. Nor do I mean that I can imagin
that this man's face might change so that, in the ordinary sense, it looke
courageous; though I may very well mean that there is a quite definit
way in which it can change into a courageous face. The reinterpreta
tion of a facial expression can be compared to the reinterpretatio
of a chord in music, when we hear it as a modulation first into thi
then into that key.

537. It is possible to say "I read timidity in this face" but at a
events the timidity does not seem to be merely associated, outwardl
connected, with the face; but fear is there, alive, in the features. If th
features change slightly, we can speak of a corresponding change in th

ear. If we were asked "Can you think of this face as an expression of courage too?"—we should, as it were, not know how to lodge courage n these features. Then perhaps I say "I don't know what it would mean for this to be a courageous face." But what would an answer to uch a question be like? Perhaps one says: "Yes, now I understand: he face as it were shews indifference to the outer world." So we nave somehow read courage into the face. Now once more, one might ay, courage *fits* this face. But *what* fits *what* here?

538.   There is a related case (though perhaps it will not seem so) when, for example, we (Germans) are surprised that in French the predicative adjective agrees with the substantive in gender, and when we explain it to ourselves by saying: they mean: "the man is *a good ne*."

539.   I see a picture which represents a smiling face. What do I lo if I take the smile now as a kind one, now as malicious? Don't I often imagine it with a spatial and temporal context which is one either of kindness or malice? Thus I might supply the picture with the ancy that the smiler was smiling down on a child at play, or again on he suffering of an enemy.

This is in no way altered by the fact that I can also take the at first ight gracious situation and interpret it differently by putting it into a wider context.—If no special circumstances reverse my interpretation shall conceive a particular smile as kind, call it a "kind" one, react correspondingly.

((Probability, frequency.))

540.   "Isn't it very odd that I should be unable—even *without* the institution of language and all its surroundings—to think that it will soon stop raining?"—Do you want to say that it is queer that you should be unable to say these words and *mean* them without those surroundings?

Suppose someone were to point at the sky and come out with a number of unintelligible words. When we ask him what he means ne explains that the words mean "Thank heaven, it'll soon stop raining." He even explains to us the meaning of the individual words. —I will suppose him suddenly to come to himself and say that the sentence was completely senseless, but that when he spoke it it had seemed to him like a sentence in a language he knew. (Positively like a familiar quotation.)—What am I to say now? Didn't he understand the sentence as he was saying it? Wasn't the whole meaning there in the sentence?

541.   But what did his understanding, and the meaning, consist in? He uttered the sounds in a cheerful voice perhaps, pointing to the sky, while it was still raining but was already beginning to clear up; *later* he made a connexion between his words and the English words.

542.   "But the point is, the words felt to him like the words of a language he knew well."—Yes: a criterion for that is that he later said just *that*. And now do *not* say: "The feel of the words in a language we know is of a quite particular kind." (What is the *expression* of this feeling?)

543.   Can I not say: a cry, a laugh, are full of meaning?
And that means, roughly: much can be gathered from them.

544.   When longing makes me cry "Oh, if only he would come!" the feeling gives the words 'meaning'. But does it give the individual words their meanings?
But here one could also say that the feeling gave the words *truth*. And from this you can see how the concepts merge here. (This recalls the question: what is the *meaning* of a mathematical proposition?)

545.   But when one says "I *hope* he'll come"—doesn't the feeling give the word "hope" its meaning? (And what about the sentence "I do *not* hope for his coming any longer"?) The feeling does perhaps give the word "hope" its special ring; that is, it is expressed in that ring.—If the feeling gives the word its meaning, then here "meaning" means *point*. But why is the feeling the point?
Is hope a feeling? (Characteristic marks.)

546.   In this way I should like to say the words "Oh, *let* him come!" are charged with my desire. And words can be wrung from us,—like a cry. Words can be *hard* to say: such, for example, as are used to effect a renunciation, or to confess a weakness. (Words are also deeds.)

547.   Negation: a 'mental activity'. Negate something and observe what you are doing.—Do you perhaps inwardly shake your head? And if you do—is this process more deserving of our interest than, say,

that of writing a sign of negation in a sentence? Do you now know the *essence* of negation?

548.   What is the difference between the two processes: wishing that something should happen—and wishing that the same thing should *not* happen?

If we want to represent it pictorially, we shall treat the picture of the event in various ways: cross it out, put a line round it, and so on. But this strikes us as a *crude* method of expression. In word-language indeed we use the sign "not". But this is like a clumsy expedient. We think that in *thought* it is arranged differently.

549.   "How can the word 'not' negate?"—"The sign 'not' indicates that you are to take what follows negatively." We should like to say: The sign of negation is our occasion for doing something—possibly something very complicated. It is as if the negation-sign occasioned our doing something. But what? That is not said. It is as if it only needed to be hinted at; as if we already knew. As if no explanation were needed, for we are in any case already acquainted with the matter.

550.   Negation, one might say, is a gesture of exclusion, of rejection. But such a gesture is used in a great variety of cases!

551.   "Does the *same* negation occur in: 'Iron does not melt at a hundred degrees Centigrade' and 'Twice two is not five'?" Is this to be decided by introspection; by trying to see what we are *thinking* as we utter the two sentences?

552.   Suppose I were to ask: is it clear to us, while we are uttering the sentences "This rod is one yard long" and "Here is one soldier",

---

(a) "The fact that three negatives yield a negative again must already be contained in the single negative that I am using now." (The temptation to invent a myth of 'meaning'.)

It looks as if it followed from the nature of negation that a double negative is an affirmative. (And there is something right about this. What? *Our* nature is connected with both.)

(b) There cannot be a question whether these or other rules are the correct ones for the use of "not". (I mean, whether they accord with its meaning.) For without these rules the word has as yet no meaning; and if we change the rules, it now has another meaning (or none), and in that case we may just as well change the word too.

that we mean different things by "one", that "one" has different meanings?—Not at all.—Say e.g. such a sentence as "One yard is occupied by one soldier, and so two yards are occupied by two soldiers." Asked "Do you mean the same thing by both 'ones'?" one would perhaps answer: "Of course I mean the same thing: one!" (Perhaps raising one finger.)

553. Now has "1" a different meaning when it stands for a measure and when it stands for a number? If the question is framed in *this* way, one will answer in the affirmative.

554. We can easily imagine human beings with a 'more primitive' logic, in which something corresponding to our negation is applied only to certain sorts of sentence; perhaps to such as do not themselves contain any negation. It would be possible to negate the proposition "He is going into the house", but a negation of the negative proposition would be meaningless, or would count only as a repetition of the negation. Think of means of expressing negation different from ours: by the pitch of one's voice, for instance. What would a double negation be like there?

555. The question whether negation had the same meaning to these people as to us would be analogous to the question whether the figure "5" meant the same to people whose numbers ended at 5 as to us.

556. Imagine a language with two different words for negation, "X" and "Y". Doubling "X" yields an affirmative, doubling "Y" a strengthened negative. For the rest the two words are used alike.— Now have "X" and "Y" the same meaning in sentences where they occur without being repeated?—We could give various answers to this.

(a) The two words have different uses. So they have different meanings. But sentences in which they occur without being repeated and which for the rest are the same make the same sense.

(b) The two words have the same function in language-games, except for this one difference, which is just a trivial convention. The use of the two words is taught in the same way, by means of the same actions, gestures, pictures and so on; and in explanations of the words the difference in the ways they are used is appended as something incidental, as one of the capricious features of the language. For this reason we shall say that "X" and "Y" have the same meaning.

(c) We connect different images with the two negatives. "X" as it were turns the sense through 180°. And *that* is why two such negatives restore the sense to its former position. "Y" is like a shake of the head. And just as one does not annul a shake of the head by shaking it again, so also one doesn't cancel one "Y" by a second one. And so even if, practically speaking, sentences with the two signs of negation come to the same thing, still "X" and "Y" express different ideas.

557. Now, when I uttered the double negation, what constituted my meaning it as a strengthened negative and not as an affirmative? There is no answer running: "It consisted in the fact that . . . . ." In certain circumstances instead of saying "This duplication is meant as a strengthening," I can *pronounce* it as a strengthening. Instead of saying "The duplication of the negative is meant to cancel it" I can e.g. put brackets.—"Yes, but after all these brackets may themselves have various roles; for who says that they are to be taken as *brackets*?" No one does. And haven't you explained your own conception in turn by means of words? The meaning of the brackets lies in the technique of applying them. The question is: under what circumstances does it make sense to say "I meant . . . .", and what circumstances justify me in saying "He meant . . . ."?

558. What does it mean to say that the "is" in "The rose is red" has a different meaning from the "is" in "twice two is four"? If it is answered that it means that different rules are valid for these two words, we can say that we have only *one* word here.—And if all I am attending to is grammatical rules, these do allow the use of the word "is" in both connexions.—But the rule which shews that the word "is" has different meanings in these sentences is the one allowing us to replace the word "is" in the second sentence by the sign of equality, and forbidding this substitution in the first sentence.

559. One would like to speak of the function of a word in *this* sentence. As if the sentence were a mechanism in which the word had a particular function. But what does this function consist in? How does it come to light? For there isn't anything hidden—don't we see the whole sentence? The function must come out in operating with the word. ((Meaning-body.))

560. "The meaning of a word is what is explained by the explanation of the meaning." I.e.: if you want to understand the use of the word "meaning", look for what are called "explanations of meaning".

561. Now isn't it queer that I say that the word "is" is used with two different meanings (as the copula and as the sign of equality), and should not care to say that its meaning is its use; its use, that is, as the copula and the sign of equality?

One would like to say that these two kinds of use do not yield a *single* meaning; the union under one head is an accident, a mere inessential.

562. But how can I decide what is an essential, and what an inessential, accidental, feature of the notation? Is there some reality lying behind the notation, which shapes its grammar?

Let us think of a similar case in a game: in draughts a king is marked by putting one piece on top of another. Now won't one say it is inessential to the game for a king to consist of two pieces?

563. Let us say that the meaning of a piece is its role in the game.—Now let it be decided by lot which of the players gets white before any game of chess begins. To this end one player holds a king in each closed fist while the other chooses one of the two hands at random. Will it be counted as part of the role of the king in chess that it is used to draw lots in this way?

564. So I am inclined to distinguish between the essential and the inessential in a game too. The game, one would like to say, has not only rules but also a *point*.

565. Why the same word? In the calculus we make no use of this identity!—Why the same piece for both purposes?—But what does it mean here to speak of "making use of the identity"? For isn't it a use, if we do in fact use the same word?

566. And now it looks as if the use of the same word or the same piece, had a *purpose*—if the identity is not accidental, inessential. And as if the purpose were that one should be able to recognize the piece and know how to play.—Are we talking about a physical or a logical possibility here? If the latter then the identity of the piece is something to do with the game.

567. But, after all, the game is supposed to be defined by the rules! So, if a rule of the game prescribes that the kings are to be used for drawing lots before a game of chess, then that is an essential part of the game. What objection might one make to this? That one does not see the point of this prescription. Perhaps as one wouldn't see the point either of a rule by which each piece had to be turned round three times

before one moved it. If we found this rule in a board-game we should be surprised and should speculate about the purpose of the rule. ("Was this prescription meant to prevent one from moving without due consideration?")

568. If I understand the character of the game aright—I might say—then this isn't an essential part of it.

((Meaning is a physiognomy.))

569. Language is an instrument. Its concepts are instruments. Now perhaps one thinks that it can make no *great* difference *which* concepts we employ. As, after all, it is possible to do physics in feet and inches as well as in metres and centimetres; the difference is merely one of convenience. But even this is not true if, for instance, calculations in some system of measurement demand more time and trouble than it is possible for us to give them.

570. Concepts lead us to make investigations; are the expression of our interest, and direct our interest.

571. Misleading parallel: psychology treats of processes in the psychical sphere, as does physics in the physical.

Seeing, hearing, thinking, feeling, willing, are not the subject of psychology *in the same sense* as that in which the movements of bodies, the phenomena of electricity etc., are the subject of physics. You can see this from the fact that the physicist sees, hears, thinks about, and informs us of these phenomena, and the psychologist observes the *external reactions* (the behaviour) of the subject.

572. Expectation is, grammatically, a state; like: being of an opinion, hoping for something, knowing something, being able to do something. But in order to understand the grammar of these states it is necessary to ask: "What counts as a criterion for anyone's being in such a state?" (States of hardness, of weight, of fitting.)

573. To have an opinion is a state.—A state of what? Of the soul? Of the mind? Well, of what object does one say that it has an opinion? Of Mr. N.N. for example. And that is the correct answer.

One should not expect to be enlightened by the answer to *that* question. Others go deeper: What, in particular cases, do we regard as criteria for someone's being of such-and-such an opinion? When do we say: he reached this opinion at that time? When: he has altered his opinion? And so on. The picture which the answers to these questions give us shews *what* gets treated grammatically as a *state* here.

574. A proposition, and hence in another sense a thought, can be the 'expression' of belief, hope, expectation, etc. But believing is not thinking. (A grammatical remark.) The concepts of believing, expecting, hoping are less distantly related to one another than they are to the concept of thinking.

575. When I sat down on this chair, of course I believed it would bear me. I had no thought of its possibly collapsing.
But: "In spite of everything that he did, I held fast to the belief . . . ." Here there is thought, and perhaps a constant struggle to renew an attitude.

576. I watch a slow match burning, in high excitement follow the progress of the burning and its approach to the explosive. Perhaps I don't think anything at all or have a multitude of disconnected thoughts. This is certainly a case of expecting.

577. We say "I am expecting him", when we believe that he will come, though his coming does not *occupy our thoughts*. (Here "I am expecting him" would mean "I should be surprised if he didn't come" and that will not be called the description of a state of mind.) But we also say "I am expecting him" when it is supposed to mean: I am eagerly awaiting him. We could imagine a language in which different verbs were consistently used in these cases. And similarly more than one verb where we speak of 'believing', 'hoping' and so on. Perhaps the concepts of such a language would be more suitable for understanding psychology than the concepts of our language.

578. Ask yourself: What does it mean to *believe* Goldbach's theorem? What does this belief consist in? In a feeling of certainty as we state, hear, or think the theorem? (That would not interest us.) And what are the characteristics of this feeling? Why, I don't even know how far the feeling may be caused by the proposition itself.
Am I to say that belief is a particular colouring of our thoughts? Where does this idea come from? Well, there is a tone of belief, as of doubt.
I should like to ask: how does the belief connect with this proposition? Let us look and see what are the consequences of this belief, where it takes us. "It makes me search for a proof of the proposition." —Very well; and now let us look and see what your searching really consists in. Then we shall know what belief in the proposition amounts to.

579. The feeling of confidence. How is this manifested in behaviour?

580. An 'inner process' stands in need of outward criteria.

581. An expectation is imbedded in a situation, from which it arises. The expectation of an explosion may, for example, arise from a situation in which an explosion *is to be expected*.

582. If someone whispers "It'll go off now", instead of saying "I expect the explosion any moment", still his words do not describe a feeling; although they and their tone may be a manifestation of his feeling.

583. "But you talk as if I weren't really expecting, hoping, *now*— as I thought I was. As if what were happening *now* had no deep significance."—What does it mean to say "What is happening now has significance" or "has deep significance"? What is a *deep* feeling? Could someone have a feeling of ardent love or hope for the space of one second—*no matter what* preceded or followed this second?—— What is happening now has significance—in these surroundings. The surroundings give it its importance. And the word "hope" refers to a phenomenon of human life. (A smiling mouth *smiles* only in a human face.)

584. Now suppose I sit in my room and hope that N.N. will come and bring me some money, and suppose one minute of this state could be isolated, cut out of its context; would what happened in it then not be hope?—Think, for example, of the words which you perhaps utter in this space of time. They are no longer part of this language. And in different surroundings the institution of money doesn't exist either.

A coronation is the picture of pomp and dignity. Cut one minute of this proceeding out of its surroundings: the crown is being placed on the head of the king in his coronation robes.—But in different surroundings gold is the cheapest of metals, its gleam is thought vulgar. There the fabric of the robe is cheap to produce. A crown is a parody of a respectable hat. And so on.

585. When someone says "I hope he'll come"—is this a *report* about his state of mind, or a *manifestation* of his hope?—I can, for example, say it to myself. And surely I am not giving myself a report. It may be a sigh; but it need not. If I tell someone "I can't keep my mind on my work today; I keep on thinking of his coming"— *this* will be called a description of my state of mind.

586. "I have heard he is coming; I have been waiting for him all day." That is a report on how I have spent the day.——In conversation I came to the conclusion that a particular event is to be expected, and I draw this conclusion in the words: "So now I must expect him to come". This may be called the first thought, the first act, of this expectation.——The exclamation "I'm longing to see him!" may be called an act of expecting. But I can utter the same words as the result of self-observation, and then they might mean: "So, after all that has happened, I am still longing to see him." The point is: what led up to these words?

587. Does it make sense to ask "How do you know that you believe?"—and is the answer: "I know it by introspection"?

In *some* cases it will be possible to say some such thing, in most not.

It makes sense to ask: "Do I really love her, or am I only pretending to myself?" and the process of introspection is the calling up of memories; of imagined possible situations, and of the feelings that one would have if . . . .

588. "I am revolving the decision to go away to-morrow." (This may be called a description of a state of mind.)——"Your arguments don't convince me; now as before it is my intention to go away to-morrow." Here one is tempted to call the intention a feeling. The feeling is one of a certain rigidity; of unalterable determination. (But there are many different characteristic feelings and attitudes here.)—— I am asked: "How long are you staying here?" I reply: "To-morrow I am going away; it's the end of my holidays."—But over against this: I say at the end of a quarrel "All right! Then I leave to-morrow!"; I make a decision.

589. "In my heart I have determined on it." And one is even inclined to point to one's breast as one says it. Psychologically this way of speaking should be taken seriously. Why should it be taken less seriously than the assertion that belief is a state of mind? (Luther: "Faith is under the left nipple.")

590. Someone might learn to understand the meaning of the expression "seriously *meaning* what one says" by means of a gesture of pointing at the heart. But now we must ask: "How does it come out that he has learnt it?"

591. Am I to say that any one who has an intention has an experience of tending towards something? That there are particular experiences of 'tending'?—Remember this case: if one urgently wants to make some remark, some objection, in a discussion, it often happens that one opens one's mouth, draws a breath and holds it; if one then decides to let the objection go, one lets the breath out. The experience of this process is evidently the experience of veering towards saying something. Anyone who observes me will know that I wanted to say something and then thought better of it. In *this* situation, that is.— In a different one he would not so interpret my behaviour, however characteristic of the intention to speak it may be in the present situation. And is there any reason for assuming that this same experience could not occur in some quite different situation—in which it has nothing to do with any 'tending'?

592. "But when you say 'I intend to go away', you surely mean it! Here again it just is the mental act of meaning that gives the sentence life. If you merely repeat the sentence after someone else, say in order to mock his way of speaking, then you say it without this act of meaning."—When we are doing philosophy it can sometimes look like that. But let us really think out various *different* situations and conversations, and the ways in which that sentence will be uttered in them.—"I always discover a mental undertone; perhaps not always the *same* one." And was there no undertone there when you repeated the sentence after someone else? And how is the 'undertone' to be separated from the rest of the experience of speaking?

593. A main cause of philosophical disease—a one-sided diet: one nourishes one's thinking with only one kind of example.

594. "But the words, significantly uttered, have after all not only a surface, but also the dimension of depth!" After all, it just is the case that something different takes place when they are uttered significantly from when they are merely uttered.—How I express this is not the point. Whether I say that in the first case they have depth; or that something goes on in me, inside my mind, as I utter them; or that they have an atmosphere—it always comes to the same thing.

"Well, if we all agree about it, won't it be true?"

(I cannot accept someone else's testimony, because it is not *testimony*. It only tells me what he is *inclined* to say.)

595. It is natural for us to say a sentence in such-and-such surroundings, and unnatural to say it in isolation. Are we to say that

there is a particular feeling accompanying the utterance of every sentence when we say it naturally?

596.   The feeling of 'familiarity' and of 'naturalness'. It is easier to get at a feeling of unfamiliarity and of unnaturalness. Or, at *feelings*. For not everything which is unfamiliar to us makes an impression of unfamiliarity upon us. Here one has to consider what we call "unfamiliar". If a boulder lies on the road, we know it for a boulder, but perhaps not for the one which has always lain there. We recognize a man, say, as a man, but not as an acquaintance. There are feelings of old acquaintance: they are sometimes expressed by a particular way of looking or by the words: "The same old room!" (which I occupied many years before and now returning find unchanged). Equally there are feelings of strangeness. I stop short, look at the object or man questioningly or mistrustfully, say "I find it all strange."— But the existence of this feeling of strangeness does not give us a reason for saying that every object which we know well and which does not seem strange to us gives us a feeling of familiarity.—We think that, as it were, the place once filled by the feeling of strangeness must surely be occupied *somehow*. The place for this kind of atmosphere is there, and if one of them is not in possession of it, then another is.

597.   Just as Germanisms creep into the speech of a German who speaks English well although he does not first construct the German expression and then translate it into English; just as this makes him speak English *as if he were translating* 'unconsciously' from the German —so we often think as if our thinking were founded on a thought-schema: as if we were translating from a more primitive mode of thought into ours.

598.   When we do philosophy, we should like to hypostatize feelings where there are none. They serve to explain our thoughts to us.

'*Here* explanation of our thinking demands a feeling!' It is as if our conviction were simply consequent upon this requirement.

599.   In philosophy we do not draw conclusions. "But it must be like this!" is not a philosophical proposition. Philosophy only states what everyone admits.

600.   Does everything that we do not find conspicuous make an impression of inconspicuousness? Does what is ordinary always make the *impression* of ordinariness?

601. When I talk about this table,—am I *remembering* that this object is called a "table"?

602. Asked "Did you recognize your desk when you entered your room this morning?"—I should no doubt say "Certainly!" And yet it would be misleading to say that an act of recognition had taken place. Of course the desk was not strange to me; I was not surprised to see it, as I should have been if another one had been standing there, or some unfamiliar kind of object.

603. No one will say that every time I enter my room, my long-familiar surroundings, there is enacted a recognition of all that I see and have seen hundreds of times before.

604. It is easy to have a false picture of the processes called "recognizing"; as if recognizing always consisted in comparing two impressions with one another. It is as if I carried a picture of an object with me and used it to perform an identification of an object as the one represented by the picture. Our memory seems to us to be the agent of such a comparison, by preserving a picture of what has been seen before, or by allowing us to look into the past (as if down a spy-glass).

605. And it is not so much as if I were comparing the object with a picture set beside it, but as if the object *coincided* with the picture. So I see only one thing, not two.

606. We say "The expression in his voice was *genuine*". If it was spurious we think as it were of another one behind it.—*This* is the face he shews the world, inwardly he has another one.—But this does not mean that when his expression is *genuine* he has two the same.
(("A quite particular expression."))

607. How does one judge what time it is? I do not mean by external evidences, however, such as the position of the sun, the lightness of the room, and so on.—One asks oneself, say, "What time can it be?", pauses a moment, perhaps imagines a clock-face, and then says a time.—Or one considers various possibilities, thinks first of one time, then of another, and in the end stops at one. That is the kind of way it is done.——But isn't the idea accompanied by a feeling of conviction; and doesn't that mean that it accords with an inner clock?—No, I don't read the time off from any clock; there is a feeling of conviction inasmuch as I say a time to myself *without* feeling any doubt, with calm assurance.—But doesn't something click as I say

this time?—Not that I know of; unless that is what you call the coming-to-rest of deliberation, the stopping at one number. Nor should I ever have spoken of a 'feeling of conviction' here, but should have said: I considered a while and then plumped for its being quarter past five.— But what did I go by? I might perhaps have said: "simply by feel", which only means that I left it to what should suggest itself.—— But you surely must at least have disposed yourself in a definite way in order to guess the time; and you don't take just any idea of a time of day as yielding the correct time!—To repeat: I *asked* myself "I wonder what time it is?" That is, I did not, for example, read this question in some narrative, or quote it as someone else's utterance; nor was I practising the pronunciation of these words; and so on. *These* were not the circumstances of my saying the words.—But then, *what* were the circumstances?—I was thinking about my breakfast and wondering whether it would be late today. These were the kind of circumstances.—But do you really not see that you were all the same disposed in a way which, though impalpable, is characteristic of guessing the time, like being surrounded by a characteristic atmosphere?— Yes; what was characteristic was that I said to myself "I wonder what time it is?"—And if this sentence has a particular atmosphere, how am I to separate it from the sentence itself? It would never have occurred to me to think the sentence had such an aura if I had not thought of how one might say it differently—as a quotation, as a joke, as practice in elocution, and so on. And *then* all at once I wanted to say, then all at once it seemed to me, that I must after all have *meant* the words somehow specially; differently, that is, from in those other cases. The picture of the special atmosphere forced itself upon me; I can see it quite clear before me—so long, that is, as I do not look at what my memory tells me really happened.

And as for the feeling of certainty: I sometimes say to myself "I am sure it's . . . o'clock", and in a more or less confident tone of voice, and so on. If you ask me the *reason* for this certainty I have none.

If I say, I read it off from an inner clock,—that is a picture, and the only thing that corresponds to it is that I said it was such-and-such a time. And the purpose of the picture is to assimilate this case to the other one. I am refusing to acknowledge two different cases here.

608. The idea of the intangibility of that mental state in estimating the time is of the greatest importance. Why is it *intangible*? Isn't it

ecause we refuse to count what is tangible about our state as part of
ιe specific state which we are postulating?

609. The description of an atmosphere is a special application of
ιnguage, for special purposes.

((Interpreting 'understanding' as atmosphere; as a mental act. One
ιn construct an atmosphere to attach to anything. 'An indescribable
ιaracter.'))

610. Describe the aroma of coffee.—Why can't it be done? Do we
ιck the words? And *for what* are words lacking?—But how do we get
ιe idea that such a description must after all be possible? Have you
ver felt the lack of such a description? Have you tried to describe
ιe aroma and not succeeded?

(((I should like to say: "These notes say something glorious, but I
ο not know what." These notes are a powerful gesture, but I cannot
ut anything side by side with it that will serve as an explanation.
ι grave nod. James: "Our vocabulary is inadequate." Then why
on't we introduce a new one? What would have to be the case for us
ο be able to?))

611. "Willing too is merely an experience," one would like to say
he 'will' too only 'idea'). It comes when it comes, and I cannot bring
about.
Not bring it about?—Like *what*? What can I bring about, then?
Ɍhat am I comparing willing with when I say this?

612. I should not say of the movement of my arm, for example:
comes when it comes, etc. . And this is the region in which we say
gnificantly that a thing doesn't simply happen to us, but that we *do*
. "I don't need to wait for my arm to go up—I can raise it." And
ιre I am making a contrast between the movement of my arm and,
ιy, the fact that the violent thudding of my heart will subside.

613. In the sense in which I can ever bring anything about (such
ι stomach-ache through over-eating), I can also bring about an act
f willing. In this sense I bring about the act of willing to swim by
ιmping into the water. Doubtless I was trying to say: I can't will
ιlling; that is, it makes no sense to speak of willing willing. "Willing"
ι not the name of an action; and so not the name of any voluntary
ιtion either. And my use of a wrong expression came from our
ιanting to think of willing as an immediate non-causal bringing-
bout. A misleading analogy lies at the root of this idea; the causal

nexus seems to be established by a mechanism connecting two parts o
a machine. The connexion may be broken if the mechanism is dis
turbed. (We think only of the disturbances to which a mechanism i
normally subject, not, say, of cog-wheels suddenly going soft, o
passing through one another, and so on.)

614. When I raise my arm 'voluntarily' I do not use any instru
ment to bring the movement about. My wish is not such an instrumen
either.

615. "Willing, if it is not to be a sort of wishing, must be th
action itself. It cannot be allowed to stop anywhere short of the action."
If it is the action, then it is so in the ordinary sense of the word
so it is speaking, writing, walking, lifting a thing, imagining some
thing. But it is also trying, attempting, making an effort,—to speak
to write, to lift a thing, to imagine something etc. .

616. When I raise my arm, I have *not* wished it might go up
The voluntary action excludes this wish. It is indeed possible to say
"I hope I shall draw the circle faultlessly". And that is to express a wis
that one's hand should move in such-and-such a way.

617. If we cross our fingers in a certain special way we are some
times unable to move a particular finger when someone tells us to d
so, if he only *points* to the finger—merely shews it to the eye. If o
the other hand he touches it, we can move it. One would like t
describe this experience as follows: we are unable to *will* to move th
finger. The case is quite different from that in which we are not abl
to move the finger because someone is, say, holding it. One now feel
inclined to describe the former case by saying: one can't find any poir
of application for the will till the finger is touched. Only when on
feels the finger can the will know where it is to catch hold.—But thi
kind of expression is misleading. One would like to say: "How ar
I to know where I am to catch hold with the will, if feeling does nc
shew the place?" But then how is it known to what point I am t
direct the will when the feeling is there?

That in this case the finger is as it were paralysed until we feel
touch on it is shewn by experience; it could not have been seen
priori.

618. One imagines the willing subject here as something withou
any mass (without any inertia); as a motor which has no inertia i
itself to overcome. And so it is only mover, not moved. That i

One can say "I will, but my body does not obey me"—but not: "My will does not obey me." (Augustine.)

But in the sense in which I cannot fail to will, I cannot try to will either.

619. And one might say: "I can always will only inasmuch as I can never try to will."

620. *Doing* itself seems not to have any volume of experience. It seems like an extensionless point, the point of a needle. This point seems to be the real agent. And the phenomenal happenings only to be consequences of this acting. "I *do* . . ." seems to have a definite sense, separate from all experience.

621. Let us not forget this: when 'I raise my arm', my arm goes up. And the problem arises: what is left over if I subtract the fact that my arm goes up from the fact that I raise my arm?

((Are the kinaesthetic sensations my willing?))

622. When I raise my arm I do not usually *try* to raise it.

623. "At all costs I will get to that house."—But if there is no difficulty about it—*can* I try at all costs to get to the house?

624. In the laboratory, when subjected to an electric current, for example, someone says with his eyes shut "I am moving my arm up and down"—though his arm is not moving. "So," we say, "he has the special feeling of making that movement."—Move your arm to and fro with your eyes shut. And now try, while you do so, to tell yourself that your arm is staying still and that you are only having certain queer feelings in your muscles and joints!

625. "How do you know that you have raised your arm?"—"I feel it." So what you recognize is the feeling? And are you certain that you recognize it right?—You are certain that you have raised your arm; isn't this the criterion, the measure, of the recognition?

626. "When I touch this object with a stick I have the sensation of touching in the tip of the stick, not in the hand that holds it." When someone says "The pain isn't here in my hand, but in my wrist", this has the consequence that the doctor examines the wrist. But what difference does it make if I say that I feel the hardness of the

object in the tip of the stick or in my hand? Does what I say mean "It is as if I had nerve-endings in the tip of the stick?" *In what sense* is it like that?—Well, I am at any rate inclined to say "I feel the hardness etc. in the tip of the stick." What goes with this is that when I touch the object I look not at my hand but at the tip of the stick; that I describe what I feel by saying "I feel something hard and round there"—not "I feel a pressure against the tips of my thumb, middle finger, and index finger . . . ." If, for example, someone asks me "What are you now feeling in the fingers that hold the probe?" I might reply: "I don't know——I feel something hard and rough *over there*."

627.   Examine the following description of a voluntary action: "I form the decision to pull the bell at 5 o'clock, and when it strikes 5, my arm makes this movement."—Is that the correct description, and not *this* one: " . . . . . and when it strikes 5, I raise my arm"?——One would like to supplement the first description: "and see! my arm goes up when it strikes 5." And this "and see!" is precisely what doesn't belong here. I do *not* say "See, my arm is going up!" when I raise it.

628.   So one might say: voluntary movement is marked by the absence of surprise. And now I do not mean you to ask "But *why* isn't one surprised here?"

629.   When people talk about the possibility of foreknowledge of the future they always forget the fact of the prediction of one's own voluntary movements.

630.   Examine these two language-games:

(a) Someone gives someone else the order to make particular movements with his arm, or to assume particular bodily positions (gymnastics instructor and pupil). And here is a variation of this language-game: the pupil gives himself orders and then carries them out.

(b) Someone observes certain regular processes—for example, the reactions of different metals to acids—and thereupon makes predictions about the reactions that will occur in certain particular cases.

There is an evident kinship between these two language-games, and also a fundamental difference. In both one might call the spoken words "predictions". But compare the training which leads to the first technique with the training for the second one.

631. "I am going to take two powders now, and in half-an-hour I shall be sick."—It explains nothing to say that in the first case I am the agent, in the second merely the observer. Or that in the first case I see the causal connexion from inside, in the second from outside. And much else to the same effect.

Nor is it to the point to say that a prediction of the first kind is no more infallible than one of the second kind.

It was not on the ground of observations of my behaviour that I said I was going to take two powders. The antecedents of this proposition were different. I mean the thoughts, actions and so on which led up to it. And it can only mislead you to say: "The only essential presupposition of your utterance was just your decision."

632. I do not want to say that in the case of the expression of intention "I am going to take two powders" the prediction is a cause—and its fulfilment the effect. (Perhaps a physiological investigation could determine this.) So much, however, is true: we can often predict a man's actions from his expression of a decision. An important language-game.

633. "You were interrupted a while ago; do you still know what you were going to say?"—If I do know now, and say it—does that mean that I had already thought it before, only not said it? No. Unless you take the certainty with which I continue the interrupted sentence as a criterion of the thought's already having been completed at that time.—But, of course, the situation and the thoughts which I had contained all sorts of things to help the continuation of the sentence.

634. When I continue the interrupted sentence and say that *this* was how I had been going to continue it, this is like following out a line of thought from brief notes.

Then don't I *interpret* the notes? Was only one continuation possible in these circumstances? Of course not. But I did not *choose* between interpretations. I *remembered* that I was going to say this.

635. "I was going to say . . . . . "—You remember various details. But not even all of them together shew your intention. It is as if a snapshot of a scene had been taken, but only a few scattered details of it were to be seen: here a hand, there a bit of a face, or a hat—the rest is dark. And now it is as if we knew quite certainly what the whole picture represented. As if I could read the darkness.

636.   These 'details' are not irrelevant in the sense in which other circumstances which I can remember equally well are irrelevant. But if I tell someone "For a moment I was going to say . . . ." he does not learn those details from this, nor need he guess them. He need not know, for instance, that I had already opened my mouth to speak. But he *can* 'fill out the picture' in this way. (And this capacity is part of understanding what I tell him.)

637.   "I know exactly what I was going to say!" And yet I did not say it.—And yet I don't read it off from some other process which took place then and which I remember.

Nor am I *interpreting* that situation and its antecedents. For I don't consider them and don't judge them.

638.   How does it come about that in spite of this I am inclined to see an interpretation in saying "For a moment I was going to deceive him"?

"How can you be certain that for the space of a moment you were going to deceive him? Weren't your actions and thoughts much too rudimentary?"

For can't the evidence be too scanty? Yes, when one follows it up it seems extraordinarily scanty; but isn't this because one is taking no account of the history of this evidence? Certain antecedents were necessary for me to have had a momentary intention of pretending to someone else that I was unwell.

If someone says "For a moment . . . . ." is he really only describing a momentary process?

But not even the whole story was my evidence for saying "For a moment . . . . ."

639.   One would like to say that an opinion *develops*. But there is a mistake in this too.

640.   "This thought ties on to thoughts which I have had before."—How does it do so? Through a *feeling* of such a tie? But how can a feeling really tie thoughts together?—The word "feeling" is very misleading here. But it is sometimes possible to say with certainty: "This thought is connected with those earlier thoughts", and yet be unable to shew the connexion. Perhaps that comes later.

641.   "My intention was no less certain as it was than it would have been if I had said 'Now I'll deceive him'."—But if you had said the words, would you necessarily have meant them quite seriously? (Thus

the most explicit expression of intention is by itself insufficient evidence of intention.)

642. "At that moment I hated him."—What happened here? Didn't it consist in thoughts, feelings, and actions? And if I were to rehearse that moment to myself I should assume a particular expression, think of certain happenings, breathe in a particular way, arouse certain feelings in myself. I might think up a conversation, a whole scene in which that hatred flared up. And I might play this scene through with feelings approximating to those of a real occasion. That I have actually experienced something of the sort will naturally help me to do so.

643. If I now become ashamed of this incident, I am ashamed of the whole thing: of the words, of the poisonous tone, etc. .

644. "I am not ashamed of what I did then, but of the intention which I had."—And didn't the intention lie *also* in what I did? What justifies the shame? The whole history of the incident.

645. "For a moment I meant to . . . ." That is, I had a particular feeling, an inner experience; and I remember it.——And now remember *quite precisely*! Then the 'inner experience' of intending seems to vanish again. Instead one remembers thoughts, feelings, movements, and also connexions with earlier situations.

It is as if one had altered the adjustment of a microscope. One did not see before what is now in focus.

646. "Well, that only shews that you have adjusted your microscope wrong. You were supposed to look at a particular section of the culture, and you are seeing a different one."

There is something right about that. But suppose that (with a particular adjustment of the lenses) I did remember a *single* sensation; how have I the right to say that it is what I call the "intention"? It might be that (for example) a particular tickle accompanied every one of my intentions.

647. What is the natural expression of an intention?—Look at a cat when it stalks a bird; or a beast when it wants to escape.

((Connexion with propositions about sensations.))

648. "I no longer remember the words I used, but I remember my intention precisely; I meant my words to quiet him." What does my memory *shew* me; what does it bring before my mind? Suppose it did

nothing but suggest those words to me!—and perhaps others which fill out the picture still more exactly.—("I don't remember my words any more, but I certainly remember their spirit.")

649.   "So if a man has not learned a language, is he unable to have certain memories?" Of course—he cannot have verbal memories, verbal wishes or fears, and so on. And memories etc., in language, are not mere threadbare representations of the *real* experiences; for is what is linguistic not an experience?

650.   We say a dog is afraid his master will beat him; but not, he is afraid his master will beat him to-morrow. Why not?

651.   "I remember that I should have been glad then to stay still longer."—What picture of this wish came before my mind? None at all. What I see in my memory allows no conclusion as to my feelings. And yet I remember quite clearly that they were there.

652.   "He measured him with a hostile glance and said . . . ." The reader of the narrative understands this; he has no doubt in his mind. Now you say: "Very well, he supplies the meaning, he guesses it."—Generally speaking: no. Generally speaking he supplies nothing, guesses nothing.—But it is also possible that the hostile glance and the words later prove to have been pretence, or that the reader is kept in doubt whether they are so or not, and so that he really does guess at a possible interpretation.—But then the main thing he guesses at is a context. He says to himself for example: The two men who are here so hostile to one another are in reality friends, etc. etc.

(("If you want to understand a sentence, you have to imagine the psychical significance, the states of mind involved."))

653.   Imagine this case: I tell someone that I walked a certain route, going by a map which I had prepared beforehand. Thereupon I shew him the map, and it consists of lines on a piece of paper; but I cannot explain how these lines are the map of my movements, I cannot tell him any rule for interpreting the map. Yet I did follow the drawing with all the characteristic tokens of reading a map. I might call such a drawing a 'private' map; or the phenomenon that I have described "following a private map". (But this expression would, of course, be very easy to misunderstand.)
Could I now say: "I read off my having then meant to do such-and-

such, as if from a map, although there is no map"? But that means
nothing but: *I am now inclined to say* "I read the intention of acting
thus in certain states of mind which I remember."

654. Our mistake is to look for an explanation where we ought to
look at what happens as a 'proto-phenomenon'. That is, where we
ought to have said: *this language-game is played.*

655. The question is not one of explaining a language-game by
means of our experiences, but of noting a language-game.

656. What is the purpose of telling someone that a time ago I
had such-and-such a wish?—Look on the language-game as the *primary*
thing. And look on the feelings, etc., as you look on a way of
regarding the language-game, as interpretation.
It might be asked: how did human beings ever come to make
the verbal utterances which we call reports of past wishes or past
intentions?

657. Let us imagine these utterances always taking this form: "I
said to myself: 'if only I could stay longer!' " The purpose of such a
statement might be to acquaint someone with my reactions. (Compare
the grammar of "mean" and "vouloir dire".)

658. Suppose we expressed the fact that a man had an intention
by saying "He as it were said to himself 'I will . . . .' "—That is the
picture. And now I want to know: how does one employ the expression "as it were to say something to oneself"? For it does not mean:
to say something to oneself.

659. Why do I want to tell him about an intention too, as well as
telling him what I did?—Not because the intention was also something
which was going on at that time. But because I want to tell him
something about *myself*, which goes beyond what happened at that
time.
I reveal to him something of myself when I tell him what I was going
to do.—Not, however, on grounds of self-observation, but by way of
response (it might also be called an intuition).

660. The grammar of the expression "I was then going to say . . . ."
is related to that of the expression "I could then have gone on."
In the one case I remember an intention, in the other I remember
having understood.

661.   I remember having meant *him*. Am I remembering a process or state?—When did it begin, what was its course; etc.?

662.   In an only slightly different situation, instead of silently beckoning, he would have said to someone "Tell N. to come to me." One can now say that the words "I wanted N. to come to me" describe the state of my mind at that time; and again one may *not* say so.

663.   If I say "I meant *him*" very likely a picture comes to my mind, perhaps of how I looked at him, etc.; but the picture is only like an illustration to a story. From it alone it would mostly be impossible to conclude anything at all; only when one knows the story does one know the significance of the picture.

664.   In the use of words one might distinguish 'surface grammar' from 'depth grammar'. What immediately impresses itself upon us about the use of a word is the way it is used in the construction of the sentence, the part of its use—one might say—that can be taken in by the ear.——And now compare the depth grammar, say of the word "to mean", with what its surface grammar would lead us to suspect. No wonder we find it difficult to know our way about.

665.   Imagine someone pointing to his cheek with an expression of pain and saying "abracadabra!"—We ask "What do you mean?" And he answers "I meant toothache".—You at once think to yourself, How can one 'mean toothache' by that word? Or what did it *mean to mean* pain by that word? And yet, in a different context, you would have asserted that the mental activity of *meaning* such-and-such was just what was most important in using language.

But—can't I say "By 'abracadabra' I mean toothache"? Of course I can; but this is a definition; not a description of what goes on in me when I utter the word.

666.   Imagine that you were in pain and were simultaneously hearing a nearby piano being tuned. You say "It'll soon stop." It certainly makes quite a difference whether you mean the pain or the piano-tuning!—Of course; but what does this difference consist in? I admit, in many cases some direction of the attention will correspond to your meaning one thing or another, just as a look often does, or gesture, or a way of shutting one's eyes which might be called "looking into oneself".

667. Imagine someone simulating pain, and then saying "It'll get better soon". Can't one say he means the pain? and yet he is not concentrating his attention on any pain.—And what about when I finally say "It's stopped now"?

668. But can't one also lie in this way: one says "It'll stop soon", and means pain—but when asked "What did you mean?" one answers "The noise in the next room"? In this sort of case one may say: "I was going to answer.... but thought better of it and did answer....."

669. One can refer to an object when speaking by pointing to it. Here pointing is a part of the language-game. And now it seems to us as if one spoke *of* a sensation by directing one's attention to it. But where is the analogy? It evidently lies in the fact that one can point to a thing by *looking* or *listening*.

But in certain circumstances, even *pointing* to the object one is talking about may be quite inessential to the language-game, to one's thought.

670. Imagine that you were telephoning someone and you said to him: "This table is too tall", and pointed to the table. What is the role of pointing here? Can I say: I *mean* the table in question by pointing to it? What is this pointing for, and what are these words and whatever else may accompany them for?

671. And what do I point to by the inner activity of listening? To the sound that comes to my ears, and to the silence when I hear *nothing*?

Listening as it were *looks for* an auditory impression and hence can't point to it, but only to the *place* where it is looking for it.

672. If a receptive attitude is called a kind of 'pointing' to something—then that something is not the sensation which we get by means of it.

673. The mental attitude doesn't '*accompany*' what is said in the sense in which a gesture accompanies it. (As a man can travel alone, and yet be accompanied by my good wishes; or as a room can be empty, and yet full of light.)

674. Does one say, for example: "I didn't really mean my pain just now; my mind wasn't on it enough for that?" Do I ask myself, say: "What did I mean by this word just now? My attention was divided between my pain and the noise—"?

675.　"Tell me, what was going on in you when you uttered the words . . . .?"—The answer to this is not: "I was meaning . . . . ."

676.　"I meant *this* by that word" is a statement which is differently used from one about an affection of the mind.

677.　On the other hand: "When you were swearing just now, die you really mean it?" This is perhaps as much as to say: "Were you really angry?"—And the answer may be given as a result of intro spection and is often some such thing as: "I didn't mean it very seriously", "I meant it half jokingly" and so on. There are difference of degree here.

And one does indeed also say "I was half thinking of him when said that."

678.　What does this act of meaning (the pain, or the piano-tuning consist in? No answer comes—for the answers which at first sigh suggest themselves are of no use.—"And yet at the time I *meant* the one thing and not the other." Yes,—now you have only repeated with emphasis something which no one has contradicted anyway.

679.　"But can you doubt that you meant *this*?"—No; but neithe can I be certain of it, know it.

680.　When you tell me that you cursed and meant N. as you di so it is all one to me whether you looked at a picture of him, o imagined him, uttered his name, or what. The conclusions from thi fact that interest me have nothing to do with these things. O the other hand, however, someone might explain to me that cursin was *effective* only when one had a clear image of the man or spoke hi name out loud. But we should not say "The point is how the ma who is cursing *means* his victim."

681.　Nor, of course, does one ask: "Are you sure that you curse *him*, that the connexion with him was established?"

Then this connexion must be very easy to establish, if one can b so sure of it?! Can know that it doesn't fail of its object!—Well, ca it happen to me, to intend to write to one person and in fact writ to another? and how might it happen?

682.　"You said, 'It'll stop soon'.—Were you thinking of the nois or of your pain?" If he answers "I was thinking of the piano-tuning"— is he observing that the connexion existed, or is he making it by mear of these words?—Can't I say *both*? If what he said was true, didn't the connexion exist—and is he not for all that making one which did not exist?

683. I draw a head. You ask "Whom is that supposed to represent?"—I: "It's supposed to be N."—You: "But it doesn't look like him; if anything, it's rather like M."—When I said it represented N.— was I establishing a connexion or reporting one? And what connexion did exist?

684. What is there in favour of saying that my words describe an existing connexion? Well, they relate to various things which didn't simply make their appearance with the words. They say, for example, that I *should have* given a particular answer then, if I had been asked. And even if this is only conditional, still it does say something about the past.

685. "Look for A" does not mean "Look for B"; but I may do just the same thing in obeying the two orders.

To say that something different must happen in the two cases would be like saying that the propositions "Today is my birthday" and "My birthday is on April 26th" must refer to different days, because they do not make the same sense.

686. "Of course I meant B; I didn't think of A at all!"

"I wanted B to come to me, so as to . . ."—All this points to a wider context.

687. Instead of "I meant him" one can, of course, sometimes say "I thought of him"; sometimes even "Yes, we were speaking of him." Ask yourself what 'speaking of him' consists in.

688. In certain circumstances one can say "As I was speaking, I felt I was saying it *to you*". But I should not say this if I were in any case talking with you.

689. "I am thinking of N." "I am speaking of N."

How do I speak *of* him? I say, for instance, "I must go and see N today"——But surely that is not enough! After all, when I say "N" I might mean various people of this name.—"Then there must surely be a further, different connexion between my talk and N, for otherwise I should *still* not have meant HIM.

Certainly such a connexion exists. Only not as you imagine it: namely by means of a mental *mechanism*.

(One compares "meaning him" with "aiming at him".)

690. What about the case where I at one time make an apparently innocent remark and accompany it with a furtive sidelong glance at someone; and at another time, without any such glance, speak of somebody present openly, mentioning his name—am I really thinking *specially* about him as I use his name?

691. When I make myself a sketch of N's face from memory, I can surely be said to *mean* him by my drawing. But which of the processes taking place while I draw (or before or afterwards) could I call meaning him?

For one would naturally like to say: when he meant him, he aimed at him. But how is anyone doing that, when he calls someone else's face to mind?

I mean, how does he call HIM to mind?

How does he call him?

692. Is it correct for someone to say: "When I gave you this rule, I meant you to . . . . . in this case"? Even if he did not think of this case at all as he gave the rule? Of course it is correct. For "to mean it" did not mean: to think of it. But now the problem is: how are we to judge whether someone meant such-and-such?—The fact that he has, for example, mastered a particular technique in arithmetic and algebra, and that he taught someone else the expansion of a series in the usual way, is such a criterion.

693. "When I teach someone the formation of the series . . . . I surely mean him to write . . . . at the hundredth place."—Quite right, you mean it. And evidently without necessarily even thinking of it. This shews you how different the grammar of the verb "to mean" is from that of "to think". And nothing is more wrong-headed than calling meaning a mental activity! Unless, that is, one is setting out to produce confusion. (It would also be possible to speak of an activity of butter when it rises in price, and if no problems are produced by this it is harmless.)

PART II

One can imagine an animal angry, frightened, unhappy, happy, startled. But hopeful? And why not?

A dog believes his master is at the door. But can he also believe his master will come the day after to-morrow?—And *what* can he not do here?—How do I do it?—How am I supposed to answer this?

Can only those hope who can talk? Only those who have mastered the use of a language. That is to say, the phenomena of hope are modes of this complicated form of life. (If a concept refers to a character of human handwriting, it has no application to beings that do not write.

"Grief" describes a pattern which recurs, with different variations, in the weave of our life. If a man's bodily expression of sorrow and of joy alternated, say with the ticking of a clock, here we should not have the characteristic formation of the pattern of sorrow or of the pattern of joy.

"For a second he felt violent pain."—Why does it sound queer to say: "For a second he felt deep grief"? Only because it so seldom happens?

But don't you feel grief *now*? ("But aren't you playing chess *now*?") The answer may be affirmative, but that does not make the concept of grief any more like the concept of a sensation.—The question was really, of course, a temporal and personal one, not the logical question which we wanted to raise.

"I must tell you: I am frightened."
"I must tell you: it makes me shiver."—
And one can say this in a *smiling* tone of voice too.

And do you mean to tell me he doesn't feel it? How else does he *know* it?—But even when he says it as a piece of information he does not learn it from his sensations.

For think of the sensations produced by physically shuddering: the words "it makes me shiver" are themselves such a shuddering re-action; and if I hear and feel them as I utter them, this belongs among the rest of those sensations. Now why should the wordless shudder be the ground of the verbal one?

ii

In saying "When I heard this word, it meant .... to me" one refers to a *point of time* and to a *way of using the word.* (Of course, it is this combination that we fail to grasp.)

And the expression "I was then going to say....." refers to a *point of time* and to an *action.*

I speak of the essential *references* of the utterance in order to distinguish them from other peculiarities of the expression we use. The references that are essential to an utterance are the ones which would make us translate some otherwise alien form of expression into this, our customary form.

If you were unable to say that the word "till" could be both a verb and a conjunction, or to construct sentences in which it was now the one and now the other, you would not be able to manage simple schoolroom exercises. But a schoolboy is not asked to *conceive* the word in one way or another out of any context, or to report how he has conceived it.

The words "the rose is red" are meaningless if the word "is" has the meaning "is identical with".—Does this mean: if you say this sentence and mean the "is" as the sign of identity, the sense disintegrates?

We take a sentence and tell someone the meaning of each of its words; this tells him how to apply them and so how to apply the sentence too. If we had chosen a senseless sequence of words instead of the sentence, he would not learn how to apply the *sequence.* And if we explain the word "is" as the sign of identity, then he does not learn how to use the sentence "the rose is red".

And yet there is something right about this 'disintegration of the sense'. You get it in the following example: one might tell someone: if you want to pronounce the salutation "Hail!" expressively, you had better not think of hailstones as you say it.

Experiencing a meaning and experiencing a mental image. "In both cases", we should like to say, "we are *experiencing* something, only something different. A different content is proffered—is present—to consciousness."—What is the content of the experience of imagining? The answer is a picture, or a description. And what is the content of the experience of meaning? I don't know what I am supposed to say to this.—If there is any sense in the above remark, it is that the two concepts are related like those of 'red' and 'blue'; and that is wrong

Can one keep hold of an understanding of meaning as one can keep hold of a mental image? That is, if one meaning of a word suddenly strikes me,—can it also stay there in my mind?

"The whole scheme presented itself to my mind in a flash and stayed there like that for five minutes." Why does this sound odd? One would like to think: what flashed on me and what stayed there in my mind can't have been the same.

I exclaimed "Now I have it!"—a sudden start, and then I was able to set the scheme forth in detail. What is supposed to have stayed in this case? A picture, perhaps. But "Now I have it" did not mean, I have the picture.

If a meaning of a word has occurred to you and you have not *forgotten* it again, you can now use the word in such-and-such a way.
If the meaning has occurred to you, now you *know* it, and the knowing began when it occurred to you. Then how is it like an experience of imagining something?

If I say "Mr. Scot is not a Scot", I mean the first "Scot" as a proper name, the second one as a common name. Then do different things have to go on in my mind at the first and second "Scot"? (Assuming that I am not uttering the sentence 'parrot-wise'.)—Try to mean the first "Scot" as a common name and the second one as a proper name.— How is it done? When *I* do it, I blink with the effort as I try to parade the right meanings before my mind in saying the words.—But do I parade the meanings of the words before my mind when I make the ordinary use of them?

When I say the sentence with this exchange of meanings I feel that its sense disintegrates.—Well, *I* feel it, but the person I am saying it to does not. So what harm is done?——"But the point is, when one utters the sentence in the usual way something *else*, quite definite, takes place."—What takes place is *not* this 'parade of the meanings before one's mind'.

What makes my image of him into an image of *him*?
Not its looking like him.

The same question applies to the expression "I see him now vividly before me" as to the image. What makes this utterance into an utterance about *him*?—Nothing in it or simultaneous with it ('behind it'). If you want to know whom he meant, ask him.

(But it is also possible for a face to come before my mind, and even for me to be able to draw it, without my knowing whose it is or where I have seen it.)

Suppose, however, that someone were to draw while he had an image or instead of having it, though it were only with his finger in the air. (This might be called "motor imagery.") He could be asked: "Whom does that represent?" And his answer would be decisive.— It is quite as if he had given a verbal description: and such a description can also simply take the *place* of the image.

iv

"I believe that he is suffering."——Do I also *believe* that he isn't an automaton?

It would go against the grain to use the word in both connexions. (Or is it like this: I believe that he is suffering, but am certain that he is not an automaton? Nonsense!)

Suppose I say of a friend: "He isn't an automaton".—What information is conveyed by this, and to whom would it be information? To a *human being* who meets him in ordinary circumstances? What information *could* it give him? (At the very most that this man always behaves like a human being, and not occasionally like a machine.)

"I believe that he is not an automaton", just like that, so far makes no sense.

My attitude towards him is an attitude towards a soul. I am not of the *opinion* that he has a soul.

Religion teaches that the soul can exist when the body has disintegrated. Now do I understand this teaching?—Of course I understand it——I can imagine plenty of things in connexion with it. And haven't pictures of these things been painted? And why should such a picture be only an imperfect rendering of the spoken doctrine? Why should it not do the *same* service as the words? And it is the service which is the point.

If the picture of thought in the head can force itself upon us, then why not much more that of thought in the soul?

The human body is the best picture of the human soul.

And how about such an expression as: "In my heart I understood when you said that", pointing to one's heart? Does one, perhaps, not *mean* this gesture? Of course one means it. Or is one conscious of using a *mere* figure? Indeed not.—It is not a figure that we choose, not a simile, yet it is a figurative expression.

V

Suppose we were observing the movement of a point (for example, a point of light on a screen). It might be possible to draw important consequences of the most various kinds from the behaviour of this point. And what a variety of observations can be made here!—The path of the point and certain of its characteristic measures (amplitude and wave-length for instance), or the velocity and the law according to which it varies, or the number or position of the places at which it changes discontinuously, or the curvature of the path at these places, and innumerable other things.—Any of these features of its behaviour might be the only one to interest us. We might, for example, be indifferent to everything about its movements except for the number of loops it made in a certain time.—And if we were interested, not in just *one* such feature, but in several, each might yield us special information, different in kind from all the rest. This is how it is with the behaviour of man; with the different characteristic features which we observe in this behaviour.

Then psychology treats of behaviour, not of the mind?

What do psychologists record?—What do they observe? Isn't it the behaviour of human beings, in particular their utterances? But *these* are not about behaviour.

"I noticed that he was out of humour." Is this a report about his behaviour or his state of mind? ("The sky looks threatening": is this about the present or the future?) Both; not side-by-side, however, but about the one *via* the other.

A doctor asks: "How is he feeling?" The nurse says: "He is groaning". A report on his behaviour. But need there be any question for them whether the groaning is really genuine, is really the expression of anything? Might they not, for example, draw the conclusion "If he groans, we must give him more analgesic"—without suppressing a middle term? Isn't the point the service to which they put the description of behaviour?

"But then they make a tacit presupposition." Then what we do in our language-game always rests on a tacit presupposition.

I describe a psychological experiment: the apparatus, the questions of the experimenter, the actions and replies of the subject—and then I say that it is a scene in a play.—Now everything is different. So it will be said: If this experiment were described in the same way in a book on psychology, then the behaviour described would be understood as the expression of something mental just because it is *presupposed* that the subject is not taking us in, hasn't learnt the replies by heart, and other things of the kind.—So we are making a presupposition?

Should we ever really express ourselves like this: "Naturally I am presupposing that . . . . ."?—Or do we not do so only because the other person already knows that?

Doesn't a presupposition imply a doubt? And doubt may be entirely lacking. Doubting has an end.

It is like the relation: physical object—sense-impressions. Here we have two different language-games and a complicated relation between them.—If you try to reduce their relations to a *simple* formula you go wrong.

vi

Suppose someone said: every familiar word, in a book for example, actually carries an atmosphere with it in our minds, a 'corona' of lightly indicated uses.—Just as if each figure in a painting were surrounded by delicate shadowy drawings of scenes, as it were in another dimension, and in them we saw the figures in different contexts.—Only let us take this assumption seriously!—Then we see that it is not adequate to explain *intention*.

For if it is like this, if the possible uses of a word do float before us in half-shades as we say or hear it—this simply goes for *us*. But we communicate with other people without knowing if they have this experience too.

How should we counter someone who told us that with *him* understanding was an inner process?——How should we counter him if he said that with him knowing how to play chess was an inner process?—We should say that when we want to know if he can play chess we aren't interested in anything that goes on inside him.—And if he replies that this is in fact just what we are interested in, that is, we are interested in whether he can play chess—then we shall have to draw his attention to the criteria which would demonstrate his capacity, and on the other hand to the criteria for the 'inner states'.

Even if someone had a particular capacity only when, and only as long as, he had a particular feeling, the feeling would not be the capacity.

The meaning of a word is not the experience one has in hearing or saying it, and the sense of a sentence is not a complex of such experiences.—(How do the meanings of the individual words make up the sense of the sentence "I still haven't seen him yet"?) The sentence is composed of the words, and that is enough.

Though—one would like to say—every word has a different character in different contexts, at the same time there is *one* character it always has: a single physiognomy. It looks at us.—But a face in a *painting* looks at us too.

Are you sure that there is a single if-feeling, and not perhaps several? Have you tried saying the word in a great variety of contexts? For example, when it bears the principal stress of the sentence, and when the word next to it does.

Suppose we found a man who, speaking of how words felt to him, told us that "if" and "but" felt the *same*.—Should we have the right to disbelieve him? We might think it strange. "He doesn't play our game at all", one would like to say. Or even: "This is a different type of man."
If he *used* the words "if" and "but" as we do, shouldn't we think he understood them as we do?

One misjudges the psychological interest of the if-feeling if one regards it as the obvious correlate of a meaning; it needs rather to be seen in a different context, in that of the special circumstances in which it occurs.

Does a person never have the if-feeling when he is not uttering the word "if"? Surely it is at least remarkable if this cause alone produces this feeling. And this applies generally to the 'atmosphere' of a word;—why does one regard it so much as a matter of course that only *this* word has this atmosphere?

The if-feeling is not a feeling which accompanies the word "if".

The if-feeling would have to be compared with the special 'feeling' which a musical phrase gives us. (One sometimes describes such a feeling by saying "Here it is as if a conclusion were being drawn", or "I should like to say '*hence* . . . . .' ", or "Here I should always like to make a gesture—" and then one makes it.)

But can this feeling be separated from the phrase? And yet it is not the phrase itself, for that can be heard without the feeling.

Is it in this respect like the 'expression' with which the phrase is played?

We say this passage gives us a quite special feeling. We sing it to ourselves, and make a certain movement, and also perhaps have some special sensation. But in a different context we should not recognize these accompaniments—the movement, the sensation—at all. They are quite empty except just when we are singing this passage.

"I sing it with a quite particular expression." This expression is not something that can be separated from the passage. It is a different concept. (A different game.)

The experience is this passage played like *this* (that is, as I am doing it, for instance; a description could only *hint* at it).

Thus the atmosphere that is inseparable from its object—is not an atmosphere.

Closely associated things, things which we *have* associated, seem to fit one another. But what is this seeming to fit? How is their seeming to fit manifested? Perhaps like this: we cannot imagine the man who had this name, this face, this handwriting, not to have produced *these* works, but perhaps quite different ones instead (those of another great man).

We cannot imagine it? Do we try?—

Here is a possibility: I hear that someone is painting a picture "Beethoven writing the ninth symphony". I could easily imagine the kind of thing such a picture would shew us. But suppose someone wanted to represent what Goethe would have looked like writing the ninth symphony? Here I could imagine nothing that would not be embarrassing and ridiculous.

People who on waking tell us certain incidents (that they have been in such-and-such places, etc.). Then we teach them the expression "I dreamt", which precedes the narrative. Afterwards I sometimes ask them "did you dream anything last night?" and am answered yes or no, sometimes with an account of a dream, sometimes not. That is the language-game. (I have assumed here that I do not dream myself. But then, nor do I ever have the feeling of an invisible presence; other people do, and I can question them about their experiences.)

Now must I make some assumption about whether people are deceived by their memories or not; whether they really had these images while they slept, or whether it merely seems so to them on waking? And what meaning has this question?—And what interest? Do we ever ask ourselves this when someone is telling us his dream? And if not—is it because we are sure his memory won't have deceived him? (And suppose it were a man with a quite specially bad memory?—)

Does this mean that it is nonsense ever to raise the question whether dreams really take place during sleep, or are a memory phenomenon of the awakened? It will turn on the use of the question.

"The mind seems able to give a word meaning"—isn't this as if I were to say "The carbon atoms in benzene seem to lie at the corners of a hexagon"? But this is not something that seems to be so; it is a picture.

The evolution of the higher animals and of man, and the awakening of consciousness at a particular level. The picture is something like this: Though the ether is filled with vibrations the world is dark. But one day man opens his seeing eye, and there is light.

What this language primarily describes is a picture. What is to be done with the picture, how it is to be used, is still obscure. Quite clearly, however, it must be explored if we want to understand the sense of what we are saying. But the picture seems to spare us this work: it already points to a particular use. This is how it takes us in.

"My kinaesthetic sensations advise me of the movement and position of my limbs."

I let my index finger make an easy pendulum movement of small amplitude. I either hardly feel it, or don't feel it at all. Perhaps a little in the tip of the finger, as a slight tension. (Not at all in the joint.) And this sensation advises me of the movement?—for I can describe the movement exactly.

"But after all, you must feel it, otherwise you wouldn't know (without looking) how your finger was moving." But "knowing" it only means: being able to describe it.—I may be able to tell the direction from which a sound comes only because it affects one ear more strongly than the other, but I don't feel this in my ears; yet it has its effect: I *know* the direction from which the sound comes; for instance, I look in that direction.

It is the same with the idea that it must be some feature of our pain that advises us of the whereabouts of the pain in the body, and some feature of our memory image that tells us the time to which it belongs.

A sensation *can* advise us of the movement or position of a limb. (For example, if you do not know, as a normal person does, whether your arm is stretched out, you might find out by a piercing pain in the elbow.)—In the same way the character of a pain can tell us where the injury is. (And the yellowness of a photograph how old it is.)

What is the criterion for my learning the shape and colour of an object from a sense-impression?

What sense-impression? Well, *this* one; I use words or a picture to describe it.

And now: what do you feel when your fingers are in this position?— "How is one to define a feeling? It is something special and indefinable." But it must be possible to teach the use of the words!

What I am looking for is the grammatical difference.

Let us leave the kinaesthetic feeling out for the moment.—I want to describe a feeling to someone, and I tell him "Do *this*, and then you'll get it," and I hold my arm or my head in a particular position. Now is this a description of a feeling? and when shall I say that he has understood what feeling I meant?—He will have to give a *further* description of the feeling afterwards. And what kind of description must it be?

I say "Do *this*, and you'll get it". Can't there be a doubt here? Mustn't there be one, if it is a feeling that is meant?

This looks *so*; *this* tastes *so*; *this* feels *so*. "This" and "so" must be differently explained.

Our interest in a 'feeling' is of a quite *particular* kind. It includes, for instance, the 'degree of the feeling', its 'place', and the extent to which one feeling can be submerged by another. (When a movement is very painful, so that the pain submerges every other slight sensation in the same place, does this make it uncertain whether you have really made this movement? Could it lead you to find out by looking?)

ix

If you observe your own grief, which senses do you use to observe it? A particular sense; one that *feels* grief? Then do you feel it *differently* when you are observing it? And what is the grief that you are observing—is it one which is there only while it is being observed?

'Observing' does not produce what is observed. (That is a conceptual statement.)

Again: I do not 'observe' what only comes into being through observation. The object of observation is something *else*.

A touch which was still painful yesterday is no longer so today.

Today I feel the pain only when I think about it. (That is: in certain circumstances.)

My grief is no longer the same; a memory which was still unbearable to me a year ago is now no longer so.

That is a result of observation.

When do we say that any one is observing? Roughly: when he puts himself in a favourable position to receive certain impressions in order (for example) to describe what they tell him.

If you trained someone to emit a particular sound at the sight of something red, another at the sight of something yellow, and so on for other colours, still he would not yet be describing objects by their colours. Though he might be a help to us in giving a description. A description is a representation of a distribution in a space (in that of time, for instance).

If I let my gaze wander round a room and suddenly it lights on an object of a striking red colour, and I say "Red!"—that is not a description.

Are the words "I am afraid" a description of a state of mind?

I say "I am afraid"; someone else asks me: "What was that? A cry of fear; or do you want to tell me how you feel; or is it a reflection on your present state?"—Could I always give him a clear answer? Could I never give him one?

187e

We can imagine all sorts of things here, for example:

"No, no! I am afraid!"

"I am afraid. I am sorry to have to confess it."

"I am still a bit afraid, but no longer as much as before."

"At bottom I am still afraid, though I won't confess it to myself."

"I torment myself with all sorts of fears."

"Now, just when I should be fearless, I am afraid!"

To each of these sentences a special tone of voice is appropriate, and a different context.

It would be possible to imagine people who as it were thought much more definitely than we, and used different words where we use only one.

We ask "What does 'I am frightened' really mean, what am I referring to when I say it?" And of course we find no answer, or one that is inadequate.

The question is: "In what sort of context does it occur?"

I can find no answer if I try to settle the question "What am I referring to?" "What am I thinking when I say it?" by repeating the expression of fear and at the same time attending to myself, as it were observing my soul out of the corner of my eye. In a concrete case I can indeed ask "Why did I say that, what did I mean by it?"— and I might answer the question too; but not on the ground of observing what accompanied the speaking. And my answer would supplement, paraphrase, the earlier utterance.

What is fear? What does "being afraid" mean? If I wanted to define it at a *single* shewing—I should *play-act* fear.

Could I also represent hope in this way? Hardly. And what about belief?

Describing my state of mind (of fear, say) is something I do in a particular context. (Just as it takes a particular context to make a certain action into an experiment.)

Is it, then, so surprising that I use the same expression in different games? And sometimes as it were between the games?

And do I always talk with very definite purpose?—And is what I say meaningless because I don't?

When it is said in a funeral oration "We mourn our . . . ." this is surely supposed to be an expression of mourning; not to tell anything to those who are present. But in a prayer at the grave these words would in a way be used to tell someone something.

But here is the problem: a cry, which cannot be called a description, which is more primitive than any description, for all that serves as a description of the inner life.

A cry is not a description. But there are transitions. And the words "I am afraid" may approximate more, or less, to being a cry. They may come quite close to this and also be *far* removed from it.

We surely do not always say someone is *complaining*, because he says he is in pain. So the words "I am in pain" may be a cry of complaint, and may be something else.

But if "I am afraid" is not always something like a cry of complaint and yet sometimes is, then why should it *always* be a description of a state of mind?

How did we ever come to use such an expression as "I believe . . . "? Did we at some time become aware of a phenomenon (of belief)? Did we observe ourselves and other people and so discover belief?

Moore's paradox can be put like this: the expression "I believe that this is the case" is used like the assertion "This is the case"; and yet the *hypothesis* that I believe this is the case is not used like the hypothesis that this is the case.

So it *looks* as if the assertion "I believe" were not the assertion of what is supposed in the hypothesis "I believe"!

Similarly: the statement "I believe it's going to rain" has a meaning like, that is to say a use like, "It's going to rain", but the meaning of "I believed then that it was going to rain", is not like that of "It did rain then".

"But surely 'I believed' must tell of just the same thing in the past as 'I believe' in the present!"—Surely $\sqrt{-1}$ must mean just the same in relation to -1, as $\sqrt{1}$ means in relation to 1! This means nothing at all.

"At bottom, when I say 'I believe . . .' I am describing my own state of mind—but this description is indirectly an assertion of the fact believed."—As in certain circumstances I describe a photograph in order to describe the thing it is a photograph of.

But then I must also be able to say that the photograph is a good one. So here too: "I believe it's raining and my belief is reliable, so I have confidence in it."—In that case my belief would be a kind of sense-impression.

One can mistrust one's own senses, but not one's own belief.

If there were a verb meaning 'to believe falsely', it would not have any significant first person present indicative.

Don't look at it as a matter of course, but as a most remarkable thing, that the verbs "believe", "wish", "will" display all the inflexions possessed by "cut", "chew", "run".

The language-game of reporting can be given such a turn that a report is not meant to inform the hearer about its subject matter but about the person making the report.

It is so when, for instance, a teacher examines a pupil. (You can measure to test the ruler.)

Suppose I were to introduce some expression—"I believe", for instance—in this way: it is to be prefixed to reports when they serve to give information about the reporter. (So the expression need not carry with it any suggestion of uncertainty. Remember that the uncertainty of an assertion can be expressed impersonally: "He might come today".)—"I believe . . . ., and it isn't so" would be a contradiction.

"I believe . . . ." throws light on my state. Conclusions about my conduct can be drawn from this expression. So there is a *similarity* here to expressions of emotion, of mood, etc. .

If, however, "I believe it is so" throws light on my state, then so does the assertion "It is so". For the sign "I believe" can't do it, can at the most hint at it.

Imagine a language in which "I believe it is so" is expressed only by means of the tone of the assertion "It is so". In this language they say, not "He believes" but "He is inclined to say . . . ." and there exists also the hypothetical (subjunctive) "Suppose I were inclined etc.", but not the expression "I am inclined to say".

Moore's paradox would not exist in this language; instead of it, however, there would be a verb lacking one inflexion.

But this ought not to surprise us. Think of the fact that one can predict one's *own* future action by an expression of intention.

I say of someone else "He seems to believe . . . ." and other people say it of me. Now, why do I never say it of myself, not even when others *rightly* say it of me?—Do I myself not see and hear myself, then?—That can be said.

"One feels conviction within oneself, one doesn't infer it from one's own words or their tone."—What is true here is: one does not infer one's own conviction from one's own words; nor yet the actions which arise from that conviction.

"Here it *looks* as if the assertion 'I believe' were not the assertion of what is supposed in the hypothesis."—So I am tempted to look for a different development of the verb in the first person present indicative.

This is how I think of it: Believing is a state of mind. It has duration; and that independently of the duration of its expression in a sentence, for example. So it is a kind of disposition of the believing person. This is shewn me in the case of someone else by his behaviour; and by his words. And under this head, by the expression "I believe . . ." as well as by the simple assertion.—What about my own case: how do I myself recognize my own disposition?—Here it will have been necessary for me to take notice of myself as others do, to listen to myself talking, to be able to draw conclusions from what I say!

My own relation to my words is wholly different from other people's.

That different development of the verb would have been possible, if only I could say "I seem to believe".

If I listened to the words of my mouth, I might say that someone else was speaking out of my mouth.

"Judging from what I say, *this* is what I believe." Now, it is possible to think out circumstances in which these words would make sense.

And then it would also be possible for someone to say "It is raining and I don't believe it", or "It seems to me that my ego believes this, but it isn't true." One would have to fill out the picture with behaviour indicating that two people were speaking through my mouth.

Even in the *hypothesis* the pattern is not what you think.

When you say "Suppose I believe . . . ." you are presupposing the whole grammar of the word "to believe", the ordinary use, of which you are master.—You are not supposing some state of affairs which, so to speak, a picture presents unambiguously to you, so that you can tack on to this hypothetical use some assertive use other than the ordinary one.—You would not know at all what you were supposing here (i.e. what, for example, would follow from such a supposition), if you were not already familiar with the use of "believe".

Think of the expression "I say . . . .", for example in "I say it will rain today", which simply comes to the same thing as the assertion "It will . . . .". "He says it will . . . ." means approximately "He believes it will . . . .". "Suppose I say . . . ." does *not* mean: Suppose it rains today.

Different concepts touch here and coincide over a stretch. But you need not think that all lines are *circles*.

Consider the misbegotten sentence "It may be raining, but it isn't"

And here one should be on one's guard against saying that "It may be raining" really means "I think it'll be raining." For why not the other way round, why should not the latter mean the former?

Don't regard a hesitant assertion as an assertion of hesitancy.

Two uses of the word "see".

The one: "What do you see there?"—"I see *this*" (and then a description, a drawing, a copy). The other: "I see a likeness between these two faces"—let the man I tell this to be seeing the faces as clearly as I do myself.

The importance of this is the difference of category between the two 'objects' of sight.

The one man might make an accurate drawing of the two faces, and the other notice in the drawing the likeness which the former did not see.

I contemplate a face, and then suddenly notice its likeness to another. I *see* that it has not changed; and yet I see it differently. I call this experience "noticing an aspect".

Its *causes* are of interest to psychologists.

We are interested in the concept and its place among the concepts of experience.

You could imagine the illustration

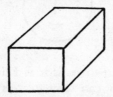

appearing in several places in a book, a text-book for instance. In the relevant text something different is in question every time: here a glass cube, there an inverted open box, there a wire frame of that shape, there three boards forming a solid angle. Each time the text supplies the interpretation of the illustration.

But we can also *see* the illustration now as one thing now as another. —So we interpret it, and *see* it as we *interpret* it.

Here perhaps we should like to reply: The description of what is got immediately, i.e. of the visual experience, by means of an interpretation—is an indirect description. "I see the figure as a box" means: I have a particular visual experience which I have found that I always have when I interpret the figure as a box or when I look at a box. But if it meant this I ought to know it. I ought to be able to refer to the experience directly, and not only indirectly. (As I can speak of red without calling it the colour of blood.)

I shall call the following figure, derived from Jastrow[1], the duck-rabbit. It can be seen as a rabbit's head or as a duck's.

And I must distinguish between the 'continuous seeing' of an aspect and the 'dawning' of an aspect.

The picture might have been shewn me, and I never have seen anything but a rabbit in it.

Here it is useful to introduce the idea of a picture-object. For instance

would be a 'picture-face'.

In some respects I stand towards it as I do towards a human face. I can study its expression, can react to it as to the expression of the human face. A child can talk to picture-men or picture-animals, can treat them as it treats dolls.

I may, then, have seen the duck-rabbit simply as a picture-rabbit from the first. That is to say, if asked "What's that?" or "What do you see here?" I should have replied: "A picture-rabbit". If I had further been asked what that was, I should have explained by pointing to all sorts of pictures of rabbits, should perhaps have pointed to real rabbits, talked about their habits, or given an imitation of them.

I should not have answered the question "What do you see here?" by saying: "Now I am seeing it as a picture-rabbit". I should simply

----

[1] *Fact and Fable in Psychology.*

have described my perception: just as if I had said "I see a red circle over there."—

Nevertheless someone else could have said of me: "He is seeing the figure as a picture-rabbit."

It would have made as little sense for me to say "Now I am seeing it as . . . " as to say at the sight of a knife and fork "Now I am seeing this as a knife and fork". This expression would not be understood.— Any more than: "Now it's a fork" or "It can be a fork too".

One doesn't 'take' what one knows as the cutlery at a meal for cutlery; any more than one ordinarily tries to move one's mouth as one eats, or aims at moving it.

If you say "Now it's a face for me", we can ask: "What change are you alluding to?"

I see two pictures, with the duck-rabbit surrounded by rabbits in one, by ducks in the other. I do not notice that they are the same. Does it follow from this that I see something different in the two cases?— It gives us a reason for using this expression here.

"I saw it quite differently, I should never have recognized it!" Now, that is an exclamation. And there is also a justification for it.

I should never have thought of superimposing the heads like that, of making this comparison between them. For they suggest a different mode of comparison.

Nor has the head seen like this the slightest similarity to the head seen like this——although they are congruent.

I am shewn a picture-rabbit and asked what it is; I say "It's a rabbit". Not "Now it's a rabbit". I am reporting my perception.—I am shewn the duck-rabbit and asked what it is; I may say "It's a duck-rabbit". But I may also react to the question quite differently.—The answer that it is a duck-rabbit is again the report of a perception; the answer "Now it's a rabbit" is not. Had I replied "It's a rabbit", the ambiguity would have escaped me, and I should have been reporting my perception.

The change of aspect. "But surely you would say that the picture is altogether different now!"
But what is different: my impression? my point of view?—Can I say? I describe the alteration like a perception; quite as if the object had altered before my eyes.

"Now I am seeing *this*", I might say (pointing to another picture, for example). This has the form of a report of a new perception.

The expression of a change of aspect is the expression of a *new* perception and at the same time of the perception's being unchanged.

I suddenly see the solution of a puzzle-picture. Before, there were branches there; now there is a human shape. My visual impression has changed and now I recognize that it has not only shape and colour but also a quite particular 'organization'.—My visual impression has changed;—what was it like before and what is it like now?—If I represent it by means of an exact copy—and isn't that a good representation of it?—no change is shewn.

And above all do *not* say "After all my visual impression isn't the *drawing*; it is *this*——which I can't shew to anyone."—Of course it is not the drawing, but neither is it anything of the same category, which I carry within myself.

The concept of the 'inner picture' is misleading, for this concept uses the *'outer* picture' as a model; and yet the uses of the words for these concepts are no more like one another than the uses of 'numeral' and 'number'. (And if one chose to call numbers 'ideal numerals', one might produce a similar confusion.)

If you put the 'organization' of a visual impression on a level with colours and shapes, you are proceeding from the idea of the visual impression as an inner object. Of course this makes this object into a chimera; a queerly shifting construction. For the similarity to a picture is now impaired.

If I know that the schematic cube has various aspects and I want to find out what someone else sees, I can get him to make a model of what he sees, in addition to a copy, or to point to such a model; even though *he* has no idea of my purpose in demanding two accounts.

But when we have a changing aspect the case is altered. Now the only possible expression of our experience is what before perhaps seemed, or even was, a useless specification when once we had the copy.

And this by itself wrecks the comparison of 'organization' with colour and shape in visual impressions.

If I saw the duck-rabbit as a rabbit, then I saw: these shapes and colours (I give them in detail)—and I saw besides something like this:

and here I point to a number of different pictures of rabbits.—This shews the difference between the concepts.

'Seeing as . . . .' is not part of perception. And for that reason it is like seeing and again not like.

I look at an animal and am asked: "What do you see?" I answer: "A rabbit".—I see a landscape; suddenly a rabbit runs past. I exclaim "A rabbit!"

Both things, both the report and the exclamation, are expressions of perception and of visual experience. But the exclamation is so in a different sense from the repoit: it is forced from us.—It is related to the experience as a cry is to pain.

But since it is the description of a perception, it can also be called the expression of thought.——If you are looking at the object, you need not think of it; but if you are having the visual experience expressed by the exclamation, you are also *thinking* of what you see.

Hence the flashing of an aspect on us seems half visual experience, half thought.

Someone suddenly sees an appearance which he does not recognize (it may be a familiar object, but in an unusual position or lighting); the lack of recognition perhaps lasts only a few seconds. Is it correct to say he has a different visual experience from someone who knew the object at once?

For might not someone be able to describe an unfamiliar shape that appeared before him just as *accurately* as I, to whom it is familiar? And isn't that the answer?—Of course it will not generally be so. And his description will run quite differently. (I say, for example, "The animal had long ears"—he: "There were two long appendages", and then he draws them.)

I meet someone whom I have not seen for years; I see him clearly, but fail to know him. Suddenly I know him, I see the old face in the altered one. I believe that I should do a different portrait of him now if I could paint.

Now, when I know my acquaintance in a crowd, perhaps after looking in his direction for quite a while,—is this a special sort of seeing? Is it a case of both seeing and thinking? or an amalgam of the two, as I should almost like to say?

The question is: *why* does one want to say this?

The very expression which is also a report of what is seen, is here a cry of recognition.

What is the criterion of the visual experience?—The criterion? What do you suppose?

The representation of 'what is seen'.

The concept of a representation of what is seen, like that of a copy, is very elastic, and so *together with it* is the concept of what is seen. The two are intimately connected. (Which is *not* to say that they are alike.)

How does one tell that human beings *see* three-dimensionally?— I ask someone about the lie of the land (over there) of which he has a view. "Is it like *this*?" (I shew him with my hand)—"Yes."—"How do you know?"—"It's not misty, I see it quite clear."—He does not give reasons for the surmise. The only thing that is natural to us is to represent what we see three-dimensionally; special practice and training are needed for two-dimensional representation whether in drawing or in words. (The queerness of children's drawings.)

If someone sees a smile and does not know it for a smile, does not understand it as such, does he see it differently from someone who understands it?—He mimics it differently, for instance.

Hold the drawing of a face upside down and you can't recognize the expression of the face. Perhaps you can see that it is smiling, but not exactly what *kind* of smile it is. You cannot imitate the smile or describe it more exactly.

And yet the picture which you have turned round may be a most exact representation of a person's face.

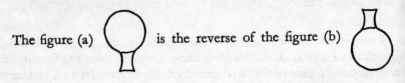

The figure (a)   is the reverse of the figure (b)

As (c)   *ǝɹnsɐǝlᗡ*   is the reverse of (d)   *Pleasure*

But—I should like to say—there is a different difference between my impressions of (c) and (d) and between those of (a) and (b). (d), for example, looks neater than (c). (Compare a remark of Lewis Carroll's.) (d) is easy, (c) hard to copy.

Imagine the duck-rabbit hidden in a tangle of lines. Now I suddenly notice it in the picture, and notice it simply as the head of a rabbit. At some later time I look at the same picture and notice the same figure, but see it as the duck, without necessarily realizing that it was the same figure both times.—If I later see the aspect change—can I say that the duck and rabbit aspects are now seen quite differently from when I recognized them separately in the tangle of lines? No.

But the change produces a surprise not produced by the recognition.

If you search in a figure (1) for another figure (2), and then find it, you see (1) in a new way. Not only can you give a new kind of description of it, but noticing the second figure was a new visual experience.

But you would not necessarily want to say "Figure (1) looks quite different now; it isn't even in the least like the figure I saw before, though they are congruent!"

There are here hugely many interrelated phenomena and possible concepts.

Then is the copy of the figure an *incomplete* description of my visual experience? No.—But the circumstances decide whether, and what, more detailed specifications are necessary.—It *may* be an incomplete description; if there is still something to ask.

Of course we can say: There are certain things which fall equally under the concept 'picture-rabbit' and under the concept 'picture-duck'. And a picture, a drawing, is such a thing.—But the *impression* is not simultaneously of a picture-duck and a picture-rabbit.

"What I really *see* must surely be what is produced in me by the influence of the object"—Then what is produced in me is a sort of copy, something that in its turn can be looked at, can be before one; almost something like a *materialization*.

And this materialization is something spatial and it must be possible to describe it in purely spatial terms. For instance (if it is a face) it can smile; the concept of friendliness, however, has no place in an account of it, but is *foreign* to such an account (even though it may observe it).

If you ask me what I saw, perhaps I shall be able to make a sketch which shews you; but I shall mostly have no recollection of the way my glance shifted in looking at it.

The concept of 'seeing' makes a tangled impression. Well, it is tangled.—I look at the landscape, my gaze ranges over it, I see all sorts of distinct and indistinct movement; *this* impresses itself sharply on me, *that* is quite hazy. After all, how completely ragged what we see can appear! And now look at all that can be meant by "description of what is seen".—But this just is what is called description of what is seen. There is not *one genuine* proper case of such description—the rest being just vague, something which awaits clarification, or which must just be swept aside as rubbish.

Here we are in enormous danger of wanting to make fine distinctions.—It is the same when one tries to define the concept of a material object in terms of 'what is really seen'.—What we have rather to do is to *accept* the everyday language-game, and to note *false* accounts of the matter *as* false. The primitive language-game which children are taught needs no justification; attempts at justification need to be rejected.

Take as an example the aspects of a triangle. This triangle

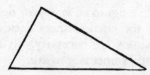

can be seen as a triangular hole, as a solid, as a geometrical drawing; as standing on its base, as hanging from its apex; as a mountain, as a wedge, as an arrow or pointer, as an overturned object which is meant to stand on the shorter side of the right angle, as a half parallelogram, and as various other things.

"You can think now of *this* now of *this* as you look at it, can regard it now as *this* now as *this*, and then you will see it now *this* way, now *this*."—*What* way? There *is* no further qualification.

But how is it possible to *see* an object according to an *interpretation*?—The question represents it as a queer fact; as if something were being forced into a form it did not really fit. But no squeezing, no forcing took place here.

When it looks as if there were no room for such a form between other ones you have to look for it in another dimension. If there is no room here, there *is* room in another dimension.

(It is in this sense too that there is no room for imaginary numbers in the continuum of real numbers. But what this means is: the application of the concept of imaginary numbers is less like that of real numbers than appears from the look of the *calculations*. It is necessary to get down to the application, and then the concept finds a different place, one which, so to speak, one never dreamed of.)

How would the following account do: "What I can see something *as*, is what it can be a picture of"?

What this means is: the aspects in a change of aspects are those ones which the figure might sometimes have *permanently* in a picture.

A triangle can really be *standing up* in one picture, be hanging in another, and can in a third be something that has fallen over.—That is, I who am looking at it say, not "It may also be something that has fallen over", but "That glass has fallen over and is lying there in fragments". This is how we react to the picture.

Could I say what a picture must be like to produce this effect? No. There are, for example, styles of painting which do not convey anything to me in this immediate way, but do to other people. I think custom and upbringing have a hand in this.

What does it mean to say that I '*see the sphere floating in the air*' in a picture?

Is it enough that this description is the first to hand, is the matter-of-course one? No, for it might be so for various reasons. This might, for instance, simply be the conventional description.

What is the expression of my not merely understanding the picture in this way, for instance, (knowing what it is *supposed* to be), but *seeing* it in this way?—It is expressed by: "The sphere seems to float", "You see it floating", or again, in a special tone of voice, "It floats!"

This, then, is the expression of taking something for something. But not being used as such.

Here we are not asking ourselves what are the causes and what produces this impression in a particular case.

And *is* it a special impression?—"Surely I see something *different* when I see the sphere floating from when I merely see it lying there."—This really means: This expression is justified!—(For taken literally it is no more than a repetition.)

(And yet my impression is not that of a real floating sphere either. There are various forms of 'three-dimensional seeing'. The three-dimensional character of a photograph and the three-dimensional character of what we see through a stereoscope.)

"And is it really a different impression?"—In order to answer this I should like to ask myself whether there is really something different there in me. But how can I find out?——I *describe* what I am seeing differently.

Certain drawings are always seen as flat figures, and others sometimes, or always, three-dimensionally.

Here one would now like to say: the visual impression of what is seen three-dimensionally is three-dimensional; with the schematic cube, for instance, it is a cube. (For the description of the impression is the description of a cube.)

And then it seems queer that with some drawings our impression should be a flat thing, and with some a three-dimensional thing. One asks oneself "Where is this going to end?"

When I see the picture of a galloping horse—do I merely *know* that this is the kind of movement meant? Is it superstition to think I *see* the horse galloping in the picture?——And does my visual impression gallop too?

What does anyone tell me by saying "Now I see it as ....."? What consequences has this information? What can I do with it?

People often associate colours with vowels. Someone might find that a vowel changed its colour when it was repeated over and over again. He finds *a* 'now blue—now red', for instance.

The expression "Now I am seeing it as ..." might have no more significance for us than: "Now I find *a* red".

(Linked with physiological observations, even this change might acquire importance for us.)

Here it occurs to me that in conversation on aesthetic matters we use the words: "You have to see it like *this*, this is how it is meant"; "When you see it like *this*, you see where it goes wrong"; "You have to hear this bar as an introduction"; "You must hear it in this key"; "You must phrase it like *this*" (which can refer to hearing as well as to playing).

This figure

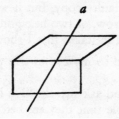

is supposed to represent a convex step and to be used in some kind
of topological demonstration. For this purpose we draw the straight
line *a* through the geometric centres of the two surfaces.—Now if
anyone's three-dimensional impression of the figure were never more
than momentary, and even so were now concave, now convex, that
might make it difficult for him to follow our demonstration. And
if he finds that the flat aspect alternates with a three-dimensional one,
that is just as if I were to shew him completely different objects in
the course of the demonstration.

What does it mean for me to look at a drawing in descriptive
geometry and say: "I know that this line appears again here, but I
can't *see* it like that"? Does it simply mean a lack of familiarity in
operating with the drawing; that I don't 'know my way about' too
well?—This familiarity is certainly one of our criteria. What tells
us that someone is seeing the drawing three-dimensionally is a certain
kind of 'knowing one's way about'. Certain gestures, for instance,
which indicate the three-dimensional relations: fine shades of behaviour.

I see that an animal in a picture is transfixed by an arrow. It has
struck it in the throat and sticks out at the back of the neck. Let the
picture be a silhouette.—Do you *see* the arrow—or do you merely *know*
that these two bits are supposed to represent part of an arrow?

(Compare Köhler's figure of the interpenetrating hexagons.)

"But this isn't *seeing*!"——"But this is seeing!"—It must be possible
to give both remarks a conceptual justification.

But this is seeing! *In what sense* is it seeing?

"The phenomenon is at first surprising, but a physiological explanation of it will certainly be found."—
Our problem is not a causal but a conceptual one.

If the picture of the transfixed beast or of the interpenetrating
hexagons were shewn to me just for a moment and then I had to
describe it, *that* would be my description; if I had to draw it I should

certainly produce a very faulty copy, but it would shew some sort of animal transfixed by an arrow, or two hexagons interpenetrating. That is to say: there are certain mistakes that I should *not* make.

The first thing to jump to my eye in this picture is: there are two hexagons.

Now I look at them and ask myself: "Do I really see them *as* hexagons?"—and for the whole time they are before my eyes? (Assuming that they have not changed their aspect in that time.)—And I should like to reply: "I am not thinking of them as hexagons the whole time."

Someone tells me: "I saw it at once as two hexagons. And that's the *whole* of *what* I saw." But how do I understand this? I think he would have given this description at once in answer to the question "What are you seeing?", nor would he have treated it as one among several possibilities. In this his description is like the answer "A face" on being shewn the figure

The best description I can give of what was shewn me for a moment is *this*: .....

"The impression was that of a rearing animal." So a perfectly definite description came out.—Was it *seeing*, or was it a thought?

Do not try to analyse your own inner experience.

Of course I might also have seen the picture first as something different, and then have said to myself "Oh, it's two hexagons!" So the aspect would have altered. And does this prove that I in fact *saw* it as something definite?

"Is it a *genuine* visual experience?" The question is: in what sense is it one?

Here it is *difficult* to see that what is at issue is the fixing of concepts. A *concept* forces itself on one. (This is what you must not forget.)

For when should I call it a mere case of knowing, not seeing?— Perhaps when someone treats the picture as a working drawing, *reads* it like a blueprint. (Fine shades of behaviour.—Why are they *important*? They have important consequences.)

"To me it is an animal pierced by an arrow." That is what I treat it as; this is my *attitude* to the figure. This is one meaning in calling it a case of 'seeing'.

But can I say in the same sense: "To me these are two hexagons"? Not in the same sense, but in a similar one.

You need to think of the role which pictures such as paintings (as opposed to working drawings) have in our lives. This role is by no means a uniform one.

A comparison: texts are sometimes hung on the wall. But not theorems of mechanics. (Our relation to these two things.)

If you see the drawing as such-and-such an animal, what I expect from you will be pretty different from what I expect when you merely know what it is meant to be.

Perhaps the following expression would have been better: we *regard* the photograph, the picture on our wall, as the object itself (the man, landscape, and so on) depicted there.

This need not have been so. We could easily imagine people who did not have this relation to such pictures. Who, for example, would be repelled by photographs, because a face without colour and even perhaps a face reduced in scale struck them as inhuman.

I say: "We regard a portrait as a human being,"—but when do we do so, and for how long? *Always*, if we see it at all (and do not, say, see it as something else)?

I might say yes to this, and that would determine the concept of regarding-as.—The question is whether yet another concept, related to this one, is also of importance to us: that, namely, of a seeing-as which only takes place while I am actually concerning myself with the picture as the object depicted.

I might say: a picture does not always *live* for me while I am seeing it.

"Her picture smiles down on me from the wall." It need not always do so, whenever my glance lights on it.

The duck-rabbit. One asks oneself: how can the eye—this *dot*—be looking in a direction?—"*See, it is looking!*" (And one 'looks' oneself as one says this.) But one does not say and do this the whole time one is looking at the picture. And now, what is this "See, it's looking!" —does it express a sensation?

(In giving all these examples I am not aiming at some kind of completeness, some classification of psychological concepts. They are only meant to enable the reader to shift for himself when he encounters conceptual difficulties.)

"Now I see it as a ....." goes with "I am trying to see it as a ...." or "I can't see it as a .... yet". But I cannot try to see a conventional picture of a lion *as* a lion, any more than an F as that letter. (Though I may well try to see it as a gallows, for example.)

Do not ask yourself "How does it work with *me*?"—Ask "What do I know about someone else?"

How does one play the game: "It could be *this* too"? (What a figure could also be—which is what it can be seen as—is not simply another

figure. If someone said "I see 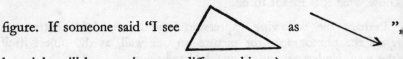 as ", he might still be meaning very different things.)

Here is a game played by children: they say that a chest, for example, is a house; and thereupon it is interpreted as a house in every detail. A piece of fancy is worked into it.

And does the child now *see* the chest as a house?
"He quite forgets that it is a chest; for him it actually is a house." (There are definite tokens of this.) Then would it not also be correct to say he *sees* it as a house?

And if you knew how to play this game, and, given a particular situation, you exclaimed with special expression "Now it's a house!"— you would be giving expression to the dawning of an aspect.

If I heard someone talking about the duck-rabbit, and *now* he spoke in a certain way about the special expression of the rabbit's face I should say, now he's seeing the picture as a rabbit.

But the expression in one's voice and gestures is the same as if the object had altered and had ended by *becoming* this or that.
I have a theme played to me several times and each time in a slower tempo. In the end I say "*Now* it's right", or "*Now* at last it's a march", "*Now* at last it's a dance".—The same tone of voice expresses the dawning of an aspect.

'Fine shades of behaviour.'—When my understanding of a theme is expressed by my whistling it with the correct expression, this is an example of such fine shades.

The aspects of the triangle: it is as if an *image* came into contact, and for a time remained in contact, with the visual impression.

In this, however, these aspects differ from the concave and convex aspects of the step (for example). And also from the aspects of the figure

(which I shall call a "double cross") as a white cross on a black ground and as a black cross on a white ground.

You must remember that the descriptions of the alternating aspects are of a different kind in each case.

(The temptation to say "I see it like *this*", pointing to the same thing for "it" and "this".) Always get rid of the idea of the private object in this way: assume that it constantly changes, but that you do not notice the change because your memory constantly deceives you.

Those two aspects of the double cross (I shall call them the aspects A) might be reported simply by pointing alternately to an isolated white and an isolated black cross.

One could quite well imagine this as a primitive reaction in a child even before it could talk.

(Thus in reporting the aspects A we point to a part of the double cross.—The duck and rabbit aspects could not be described in an analogous way.)

You only 'see the duck and rabbit aspects' if you are already conversant with the shapes of those two animals. There is no analogous condition for seeing the aspects A.

It is possible to take the duck-rabbit simply for the picture of a rabbit, the double cross simply for the picture of a black cross, but not to take the bare triangular figure for the picture of an object that has fallen over. To see this aspect of the triangle demands *imagination*.

The aspects A are not essentially three-dimensional; a black cross on a white ground is not essentially a cross with a white surface in the background. You could teach someone the idea of the black cross on a ground of different colour without shewing him anything but crosses painted on sheets of paper. Here the 'background' is simply the surrounding of the cross.

The aspects A are not connected with the possibility of illusion in the same way as are the three-dimensional aspects of the drawing of a cube or step.

I can see the schematic cube as a box;—but can I also see it now as a paper, now as a tin, box?—What ought I to say, if someone assured me *he* could?—I can set a limit to the concept here.

Yet think of the expression "*felt*" in connexion with looking at a picture. ("One feels the softness of that material.") (*Knowing* in dreams. "And I *knew* that . . . was in the room.")

How does one teach a child (say in arithmetic) "Now take *these* things together!" or "Now *these* go together"? Clearly "taking together" and "going together" must originally have had another meaning for him than that of *seeing* in this way or that.—And this is a remark about concepts, not about teaching methods.

One *kind* of aspect might be called 'aspects of organization'. When the aspect changes parts of the picture go together which before did not.

In the triangle I can see now *this* as apex, *that* as base—now *this* as apex, *that* as base.—Clearly the words "Now I am seeing *this* as the apex" cannot so far mean anything to a learner who has only just met the concepts of apex, base, and so on.—But I do not mean this as an empirical proposition.

"Now he's seeing it like *this*", "now like *that*" would only be said of someone *capable* of making certain applications of the figure quite freely.

The substratum of this experience is the mastery of a technique.

But how queer for this to be the logical condition of someone's having such-and-such an *experience*! After all, you don't say that one only 'has toothache' if one is capable of doing such-and-such.—From this it follows that we cannot be dealing with the same concept of experience here. It is a different though related concept.

It is only if someone *can do*, has learnt, is master of, such-and-such, that it makes sense to say he has had *this* experience.

And if this sounds crazy, you need to reflect that the *concept* of seeing is modified here. (A similar consideration is often necessary to get rid of a feeling of dizziness in mathematics.)

We talk, we utter words, and only *later* get a picture of their life.

For how could I see that this posture was hesitant before I knew that it was a posture and not the anatomy of the animal?

But surely that only means that I cannot use *this* concept to describe the object of sight, just because it has *more* than purely visual reference?— Might I not for all that have a purely visual concept of a hesitant posture, or of a timid face?

Such a concept would be comparable with 'major' and 'minor' which certainly have emotional value, but can also be used purely to describe a perceived structure.

The epithet "sad", as applied for example to the outline face, characterizes the grouping of lines in a circle. Applied to a human being it has a different (though related) meaning. (But this does *not* mean that a sad expression is *like* the feeling of sadness!)

Think of this too: I can only see, not hear, red and green,—but sadness I can hear as much as I can see it.

Think of the expression "I heard a plaintive melody". And now the question is: "Does he *hear* the plaint?"

And if I reply: "No, he doesn't hear it, he merely has a sense of it"— where does that get us? One cannot mention a sense-organ for this 'sense'.

Some would like to reply here: "Of course I hear it!"—Others: "I don't really *hear* it."

We can, however, establish differences of concept here.

We react to the visual impression differently from someone who does not recognize it as timid (in the *full* sense of the word).—But I do *not* want to say here that we feel this reaction in our muscles and joints and that this is the 'sensing'.—No, what we have here is a modified concept of *sensation*.

One might say of someone that he was blind to the *expression* of a face. Would his eyesight on that account be defective?

This is, of course, not simply a question for physiology. Here the physiological is a symbol of the logical.

If you feel the seriousness of a tune, what are you perceiving?— Nothing that could be conveyed by reproducing what you heard.

I can imagine some arbitrary cipher—this, for instance:

to be a strictly correct letter of some foreign alphabet. Or again, to be a faultily written one, and faulty in this way or that: for example, it might be slap-dash, or typical childish awkwardness, or like the flourishes in a legal document. It could deviate from the correctly written letter in a variety of ways.—And I can see it in various aspects according to the fiction I surround it with. And here there is a close kinship with 'experiencing the meaning of a word'.

I should like to say that what dawns here lasts only as long as I am occupied with the object in a particular way. ("See, it's looking!")—— 'I should like to say'—and *is* it so?——Ask yourself "For how long am I struck by a thing?"—For how long do I find it *new*?

The aspect presents a physiognomy which then passes away. It is almost as if there were a face there which at first I *imitate*, and then accept without imitating it.—And isn't this really explanation enough? —But isn't it too much?

"I observed the likeness between him and his father for a few minutes, and then no longer."—One might say this if his face were changing and only looked like his father's for a short time. But it can also mean that after a few minutes I stopped being struck by the likeness.

"After the likeness had struck you, how long were you aware of it?" What kind of answer might one give to this question?—"I soon stopped thinking about it", or "It struck me again from time to time", or "I several times had the thought, how like they are!", or "I marvelled at the likeness for at least a minute"—That is the sort of answer you would get.

I should like to put the question "Am I *aware* of the spatial character, the depth of an object (of this cupboard for instance), the *whole* time

I am seeing it?" Do I, so to speak, *feel* it the whole time?—But put the question in the third person.—When would you say of someone that he was aware of it the whole time, and when the opposite?—Of course, one could ask him,—but how did he learn how to answer such a question?—He knows what it means "to feel pain continuously". But that will only confuse him here (as it confuses me).

If he now says he is continuously aware of the depth—do I believe him? And if he says he is aware of it only occasionally (when talking about it, perhaps)—do I believe *that*? These answers will strike me as resting on a false foundation.—It will be different if he says that the object sometimes strikes him as flat, sometimes as three-dimensional.

Someone tells me: "I looked at the flower, but was thinking of something else and was not conscious of its colour." Do I understand this?—I can imagine a significant context, say his going on: "Then I suddenly *saw* it, and realized it was the one which . . . . . .".
Or again: "If I had turned away then, I could not have said what colour it was."
"He looked at it without seeing it."—There is such a thing. But what is the criterion for it?—Well, there is a variety of cases here.

"Just now I looked at the shape rather than at the colour." Do not let such phrases confuse you. Above all, don't wonder "What can be going on in the eyes or brain?"

The likeness makes a striking impression on me; then the impression fades.
It only struck me for a few minutes, and then no longer did.
What happened here?—What can I recall? My own facial expression comes to mind; I could reproduce it. If someone who knew me had seen my face he would have said "Something about his face struck you just now".—There further occurs to me what I say on such an occasion, out loud or to myself. And that is all.—And is this what being struck is? No. These are the phenomena of being struck; but they *are* 'what happens'.

Is being struck looking plus thinking? No. Many of our concepts *cross* here.

('Thinking' and 'inward speech'—I do not say '*to* oneself'—are different concepts.)

The colour of the visual impression corresponds to the colour of the object (this blotting paper looks pink to me, and is pink)—the shape of the visual impression to the shape of the object (it looks rectangular to me, and is rectangular)—but what I perceive in the dawning of an aspect is not a property of the object, but an internal relation between it and other objects.

It is almost as if 'seeing the sign in this context' were an echo of a thought.

"The echo of a thought in sight"—one would like to say.

Imagine a physiological explanation of the experience. Let it be this: When we look at the figure, our eyes scan it repeatedly, always following a particular path. The path corresponds to a particular pattern of oscillation of the eyeballs in the act of looking. It is possible to jump from one such pattern to another and for the two to alternate. (Aspects A.) Certain patterns of movement are physiologically impossible; hence, for example, I cannot see the schematic cube as two interpenetrating prisms. And so on. Let this be the explanation.— "Yes, that shews it is a kind of *seeing*."—You have now introduced a new, a physiological, criterion for seeing. And this can screen the old problem from view, but not solve it.—The purpose of this paragraph however, was to bring before our view what happens when a physiological explanation is offered. The psychological concept hangs out of reach of this explanation. And this makes the nature of the problem clearer.

Do I really see something different each time, or do I only interpret what I see in a different way? I am inclined to say the former. But why?—To interpret is to think, to do something; seeing is a state.

Now it is easy to recognize cases in which we are *interpreting*. When we interpret we form hypotheses, which may prove false.—"I am seeing this figure as a . . . . ." can be verified as little as (or in the same sense as) "I am seeing bright red". So there is a similarity in the use of "seeing" in the two contexts. Only do not think you knew in advance what the "*state* of seeing" means here! Let the use *teach* you the meaning.

We find certain things about seeing puzzling, because we do not find the whole business of seeing puzzling enough.

If you look at a photograph of people, houses and trees, you do not feel the lack of the third dimension in it. We should not find it easy to describe a photograph as a collection of colour-patches on a flat surface; but what we see in a stereoscope looks three-dimensional in a different way again.

(It is anything but a matter of course that we see 'three-dimensionally' with two eyes. If the two visual images are amalgamated, we might expect a blurred one as a result.)

The concept of an aspect is akin to the concept of an image. In other words: the concept 'I am now seeing it as . . . .' is akin to 'I am now having *this* image'.

Doesn't it take imagination to hear something as a variation on a particular theme? And yet one is perceiving something in so hearing it.

"Imagine this changed like this, and you have this other thing." One can use imagining in the course of proving something.

Seeing an aspect and imagining are subject to the will. There is such an order as "Imagine *this*", and also: "Now see the figure like *this*"; but not: "Now see this leaf green".

The question now arises: Could there be human beings lacking in the capacity to see something *as something*—and what would that be like? What sort of consequences would it have?—Would this defect be comparable to colour-blindness or to not having absolute pitch?— We will call it "aspect-blindness"—and will next consider what might be meant by this. (A conceptual investigation.) The aspect-blind man is supposed not to see the aspects A change. But is he also supposed not to recognize that the double cross contains both a black and a white cross? So if told "Shew me figures containing a black cross among these examples" will he be unable to manage it? No, he should be able to do that; but he will not be supposed to say: "Now it's a black cross on a white ground!"

Is he supposed to be blind to the similarity between two faces?— And so also to their identity or approximate identity? I do not want to settle this. (He ought to be able to execute such orders as "Bring me something that looks like *this*.")

Ought he to be unable to see the schematic cube as a cube?—It would not follow from that that he could not recognize it as a representation (a working drawing for instance) of a cube. But for him it would not jump from one aspect to the other.—Question: Ought he to be able to *take* it as a cube in certain circumstances, as we do?—If not, this could not very well be called a sort of blindness.

The 'aspect-blind' will have an altogether different relationship to pictures from ours.

(Anomalies of *this* kind are easy for us to imagine.)

Aspect-blindness will be *akin* to the lack of a 'musical ear'.

The importance of this concept lies in the connexion between the concepts of 'seeing an aspect' and 'experiencing the meaning of a word'. For we want to ask "What would you be missing if you did not *experience* the meaning of a word?"

What would you be missing, for instance, if you did not understand the request to pronounce the word "till" and to mean it as a verb,—or if you did not feel that a word lost its meaning and became a mere sound if it was repeated ten times over?

In a law-court, for instance, the question might be raised how someone meant a word. And this can be inferred from certain facts.—It is a question of *intention*. But could how he experienced a word—the word "bank" for instance—have been significant in the same way?

Suppose I had agreed on a code with someone; "tower" means bank. I tell him "Now go to the tower"—he understands me and acts accordingly, but he feels the word "tower" to be strange in this use, it has not yet 'taken on' the meaning.

"When I read a poem or narrative with feeling, surely something goes on in me which does not go on when I merely skim the lines for information."—What processes am I alluding to?—The sentences have a different *ring*. I pay careful attention to my intonation. Sometimes a word has the wrong intonation, I emphasize it too much or too little. I notice this and shew it in my face. I might later talk about my reading in detail, for example about the mistakes in my tone of voice. Sometimes a picture, as it were an illustration, comes to me. And this seems to help me to read with the correct expression. And I could mention a good deal more of the same kind.—I can also give a word a tone of voice which brings out the meaning of the rest, almost as if this word were a picture of the whole thing. (And this may, of course, depend on sentence-formation.)

When I pronounce this word while reading with expression it is completely filled with its meaning.—"How can this be, if meaning is the use of the word?" Well, what I said was intended figuratively. Not that I chose the figure: it forced itself on me.—But the figurative employment of the word can't get into conflict with the original one.

Perhaps it could be explained why precisely *this* picture suggests itself to me. (Just think of the expression, and the meaning of the expression: "the word that hits it off".)

But if a sentence can strike me as like a painting in words, and the very individual word in the sentence as like a picture, then it is no such marvel that a word uttered in isolation and without purpose can seem to carry a particular meaning in itself.

Think here of a special kind of illusion which throws light on these matters.—I go for a walk in the environs of a city with a friend. As we talk it comes out that I am imagining the city to lie on our right. Not only have I *no* conscious reason for this assumption, but some quite simple consideration was enough to make me realize that the city lay rather to the left ahead of us. I can at first give no answer to the question *why* I imagine the city in *this* direction. I had *no reason* to think it. But though I see no reason still I seem to see certain psychological causes for it. In particular, certain associations and memories. For example, we walked along a canal, and once before in similar circumstances I had followed a canal and that time the city lay on our right.—I might try as it were psychoanalytically to discover the causes of my unfounded conviction.

"But what is this queer experience?"—Of course it is not queerer than any other; it simply differs in kind from those experiences which we regard as the most fundamental ones, our sense impressions for instance.

"I feel as if I knew the city lay over there."—"I feel as if the name 'Schubert' fitted Schubert's works and Schubert's face."

You can say the word "March" to yourself and mean it at one time as an imperative at another as the name of a month. And now say "March!"—and then "March *no further*!"—Does the *same* experience accompany the word both times—are you sure?

If a sensitive ear shews me, when I am playing this game, that I have now *this* now *that* experience of the word—doesn't it also shew me that I often do not have *any* experience of it in the course of talking?—For the fact that I then also mean it, intend it, now like *this* now like *that*, and maybe also say so later is, of course, not in question.

But the question now remains why, in connexion with this *game* of experiencing a word, we also speak of 'the meaning' and of 'meaning it'.—This is a different kind of question.——It is the phenomenon which is characteristic of this language-game that in *this* situation we use this expression: we say we pronounced the word with *this* meaning and take this expression over from that other language-game.

Call it a dream. It does not change anything.

Given the two ideas 'fat' and 'lean', would you be rather inclined to say that Wednesday was fat and Tuesday lean, or *vice versa*? (I incline decisively towards the former.) Now have "fat" and "lean" some different meaning here from their usual one?—They have a different use.—So ought I really to have used different words? Certainly not that.—I want to use *these* words (with their familiar meanings) *here*.—Now, I say nothing about the causes of this phenomenon. They *might* be associations from my childhood. But that is a hypothesis. Whatever the explanation,—the inclination is there.

Asked "What do you really mean here by 'fat' and 'lean'?"—I could only explain the meanings in the usual way. I could *not* point to the examples of Tuesday and Wednesday.

Here one might speak of a 'primary' and 'secondary' sense of a word. It is only if the word has the primary sense for you that you use it in the secondary one.

Only if you have learnt to calculate—on paper or out loud—can you be made to grasp, by means of this concept, what calculating in the head is.

The secondary sense is not a 'metaphorical' sense. If I say "For me the vowel *e* is yellow" I do not mean: 'yellow' in a metaphorical sense,—for I could not express what I want to say in any other way than by means of the idea 'yellow'.

Someone tells me: "Wait for me by the bank". Question: Did you, *as you were saying the word*, mean this bank?—This question is of the same kind as "Did you intend to say such-and-such to him on your way to meet him?" It refers to a definite time (the time of walking, as the former question refers to the time of speaking)—but not to an *experience* during that time. Meaning is as little an experience as intending.

But what distinguishes them from experience?—They have no experience-content. For the contents (images for instance) which accompany and illustrate them are not the meaning or intending.

The intention *with which* one acts does not 'accompany' the action any more than the thought 'accompanies' speech. Thought and intention are neither 'articulated' nor 'non-articulated'; to be compared neither with a single note which sounds during the acting or speaking, nor with a tune.

'Talking' (whether out loud or silently) and 'thinking' are not concepts of the same kind; even though they are in closest connexion.

The *interest* of the experiences one has while speaking and of the intention is not the same. (The experiences might perhaps inform a psychologist about the '*unconscious*' intention.)

"At that word we both thought of him." Let us assume that each of us said the same words to himself—and how can it mean MORE than that?—But wouldn't even those words be only a *germ*? They must surely belong to a language and to a context, in order really to be the expression of the thought *of* that man.

If God had looked into our minds he would not have been able to see there whom we were speaking of.

"Why did you look at me at that word, were you thinking of . . . .?" —So there is a reaction at a certain moment and it is explained by saying "I thought of . . . ." or "I suddenly remembered . . . ."

In saying this you refer to that moment in the time you were speaking. It makes a difference whether you refer to this or to that moment.

Mere explanation of a word does not refer to an occurrence at the moment of speaking.

The language-game "I mean (or meant) *this*" (subsequent explanation of a word) is quite different from this one: "I thought of . . . . as I said it." The latter is akin to "It reminded me of . . . ."

"I have already remembered three times today that I must write to him." Of what importance is it what went on in me then?—On the other hand what is the importance, what the interest, of the statement itself?—It permits certain conclusions.

"At these words *he* occurred to me."—What is the primitive reaction with which the language-game begins—which can then be translated into these words? How do people get to use these words?

The primitive reaction may have been a glance or a gesture, but it may also have been a word.

"Why did you look at me and shake your head?"—"I wanted to give you to understand that you . . . . ." This is supposed to express not a symbolic convention but the purpose of my action.

Meaning it is not a process which accompanies a word. For no *process* could have the consequences of meaning.

(Similarly, I think, it could be said: a calculation is not an experiment, for no experiment could have the peculiar consequences of a multiplication.)

There are important accompanying phenomena of talking which are often missing when one talks without thinking, and this is characteristic of talking without thinking. But *they* are not the thinking.

"Now I know!" What went on here?————So did I *not* know, when I declared that now I knew?
You are looking at it wrong.
(What is the signal for?)
And could the 'knowing' be called an accompaniment of the exclamation?

The familiar physiognomy of a word, the feeling that it has taken up its meaning into itself, that it is an actual likeness of its meaning—there could be human beings to whom all this was alien. (They would not have an attachment to their words.)—And how are these feelings manifested among us?—By the way we choose and value words.

How do I find the 'right' word? How do I choose among words? Without doubt it is sometimes as if I were comparing them by fine differences of smell: *That* is too . . . . . ., *that* is too . . . . . ., —*this* is the right one.—But I do not always have to make judgments, give explanations; often I might only say: "It simply isn't right yet". I am dissatisfied, I go on looking. At last a word comes: "*That's* it!" *Sometimes* I can say why. This is simply what searching, this is what finding, is like here.

But doesn't the word that occurs to you somehow 'come' in a special way? Just attend and you'll see!—Careful attention is no use to me. All it could discover would be what is *now* going on in *me*.

And how can I, precisely now, listen for it at all? I ought to have to wait until a word occurs to me anew. This, however, is the queer thing: it seems as though I did not have to wait on the occasion, but could give myself an exhibition of it, even when it is not actually taking place. How?—I *act* it.—But *what* can I learn in this way? What do I reproduce?—Characteristic accompaniments. Primarily: gestures, faces, tones of voice.

It is possible—and this is important—to say a *great deal* about a fine aesthetic difference.—The first thing you say may, of course, be just: "*This* word fits, *that* doesn't"—or something of the kind. But then you can discuss all the extensive ramifications of the tie-up effected by each of the words. That first judgment is *not* the end of the matter, for it is the field of force of a word that is decisive.

"The word is on the tip of my tongue." What is going on in my consciousness? That is not the point at all. Whatever did go on was not what was meant by that expression. It is of more interest what went on in my behaviour.—"The word is on the tip of my tongue" tells you: the word which belongs here has escaped me, but I hope to find it soon. For the rest the verbal expression does no more than certain wordless behaviour.

James, in writing of this subject, is really trying to say: "What a remarkable experience! The word is not there yet, and yet in a certain sense is there,—or something is there, which *cannot* grow into anything but this word."—But this is not experience at all. *Interpreted* as experience it does indeed look odd. As does intention, when it is interpreted as the accompaniment of action; or again, like minus one interpreted as a cardinal number.

The words "It's on the tip of my tongue" are no more the expression of an experience than "Now I know how to go on!"—We use them in *certain situations*, and they are surrounded by behaviour of a special kind, and also by some characteristic experiences. In particular they are frequently followed by *finding* the word. (Ask yourself: "What would it be like if human beings *never* found the word that was on the tip of their tongue?")

Silent 'internal' speech is not a half hidden phenomenon which is as it were seen through a veil. It is not hidden *at all*, but the concept may easily confuse us, for it runs over a long stretch cheek by jowl with the concept of an 'outward' process, and yet does not coincide with it.

(The question whether the muscles of the larynx are innervated in connexion with internal speech, and similar things, may be of great interest, but not in our investigation.)

The close relationship between 'saying inwardly' and 'saying' is manifested in the possibility of telling out loud what one said inwardly, and of an outward action's *accompanying* inward speech. (I can sing inwardly, or read silently, or calculate in my head, and beat time with my hand as I do so.)

"But saying things inwardly is surely a certain activity which I have to learn!" Very well; but what is 'doing' and what is 'learning' here?

Let the use of words teach you their meaning. (Similarly one can often say in mathematics: let the *proof* teach you *what* was being proved.)

"So I don't *really* calculate, when I calculate in my head?"—After all, you yourself distinguish between calculation in the head and perceptible calculation! But you can only learn what 'calculating in the head' is by learning what 'calculating' is; you can only learn to calculate in your head by learning to calculate.

One can say things in one's head very 'distinctly', when one reproduces the tone of voice of one's sentences by humming (with closed lips). Movements of the larynx help too. But the remarkable thing is precisely that one then *hears* the talk in one's imagination and does not merely *feel* the skeleton of it, so to speak, in one's larynx. (For human beings could also well be imagined calculating silently with movements of the larynx, as one can calculate on one's fingers.)

A hypothesis, such as that such-and-such went on in our bodies when we made internal calculations, is only of interest to us in that it points to a possible use of the expression "I said .... to myself"; namely that of inferring the physiological process from the expression.

That what someone else says to himself is hidden from me is part of the *concept* 'saying inwardly'. Only "hidden" is the wrong word here; for if it is hidden from me, it ought to be apparent to him, *he* would have to *know* it. But he does not 'know' it; only, the doubt which exists for me does not exist for him.

"What anyone says to himself within himself is hidden from me" might of course also mean that I can for the most part not *guess* it, nor can I read it off from, for example, the movements of his throat (which would be a possibility.)

"I know what I want, wish, believe, feel, ..." (and so on through all the psychological verbs) is either philosophers' nonsense, or at any rate *not* a judgment *a priori*.

"I know . . ." may mean "I do not doubt . . ." but does not mean that the words "I doubt . . ." are *senseless*, that doubt is logically excluded.

One says "I know" where one can also say "I believe" or "I suspect"; where one can find out. (If you bring up against me the case of people's saying "But I must know if I am in pain!", "Only you can know what you feel", and similar things, you should consider the occasion and purpose of these phrases. "War is war" is not an example of the law of identity, either.)

It is possible to imagine a case in which I *could* find out that I had two hands. Normally, however, I *cannot* do so. "But all you need is to hold them up before your eyes!"—If I am *now* in doubt whether I have two hands, I need not believe my eyes either. (I might just as well ask a friend.)

With this is connected the fact that, for instance, the proposition "The Earth has existed for millions of years" makes clearer sense than "The Earth has existed in the last five minutes". For I should ask anyone who asserted the latter: "What observations does this proposition refer to; and what observations would count against it?"—whereas I know what ideas and observations the former proposition goes with.

"A new-born child has no teeth."—"A goose has no teeth."—"A rose has no teeth."—This last at any rate—one would like to say—is obviously true! It is even surer than that a goose has none.—And yet it is none so clear. For where should a rose's teeth have been? The goose has none in its jaw. And neither, of course, has it any in its wings; but no one means that when he says it has no teeth.—Why, suppose one were to say: the cow chews its food and then dungs the rose with it, so the rose has teeth in the mouth of a beast. This would not be absurd, because one has no notion in advance where to look for teeth in a rose. ((Connexion with 'pain in someone else's body'.))

I can know what someone else is thinking, not what I am thinking.
It is correct to say "I know what you are thinking", and wrong to say "I know what I am thinking."
(A whole cloud of philosophy condensed into a drop of grammar.)

"A man's thinking goes on within his consciousness in a seclusion in comparison with which any physical seclusion is an exhibition to public view."
If there were people who always read the silent internal discourse of others—say by observing the larynx—would they too be inclined to use the picture of complete seclusion?

If I were to talk to myself out loud in a language not understood by those present my thoughts would be hidden from them.

Let us assume there was a man who always guessed right what I was saying to myself in my thoughts. (It does not matter how he manages it.) But what is the criterion for his guessing *right*? Well, I am a truthful person and I confess that he has guessed right.—But might I not be mistaken, can my memory not deceive me? And might it not always do so when—without lying—I express what I have thought within myself?——But now it does appear that 'what went on within me' is not the point at all. (Here I am drawing a construction-line.)

The criteria for the truth of the *confession* that I thought such-and-such are not the criteria for a true *description* of a process. And the importance of the true confession does not reside in its being a correct and certain report of a process. It resides rather in the special consequences which can be drawn from a confession whose truth is guaranteed by the special criteria of *truthfulness*.

(Assuming that dreams can yield important information about the dreamer, what yielded the information would be truthful accounts of dreams. The question whether the dreamer's memory deceives him when he reports the dream after waking cannot arise, unless indeed we introduce a completely new criterion for the report's 'agreeing' with the dream, a criterion which gives us a concept of 'truth' as distinct from 'truthfulness' here.)

There is a game of 'guessing thoughts'. A variant of it would be this: I tell A something in a language that B does not understand. B is supposed to guess the meaning of what I say.—Another variant: I write down a sentence which the other person cannot see. He has to guess the words or their sense.—Yet another: I am putting a jig-saw puzzle together; the other person cannot see me but from time to time guesses my thoughts and utters them. He says, for instance, "Now where is this bit?"—"*Now* I know how it fits!"—"I have no idea what goes in here,"—"The sky is always the hardest part" and so on—but *I* need not be talking to myself either out loud or silently at the time.

All this would be guessing at thoughts; and the fact that it does not actually happen does not make thought any more hidden than the unperceived physical proceedings.

"What is *internal* is hidden from us."—The future is hidden from us. But does the astronomer think like this when he calculates an eclipse of the sun?

If I see someone writhing in pain with evident cause I do not think: all the same, his feelings are hidden from me.

We also say of some people that they are transparent to us. It is, however, important as regards this observation that one human being can be a complete enigma to another. We learn this when we come into a strange country with entirely strange traditions; and, what is more, even given a mastery of the country's language. We do not *understand* the people. (And not because of not knowing what they are saying to themselves.) We cannot find our feet with them.

"I cannot know what is going on in him" is above all a *picture*. It is the convincing expression of a conviction. It does not give the reasons for the conviction. *They* are not readily accessible.

If a lion could talk, we could not understand him.

It is possible to imagine a guessing of intentions like the guessing of thoughts, but also a guessing of what someone is actually *going to do*.

To say "He alone can know what he intends" is nonsense: to say "He alone can know what he will do", wrong. For the prediction contained in my expression of intention (for example "When it strikes five I am going home") need not come true, and someone else may know what will really happen.

Two points, however, are important: one, that in many cases someone else cannot predict my actions, whereas I foresee them in my intentions; the other, that my prediction (in my expression of intention) has not the same foundation as his prediction of what I shall do, and the conclusions to be drawn from these predictions are quite different.

I can be as *certain* of someone else's sensations as of any fact. But this does not make the propositions "He is much depressed", "25 × 25 = 625" and "I am sixty years old" into similar instruments. The explanation suggests itself that the certainty is of a different *kind*.— This seems to point to a psychological difference. But the difference is logical.

"But, if you are *certain*, isn't it that you are shutting your eyes in face of doubt?"—They are shut.

Am I less certain that this man is in pain than that twice two is four?—Does this shew the former to be mathematical certainty?—— 'Mathematical certainty' is not a psychological concept.

The kind of certainty is the kind of language-game.

"He alone knows his motives"—that is an expression of the fact that we ask *him* what his motives are.—If he is sincere he will tell us them; but I need more than sincerity to guess his motives. This is where there is a kinship with the case of *knowing*.

Let yourself be *struck* by the existence of such a thing as our language-game of: confessing the motive of my action.

We remain unconscious of the prodigious diversity of all the everyday language-games because the clothing of our language makes everything alike.

Something new (spontaneous, 'specific') is always a language-game.

What is the difference between cause and motive?—How is the motive *discovered*, and how the cause?

There is such a question as: "Is this a reliable way of judging people's motives?" But in order to be able to ask this we must know what "judging a motive" means; and we do not learn this by being told what '*motive*' is and what '*judging*' is.

One judges the length of a rod and can look for and find some method of judging it more exactly or more reliably. So—you say—*what* is judged here is independent of the method of judging it. What length *is* cannot be defined by the method of determining length.—To think like this is to make a mistake. What mistake?—To say "The height of Mont Blanc depends on how one climbs it" would be queer. And one wants to compare 'ever more accurate measurement of length' with the nearer and nearer approach to an object. But in certain cases it is, and in certain cases it is *not*, clear what "approaching nearer to the length of an object" means. What "determining the length" means is not learned by learning what *length* and *determining* are; the meaning of the word "length" is learnt by learning, among other things, what it is to determine length.

(For this reason the word "methodology" has a double meaning. Not only a physical investigation, but also a conceptual one, can be called "methodological investigation".)

We should sometimes like to call certainty and belief tones, colourings, of thought; and it is true that they receive expression in the *tone* of voice. But do not think of them as 'feelings' which we have in speaking or thinking.

Ask, not: "What goes on in us when we are certain that . . . .?"—but: How is 'the certainty that this is the case' manifested in human action?

"While you can have complete certainty about someone else's state of mind, still it is always merely subjective, not objective, certainty."—These two words betoken a difference between language-games.

There can be a dispute over the correct result of a calculation (say of a rather long addition). But such disputes are rare and of short duration. They can be decided, as we say, 'with certainty'.

Mathematicians do not in general quarrel over the result of a calculation. (This is an important fact.)—If it were otherwise, if for instance one mathematician was convinced that a figure had altered unperceived, or that his or someone else's memory had been deceived, and so on—then our concept of 'mathematical certainty' would not exist.

Even then it might always be said: "True we can never *know* what the result of a calculation is, but for all that it always has a quite definite result. (God knows it.) Mathematics is indeed of the highest certainty—though we only have a crude reflection of it."

But am I trying to say some such thing as that the certainty of mathematics is based on the reliability of ink and paper? *No*. (That would be a vicious circle.)—I have not said *why* mathematicians do not quarrel, but only *that* they do not.

It is no doubt true that you could not calculate with certain sorts of paper and ink, if, that is, they were subject to certain queer changes—but still the fact that they changed could in turn only be got from memory and comparison with other means of calculation. And how are these tested in their turn?

What has to be accepted, the given, is—so one could say—*forms of life*.

Does it make sense to say that people generally agree in their judgments of colour? What would it be like for them not to?—One man would say a flower was red which another called blue, and so on.—But what right should we have to call these people's words "red" and "blue" *our* 'colour-words'?"—

How would they learn to use these words? And is the language-game which they learn still such as we call the use of 'names of colour'? There are evidently differences of degree here.

This consideration must, however, apply to mathematics too. If there were not complete agreement, then neither would human beings be learning the technique which we learn. It would be more or less different from ours up to the point of unrecognizability.

"But mathematical truth is independent of whether human beings know it or not!"—Certainly, the propositions "Human beings believe that twice two is four" and "Twice two is four" do not mean the same. The latter is a mathematical proposition; the other, if it makes sense at all, may perhaps mean: human beings have *arrived* at the mathematical proposition. The two propositions have entirely different *uses*.—But what would *this* mean: "Even though everybody believed that twice two was five it would still be four"?—For what would it be like for everybody to believe that?—Well, I could imagine, for instance, that people had a different calculus, or a technique which we should not call "calculating". But would it be *wrong*? (Is a coronation *wrong*? To beings different from ourselves it might look extremely odd.)

Of course, in one sense mathematics is a branch of knowledge,— but still it is also an *activity*. And 'false moves' can only exist as the exception. For if what we now call by that name became the rule, the game in which they were false moves would have been abrogated.

"We all learn the same multiplication table." This might, no doubt, be a remark about the teaching of arithmetic in our schools,—but also an observation about the concept of the multiplication table. ("In a horse-race the horses generally run as fast as they can.")

There is such a thing as colour-blindness and there are ways of establishing it. There is in general complete agreement in the judgments of colours made by those who have been diagnosed normal. This characterizes the concept of a judgment of colour.

There is in general no such agreement over the question whether an expression of feeling is genuine or not.

I am sure, *sure*, that he is not pretending; but some third person is not. Can I always convince him? And if not is there some mistake in his reasoning or observations?

"You're all at sea!"—we say this when someone doubts what we recognize as clearly genuine—but we cannot prove anything.

Is there such a thing as 'expert judgment' about the genuineness of expressions of feeling?—Even here, there are those whose judgment is 'better' and those whose judgment is 'worse'.

Correcter prognoses will generally issue from the judgments of those with better knowledge of mankind.

Can one learn this knowledge? Yes; some can. Not, however, by taking a course in it, but through '*experience*'.—Can someone else be a man's teacher in this? Certainly. From time to time he gives him the right *tip*.—This is what 'learning' and 'teaching' are like here.— What one acquires here is not a technique; one learns correct judgments. There are also rules, but they do not form a system, and only experienced people can apply them right. Unlike calculating-rules.

What is most difficult here is to put this indefiniteness, correctly and unfalsified, into words.

"The genuineness of an expression cannot be proved; one has to feel it."—Very well,—but what does one go on to do with this recognition of genuineness? If someone says "Voila ce que peut dire un cœur vraiment épris"—and if he also brings someone else to the same mind,—what are the further consequences? Or are there none, and does the game *end* with one person's relishing what another does not?

There are certainly *consequences*, but of a diffuse kind. Experience, that is varied observation, can inform us of them, and they too are incapable of general formulation; only in scattered cases can one arrive at a correct and fruitful judgment, establish a fruitful connexion. And the most general remarks yield at best what looks like the fragments of a system.

It is certainly possible to be convinced by evidence that someone is in such-and-such a state of mind, that, for instance, he is not pretending. But 'evidence' here includes 'imponderable' evidence.

The question is: what does imponderable evidence *accomplish?*

Suppose there were imponderable evidence for the chemical (internal) structure of a substance, still it would have to prove itself to be evidence by certain consequences which *can* be weighed.

(Imponderable evidence might convince someone that a picture was a genuine .... But it is *possible* for this to be proved right by documentary evidence as well.)

Imponderable evidence includes subtleties of glance, of gesture, of tone.

I may recognize a genuine loving look, distinguish it from a pretended one (and here there can, of course, be a 'ponderable' confirmation of my judgment). But I may be quite incapable of describing the difference. And this not because the languages I know have no words for it. For why not introduce new words?—If I were a very talented painter I might conceivably represent the genuine and the simulated glance in pictures.

Ask yourself: How does a man learn to get a 'nose' for something? And how can this nose be used?

Pretending is, of course, only a special case of someone's producing (say) expressions of pain when he is not in pain. For if this is possible at all, why should it always be pretending that is taking place—this very special pattern in the weave of our lives?

A child has much to learn before it can pretend. (A dog cannot be a hypocrite, but neither can he be sincere.)

There might actually occur a case where we should say "This man *believes* he is pretending."

xii

If the formation of concepts can be explained by facts of nature, should we not be interested, not in grammar, but rather in that in nature which is the basis of grammar?—Our interest certainly includes the correspondence between concepts and very general facts of nature. (Such facts as mostly do not strike us because of their generality.) But our interest does not fall back upon these possible causes of the formation of concepts; we are not doing natural science; nor yet natural history—since we can also invent fictitious natural history for our purposes.

I am not saying: if such-and-such facts of nature were different people would have different concepts (in the sense of a hypothesis). But: if anyone believes that certain concepts are absolutely the correct ones, and that having different ones would mean not realizing something that we realize—then let him imagine certain very general facts of nature to be different from what we are used to, and the formation of concepts different from the usual ones will become intelligible to him.

Compare a concept with a style of painting. For is even our style of painting arbitrary? Can we choose one at pleasure? (The Egyptian, for instance.) Is it a mere question of pleasing and ugly?

xiii

When I say: "He was here half an hour ago"—that is, remembering it—this is not the description of a present experience.

Memory-*experiences* are accompaniments of remembering.

Remembering has no experiential content.—Surely this can be seen by introspection? Doesn't *it* shew precisely that there is nothing there, when I look about for a content?—But it could only shew this in this case or that. And even so it cannot shew me what the word "to remember" means, and hence *where* to look for a content!

I get the *idea* of a memory-content only because I assimilate psychological concepts. It is like assimilating two *games*. (Football has *goals*, tennis not.)

Would this situation be conceivable: someone remembers for the first time in his life and says "Yes, now I know what 'remembering' is, what it *feels like* to remember".—How does he know that this feeling is 'remembering'? Compare: "Yes, now I know what 'tingling' is". (He has perhaps had an electric shock for the first time.)—Does he know that it is memory because it is caused by something past? And how does he know what the past is? Man learns the concept of the past by remembering.

And how will he know again in the future what remembering feels like?

(On the other hand one might, perhaps, speak of a feeling "Long, long ago", for there is a tone, a gesture, which go with certain narratives of past times.)

The confusion and barrenness of psychology is not to be explained by calling it a "young science"; its state is not comparable with that of physics, for instance, in its beginnings. (Rather with that of certain branches of mathematics. Set theory.) For in psychology there are experimental methods and *conceptual confusion*. (As in the other case conceptual confusion and methods of proof.)

The existence of the experimental method makes us think we have the means of solving the problems which trouble us; though problem and method pass one another by.

An investigation is possible in connexion with mathematics which is entirely analogous to our investigation of psychology. It is just as little a *mathematical* investigation as the other is a psychological one. It will *not* contain calculations, so it is not for example logistic. It might deserve the name of an investigation of the 'foundations of mathematics'.

INDEX[1]

Numbers refer to the numbered 'Remarks' of the text except where a page reference is indicated.

[1] We are indebted to the Rev. Garth Hallett, S.J., for the compilation of this index.

234 INDEX

behaviour (*contd*)
  human –, 281, 288; p. 179
  – and inference, 486
  pain –, 244, 246, 281, 288, 304, 393
  psychologists study –, 571
  reading –, 157
  fine shades of –, pp. 203–4, 207
  – of a living thing, 357
behaviourism, 308
behaviourist, 307
belief,
  assertion that – is a state of mind, 589; pp. 191–2
  grounds of –, 481
  – in the uniformity of nature, 472–3, 477, 481
  unsatisfied –s, 439
  what – amounts to, 578
believe,
  – another is in pain, 303; p. 178
  'to – falsely', p. 190
  a dog –s, p. 174
  – Goldbach's theorem, 578
  'How do you know that you –?', 587; pp. 191–2, 221
  – a hypothesis, p. 190
  'I – . . .', pp. 190–1
  'I –' and 'I –ed', p. 190
  'I – that he is an automaton', p. 178
  – ing is not thinking, 574–5
  – one is not pretending, p. 229
  – that twice two is four, five, pp. 226–7
benzene, p. 184
blue, *cf.* colour, 33, 275; p. 18
blurred, *cf.* vague, 71, 77
boiler, 466, 469
boundary, *cf.* blurred, definite, field of force, frontier, lamp, limit, sharp, vague, 68, 71, 76, 79, 99, 163, 499
box, 293, 425; p. 193
boxer, p. 11
brain, 158, 427
brake, 6
broom, 60
'bububu', p. 18
builder, building, 2, 8–10, 15, 17, 19–21

bumps, 119
calculating, calculation,
  guidance in –, 233–4, 236
  – in the head, 364, 385–6; pp. 216, 220
  – is not an experiment, p. 218

reasons for –, 466
results of –, p. 225
– with words, 449
calculus, *cf.* law, natural law, regular, rule, 81, 136, 565; p. 14
call, *i.e.* summon, 27, 691
can, *cf.* capable, mastery, technique, 150, 183, 194, 497; p. 209
  'Now I – do, know, understand it', 151
capability, capacity,
  – of applying a figure, p. 208
  – of asking a thing's name, 6, 31
  criteria of –, 182, 385
  – to go on, 181
  – is not a feeling, p. 181
  – to learn, 143–4
  loss of – to see something as something, p. 213
  – to talk, 25
carefulness, 173
Carroll, Lewis, 13; p. 198
causal, *cf.* cause,
  – connexions not the logician's interest, 89
  experience of – connexion, 170, 631
  logical vs. – connexion, 198
  – nexus in willing, 613
  non – bringing about, 613
cause, *cf.* because, grounds, induction, influence, motive, reason,
  –s of an assumption, p. 215
  – of certainty, 325
  – of fear vs. object, 476
  – vs. ground, 325, 475
  – hens to come, 493
  –s of interest of psychologists, pp. 193, 201, 203
  – vs. motive, p. 224
  grasping sense doesn't – use, 195
  shape don't – utterance, 169
certain, certainty, 320, 324–5, 474, 607; pp. 224–6
chair, 47, 59, 60, 80, 361, 486
character (of a word), p. 181
characteristic,
  – accompaniments of a word, pp. 218–19
  – because they recur often, not always, 35
  – experience of pointing, 35
  – features of human behaviour, p. 179
  – feelings of intending, 588
  – pattern of sorrow, p. 174
  a printed line is –, 167
  – processes of understanding, 154, 321
  – sensations in reading, 159